WHAT SO PROUDLY
We Hailed

FRANCIS SCOTT KEY

Manuscript of "The Star-Spangled Banner" (*Library of Congress, Prints and Photographs Division*)

WHAT SO PROUDLY
We Hailed

FRANCIS SCOTT KEY
A Life

MARC LEEPSON

palgrave
macmillan

First published in 2014 by
PALGRAVE MACMILLAN®
in the United States—a division of St. Martin's Press LLC,
175 Fifth Avenue, New York, NY 10010.

Where this book is distributed in the UK, Europe and the rest of the world,
this is by Palgrave Macmillan, a division of Macmillan Publishers Limited,
registered in England, company number 785998, of Houndmills,
Basingstoke, Hampshire RG21 6XS.

Palgrave Macmillan is the global academic imprint of the above companies
and has companies and representatives throughout the world.

Palgrave® and Macmillan® are registered trademarks in the United States,
the United Kingdom, Europe and other countries.

ISBN: 978–1–137–27828–9

Library of Congress Cataloging-in-Publication Data

Leepson, Marc, 1945–
    What so proudly we hailed : Francis Scott Key, a life / Marc Leepson.
        pages cm
    Includes bibliographical references and index.
    ISBN 978–1–137–27828–9 (alk. paper)
        1. Key, Francis Scott, 1779–1843. 2. Poets, American—19th century—
    Biography. 3. United States—History—War of 1812—Biography.
    4. Star-spangled banner (Song) 5. Patriotic poetry, American—
    Authorship. I. Title.

PS2168.L44 2014
811′.2—dc23   2013039997
[B]

A catalogue record of the book is available from the British Library.

Design by Newgen Knowledge Works (P) Ltd., Chennai, India.

First edition: June 2014

10 9 8 7 6 5 4 3 2 1

Printed in the United States of America.

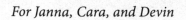

For Janna, Cara, and Devin

CONTENTS

INTRODUCTION

A CLASSICAL SPEAKER

The man could talk. The well-connected, highly successful Washington, D.C., lawyer—the scion of an aristocratic Maryland family—was known throughout the early American Republic for his multifaceted oratorical skills: in the courtroom; in front of patriotic, religious, and political gatherings; and in the salonlike atmosphere of his finely appointed Georgetown home.

"From the moment he arose" to speak at a trial in 1811, one courtroom observer wrote, "the crowd was brought back from the doors and every adjoining part of the house," drawn by his "peculiar celebrity...as an orator."[1]

The celebrated orator loved poetry. From the time he was a child, he spun out rhyming verses with prolific regularity, verses that with one giant exception were at best overly flowery and at worst embarrassingly amateurish. Verses that their author never meant to be seen or read outside the circle of his family and friends.

The giant exception was the patriotic poem he wrote on the fateful night of September 13-14, 1814, during one of the War of 1812's most ferocious and crucial engagements, the Battle of Baltimore. That night a massive British fleet of warships tried to pound the city into submission with a constant stream of bomb, mortar, and rocket shells as an intense thunderstorm punctuated the darkness.

The poem that thirty-five-year-old Francis Scott Key wrote that night—initially titled "The Defence of Ft. M'Henry"—contained lines that have melded into the fabric of American life. Put to music, the words morphed into "The Star-Spangled Banner," which became the official national anthem in 1931.

Two mysteries surround the writing of "The Star-Spangled Banner." First, did Frank Key (as he was known to family and friends) write a poem or a song that night? Described by family members as "unmusical," Key had never written a song in his life (aside from several religious hymns), which makes it unlikely that he was thinking musically in Baltimore Harbor when he scribbled the words "Oh say can you see by the dawn's early light" on the back of a letter he fished out of his pocket.

On the other hand, this poem (as well as one he had written seven years earlier) was set in rhyme and meter precisely to the tune "To Anacreon in Heaven," a well-known song of the era.

"Star-Spangled Banner" mystery number two: No one knows for certain how the poem wound up at a Baltimore printer the following morning—nor do we know how the words later found their way onto sheet music of the tune that was the theme song of the Anacreontic Society in England, a gentlemen's club that met periodically to listen to musical performances, to dine lavishly, and to belt out songs.

Compounding the mysteries is the fact that Francis Scott Key had precious little to say about the poem (or song) after he wrote it. Key did not speak of it in the one letter he wrote after the battle, in which he recounted his Baltimore mission to free an American prisoner taken after the Battle of Bladensburg. And, it appears that he spoke of the song in public only once—in a political speech in 1834, nearly twenty years later, in which Key deferentially said that the real credit for the piece went to the defenders of Baltimore, not the lawyer-poet who set down the words.

The fourth verse of "The Star-Spangled Banner" contains the lines: "Then conquer we must, when our cause it is just, / And this be our motto - 'In God is our trust.' "

Francis Scott Key, as those lines suggest, was both extremely patriotic and pious from the earliest days of his childhood in the early 1780s until his death on January 11, 1843. As a young man, he seriously considered joining the Episcopal priesthood but opted instead for the law and a secular life. Virtually everyone who came in contact with Key remarked on his piety. He peppered his letters to family and friends with references to the Bible and its teachings.

"Read your Bibles every morning and evening, never neglect private prayers both morning and evening, and throughout the day strive to think of God often, and breathe a sincere supplication to him for all things," Key wrote to his children later in his life, in a not untypical missive. "Go regularly to church, plainly [dressed] and behave reverently.... Do everything for God's sake and consider yourselves always in his service."[2]

The pious Key devoted himself to religious causes throughout his life. In him, "the Episcopal Church had one of its few great laymen," one student of Key's church life wrote.[3] Indeed, for decades Key was an influential and effective lay supporter of the Episcopal Church, taking an active role in three: Christ Church and St. John's Church in Georgetown and Trinity Church in Washington, D.C. He served as a lay rector for many years, leading services and visiting the sick. Among the scores of poems he wrote, many dealt with religious themes.

A longtime trustee of the Maryland General Theological Seminary and a founder of what became the Virginia Theological Seminary in 1823, Key also was a strong proponent of the American Bible Society and a leading advocate for government-run religious Sunday schools known as "Sabbath schools."

Although he disdained politics for much of his life, in his fifties Key became an ardent supporter of Andrew Jackson and his newly formed Democratic Party. He became a trusted adviser to Jackson after the Tennessean won the presidency in 1828. A member of Jackson's "kitchen cabinet," Key was steadfastly loyal to Old Hickory throughout his tumultuous presidency. As a reward, Jackson appointed him U.S. Attorney for Washington, a post in which he served for eight years, from 1833–41.

A slave owner from a large slave-owning family, Key was an early and ardent opponent of slave trafficking. He became one of the founders and strongest and most active proponents of the American Colonization Society, which sent freed blacks to Africa beginning in the early 1820s. Yet, Key's legacy with respect to the "peculiar institution" is cloudy.

Neither he nor the Colonization Society called for the abolition of slavery; their mission instead focused solely on sending freed blacks to Africa. That was one reason that few abolitionists had any use for the society. By all accounts, Key treated his own slaves humanely and freed several during his lifetime. What's more, he had a deserved reputation for providing free legal advice to impoverished blacks in Washington.

"If ever man was a true friend to the African race, that man was Francis Scott Key," his friend, Reverend John T. Brooke, wrote. "Throughout his own region of the country, he was proverbially the colored man's friend. He was their standing gratuitous advocate in courts of justice, pressing their rights to the extent of the law, and ready to brave odium or even personal danger in their behalf."[4]

Still, the fact remains that Francis Scott Key bought and sold other human beings throughout his adult life and that his answer to the slavery question—the American Colonization Society—did nothing whatsoever to end slavery and precious little to make life better for freed African Americans.

There were several other flies in the Francis Scott Key antislavery ointment. One was his steadfast and wrongheaded prosecution as U.S. Attorney of Reuben Crandall, a young doctor in Washington, D.C., for possession of abolitionist literature in 1835, and at the same time his pushing for the death penalty for a nineteen-year-old African American man accused of threatening a white woman. Key did so apparently out of animus toward both men after their arrests led to the first race riot in the nation's capital.

The other stain on Key's racial record is guilt by association. His longstanding, close personal and professional friend and brother-in-law, Roger B. Taney, the U.S. chief justice, issued the infamous majority opinion in the 1857 Supreme Court Dred Scott case. In that case, Taney—to his everlasting discredit—ruled that no enslaved African American or any freed African American descended from slaves could be a citizen of the United States.

"*It's no great secret that* the best subject is the ill-behaved subject," the accomplished biographer Stacy Schiff recently wrote. "The ideal one would combine Houdini's close calls, Boss Tweed's ethics, Richard Nixon's friends, and John Cheever's sexuality."[5]

If Francis Scott Key was anything, he was well behaved for virtually his entire life. Outside of being part of the ragtag militia that folded like a cheap suit, thereby allowing the British to march into Washington in

August 1814, and his long night of the soul watching the Battle of Baltimore unfold, Key never experienced any close calls. With few exceptions, he was as ethically and morally straight as a monk.

But Francis Scott Key is a great subject. He led a fascinating and full life in a portentous era of American history. One of the most famous, admired, and accomplished men in the early American Republic, Key was a patriotic, hardworking, able, and well-connected attorney in the nation's capital who played important roles in many high-profile court cases, including scores of cases before the Supreme Court.

He was a morally upright, conservative, and deeply religious family man. And he was a national player throughout his adult life in the most significant social, political, economic, and humanitarian issue of the early nation: slavery.

As the young nation came alive in the 1820s, '30s, and '40s, the slavery issue remained stubbornly unresolved. Francis Scott Key helped shape the national debate over slavery with his disdain for abolition and with his single-minded devotion to colonization as the answer to the entire question. Colonization proved to be a giant failure, doing nothing to stem the forces that brought the nation to Civil War eighteen years after Key's death.

Key believed that blacks were inferior to whites, the accepted view of nearly all Americans at the time, including Abraham Lincoln. However, he also was a persuasive and important voice for ameliorating the worst aspects of slavery.

In short, Francis Scott Key lived a full life, deeply engaged in the most important issues of his time. His burst of poetic patriotic fervor on that September night in 1814 enshrined his name in the ranks of the nation's iconic figures.

What follows is a look at the life and times of Francis Scott Key, a name virtually every American knows, yet the details of his life are largely unknown to Americans today.

1

A FAMILY OF LAWYERS

"I am in the Bible at school.... It is hard words, but I hope I shall get it."

—*Francis Scott Key, age ten*

Francis Scott Key came from a male line of ambitious and successful strivers, many of whom were members of the legal profession. The American branch of the family began when his great-grandfather Philip Key, a lawyer born in St. Paul's Parish in London's Covent Garden district in 1696, left England in 1720 to seek his fortune in the colonies.[1]

Philip Key settled in the small southern Maryland town of Chaptico in St. Mary's County near Leonardtown. Within a few years he did indeed make his fortune. He bought vast tracts of land and became one of the thriving colony's most prominent citizens—a prosperous lawyer and large plantation owner, and at various times a member of the Maryland Assembly, high sheriff of St. Mary's County, presiding justice of the county, and member of the Governor's Council.

Among Philip Key's holdings was an 1,865-acre parcel of farmland he purchased in 1752 near Pipe Creek in the gently rolling hills of sparsely populated northern Frederick County, Maryland, about fifteen miles south of the Pennsylvania line. He gave the property a Latin name, *Terra Rubra* (roughly translated "Red Land").

Philip Key was a religious Church of England man who owned scores of slaves. A year before his death in 1764, he compiled a list "of Negroes it has pleased God to bless me with." It contains the names and ages of sixty human beings, including "Rumulus, born 15 April 1755," "Tom the Smith, 45," "Harry, born 20 February 1760," "Jemmy, 69," and "Tom, son of Hanna, 11."[2]

Philip Key had seven children with his first wife, Susanna Barton Gardiner, whom he married in 1724. Five of his six sons chose the profession of the law, including Francis Key—Francis Scott Key's grandfather, for whom he was named—who was born in 1731.

Francis Key, the longtime clerk of Cecil County in the northeast corner of Maryland, married into another prosperous Maryland family when he and Ann Arnold Ross of Annapolis tied the knot in 1752. Born in Annapolis in 1727, Ann Arnold was the eldest daughter of Alicia Arnold and John Ross, a prominent Annapolis attorney. Ann Arnold Ross, the *Maryland Gazette* of Annapolis noted two days after her wedding, was "a well accomplish'd and deserving young Lady, with a pretty Fortune."[3]

That fortune had been amassed by her father, John Ross, who was born in England in 1696. Ross, the clerk of colonial Maryland's Governor's Council for many years, also served as the deputy agent for the Sixth Lord Baltimore, as an alderman and a one-term mayor of Annapolis. He owned more than seven thousand acres of land throughout Maryland, including a large tract overlooking the Severn River, seven miles from Annapolis. It is the site of the Ross mansion known as Belvoir, which has been on the National Register of Historic Places since 1971.

Alicia Arnold Ross, born in 1700, was a deeply devout woman who impressed upon her daughters the importance of fealty to God, family, and their future husbands. "I beg above all things you will take care and Serve God [and] let nothing, my Dear Girl, make you neglect your duty morning and Evening and be sure not to neglect going to Church as often as you can and to Receive Holy Sacrament," Alicia Ross wrote to her daughter Ann. "Be sure you Love and honour your father and do everything you can to please him and . . . take his advice in all things. . . . Take care not to be extravagant and to be always clean and a good Housewife."[4]

Francis Key and Ann Arnold Ross Key, who would outlive her husband by forty-one years, had three children. The first, John Ross Key—Francis Scott Key's father—was born on September 19, 1754; his younger brother Philip Barton Key was born on April 12, 1757; and his sister, Elizabeth Scott Key, came along two years later.

In keeping with family tradition, Francis Key amassed large real estate holdings, including a three-hundred-acre plantation along the Chesapeake Bay in Cecil County. In 1767 Francis and his brother-in-law, the wealthy Irish-born Annapolis physician Dr. Upton Scott (who married Francis's wife's sister Elizabeth), bought a nearly 3,700-acre parcel of farmland not far from Terra Rubra.

Francis Key died young and without a will at age thirty-nine in November 1770. Under English law, his oldest son inherited his property, which is how sixteen-year-old John Ross Key found himself the owner of Terra Rubra. That same year the family built a large brick home on the property. The Key family managed it in the manner of a southern planta-tion, complete with about two dozen slaves who worked in the fields and in the expansive manor house.[5]

John Ross Key and his younger brother Philip Barton were groomed to fol-low family tradition and become lawyers. Philip went off to England to do so, while John Ross stayed in Maryland. He received his schooling from tutors in Annapolis and at his maternal grandfather and namesake John Ross's plantation, Belvoir. On his sixteenth birthday, several weeks before his father's death, however, young John Ross wrote to his father expressing grave doubts about his future as a lawyer. "I have not yet begun the study of law," he wrote, "nor have I any desire to attempt it because I think I am not qualified for it. Unless I could be a Master of that science undertaken, it would be better never to have attempted it."[6] The boy signed the letter "Your Dutiful & Obedient Son."

The dutiful teenager would later change his mind and enjoy a long and successful legal career. In January 1778, John Ross Key became a justice of the peace in Frederick, a position he held for several years. Twenty years after writing the discouraging letter to his father, in January 1790, the one-time recalcitrant law student was appointed asso-ciate justice of the Frederick County Court, a position he held for many years.

In June 1775, two months after Lexington and Concord, word went out from the Maryland delegation in the Second Continental Congress in Philadelphia for militias to be formed throughout the state. On June 22, John Hanson, the presiding officer of Frederick County's Committee of Observation (the local governing body), organized two local rifle companies. Listed among the officers of the Western Maryland Rifles was 2nd Lieutenant John Ross Key.[7]

The records are unclear about how long the twenty-one-year-old lieutenant served in that unit under Captain Michael Cresap, who marched his men to Massachusetts on July 18. What is known is that John Ross Key was back home in Maryland on October 19, 1775, the day he married nineteen-year-old Anne Phoebe Penn Dagworthy Charlton of Frederick. The young couple set up housekeeping at Terra Rubra. A little more than a year later, he volunteered once more for the fight against the British and received a commission in Colonel Norman Bruce's battalion.

It appears that John Ross Key returned home to Terra Rubra not long after that. But in the last year of the war, on February 3, 1781, he rejoined the military a third time, receiving his commission as a lieutenant in Captain Philip Thomas's Troop of Light Horse in Frederick.[8] He soon was promoted to captain and given command of the Frederick Light Dragoons, which joined the Continental Army early in June in the Virginia campaign that led to the siege of Yorktown and the surrender of the British forces on October 19. Family lore has it that Captain John Ross Key, in command of the Frederick Company under Thomas took part in the siege of Yorktown under the command of the famed French Continental Army major general, the Marquis de Lafayette.[9]

While John Ross Key was ensuring that all of his descendants could become members of the Sons and Daughters of the American Revolution, his younger brother Philip Barton Key took a very different path. He declared himself a Loyalist and joined the British Army to fight against the Americans in July 1776, not long after the Declaration of Independence was signed. Five years later, in 1781, the General Court of the Maryland Eastern Shore found Philip Barton Key—along with all the other Marylanders who joined Loyalist regiments—guilty of treason.

In 1778 Philip Barton was serving as a captain in Lieutenant Colonel James Chalmer's Maryland Loyalist Regiment, which had been formed in 1777. The regiment, numbering as many as five hundred men, joined the British Army under General Sir Henry Clinton in June 1778 as they left Philadelphia and fought George Washington's troops at the Battle of Monmouth Courthouse in New Jersey. Philip Barton and his regiment later were sent to help the Redcoats defend Fort George in Pensacola, the capital of the British colony of West Florida. On May 9, 1781, when the British succumbed to a withering assault by Spanish forces under Bernardo de Galvez, he was among nearly 1,100 men taken prisoner and shipped to Havana in Spain's colony of Cuba. He was released soon thereafter and went to back England to continue his law studies.

Philip Barton did well in London. In 1784 he was admitted to the Middle Temple of the Inns of Court in London. After reporting that the Americans had seized all of his land in Maryland, he received a lifetime half-pay military pension.

Then in 1785 Philip Barton Key decided to return to the land of his birth. Loyalists—especially those who fought against the Continental Army—typically faced bitter enmity in the new United States after the Revolution. But Philip Barton seemed to easily mend whatever fences he had broken. The charge of treason melted away as he studied law in Annapolis under Gabriel Duvall, a noted jurist who had served in the Continental Army and later would become a U.S. Supreme Court justice.

Philip Barton Key was admitted to the Maryland bar in 1787 and began a law practice in Leonardtown in Southern Maryland. He moved to the state capital of Annapolis in 1790 and on July 4 married Ann Plater. He was thirty-three; his bride sixteen. She was a daughter of one of Southern Maryland's leading citizens, George Plater, a former member of the Continental Congress who, in 1791, was elected governor of Maryland.

The one-time Loyalist's legal practice thrived in Annapolis, where Philip Barton Key quickly became one of the city's movers and shakers. By 1800 he presided over a bustling household that included twenty-two slaves. He ran for a seat in the Maryland House of Delegates in 1794 and won, representing Annapolis in that body from 1794 to 1799. He also served as mayor of the city from 1797 to 1798. President John Adams appointed him to the Fourth U.S. Circuit Court early in 1801, where he served as chief judge until the Jefferson administration abolished that position in July 1802.

Philip Barton took his law practice to Georgetown, then an incorporated city adjoining Washington, D.C. In a short time he moved his wife and their two young daughters into a huge, three-story Federal-style house he built north of Georgetown; he named the house Woodley.[10]

In May 1802, around the time he moved to Woodley, Philip Barton bought eight slaves from Uriah Forrest, the clerk of the U.S. District

Court in Washington. For $2,565, Key received the eight human beings (including a cook named Rachel Young and a boy named Harry), along with "five featherbeds with furniture and bedsteads and two hair mattresses, dining tables, other side tables, carpets, book cases, one set of china...one four wheeled sulky and harnesses and wagon, three mules, four horses and two cows."[11]

Philip Barton thrived in the nation's capital. He ran a hugely successful law practice, and he and his growing family (seven children survived infancy) lived in baronial splendor at Woodley, attended by more than a dozen slaves who worked in the house and in the hundreds of acres of gardens and fields that surrounded it. The city's elite flocked to Woodley to be entertained in style by the hospitable Keys.

Philip Barton Key, who also owned hundreds of acres of farmland in Montgomery County, Maryland, just north of the capital, decided to run for Congress from Maryland's 3rd District. In January 1806 he officially severed his ties with England, writing to his agent in London to end his half-pay British military pension. His conversion from British Loyalist to American Federalist was complete when he won that election on October 6. He went on to win two more House elections, serving in Congress from March 1807 to March 1813.

"I had returned to my country like a prodigal son to his father," Philip Barton Key said following his first election campaign, "had felt as an American should feel, was received and forgiven, of which the most convincing proof is my election."[12]

In 1796, a seventeen-year-old newly minted graduate of St. John's College in Annapolis came to Philip Barton Key's law offices to follow family tradition and read law. He was a bright, obedient young man, eager to take advantage of the power and prestige of his father's brother's law firm. He studied law for four years in Annapolis before striking out on his own to begin a law practice that he would stick with for the rest of his life and that would bring him wealth, fame, and prestige.

This fledgling lawyer, Francis Scott Key, was born at Terra Rubra on August 1, 1779. He was a short, thin, handsome boy—and would become a handsome man, with flowing, dark curly hair, dark eyes, and a prominent, patrician nose. Although his uncle Philip Barton and his father John Ross were "large, manly looking fellows," Frankie (as the family called

him as a boy) and his sister, Anne, were "of much smaller mould," recalled
a neighbor of the family, who described her as "a beautiful little girl with
the cheerfulest face and most pleasant smile I ever saw."[13]

Frankie passed his childhood in idyllic fashion on his family's prosperous plantation in the company of adoring relatives, tended to by slaves
and surrounded by a few similar-size farms, along with a larger number
of more modest rural farmsteads. He passed countless hours playing
with his sister Anne Phoebe Charlton Key, who was three years younger.
Another sister, Anne Charlton, born in 1777, had died in infancy; a second younger sister, Catherine Charlton Key, died at six months of age in
the summer of 1782.

Looking back on his carefree childhood at Terra Rubra, Key later
wrote "To My Sister," a sentimental poem in which he rhapsodized over
"those bright hours" he shared with Anne as they played together on "The
mountain top, the meadow plain / The winding creek, the shaded lane."
Those "sunny paths were all our own," he wrote, "And thou and I were
alone / Each to the other only known / My sister!"[14]

Frankie and Anne were taught at home by their mother until he was ten
years old. Religion played an integral part in their upbringing under their
pious mother. In 1789, the Keys sent their only son to Annapolis to attend
St. John's College, which had been chartered by the state of Maryland in
1784. St. John's had absorbed Annapolis's King William's School, a prep
school that had been in existence since 1696. The new prep school and
college had opened its doors under newly hired president John McDowell,
a lawyer and professor of mathematics.

Classes took place in a building called Bladen's Folly that forty years
earlier had been intended as the official residence of Maryland's governor Thomas Bladen. Construction on the grand, three-story brick
building—today known as McDowell Hall—had been suspended, but
was completed after the state of Maryland chartered the new college.
The students and their teachers (called masters) also lived in Bladen's
Folly, the center of a four-acre campus. The young men studied Greek
and Latin, grammar, mathematics, and the sciences.[15]

The Keys did not have pay for young Francis's board, lodging, or other
residential expenses. For the next seven years while he was a student at
St. John's he lived with his great-aunt Elizabeth Ross Scott (the sister of his
grandmother, Ann Arnold Ross Key) and her husband, Dr. Upton Scott,

who were then in their mid-sixties. The Scotts easily made room for their young grand-nephew in their opulent home (which still stands today) on Shipwright Street in downtown Annapolis, two blocks from the water-front and eight short blocks from St. John's College.

Young Frankie, naturally, was homesick. "I remember when I was a little boy and was sent all the way to Annapolis, I used be very sad for a while when I first got there whenever I thought about Pipe Creek, and par-ticularly when I thought about my mother," Key wrote many years later to his youngest son, Charles. "But then when I became engaged in my studies and amused with my plays, I found these thoughts would not disturb me so often and I could be cheerful and happy."[16]

The Scotts were an upright, religious couple. Upton Scott, born in Ireland in 1724, was a medical doctor when he arrived in Maryland in the mid-1750s. He made a small fortune in the colony, served one term as mayor of Annapolis, and from 1770 to 1776 was the personal physician to Robert Eden, the twenty-third and last royal governor of Maryland. Like Philip Barton Key, Upton Scott declared himself a Loyalist during the American Revolution, went to England during the war, and returned to Maryland after the hostilities ended. Dr. Scott, too, had no reentry prob-lems into the new United States. He remained a prominent, prosperous, slaving-owning citizen of Annapolis until his death in 1814.[17]

In his free time during the school year, Frankie paid regular vis-its to his grandmother Ann Arnold Ross Key, who was blind and lived with her daughter at Belvoir outside Annapolis. The family story is that Grandmother Ann Arnold lost her sight when she came to the aid of house slaves (called "servants" by the family) trapped by a fire inside one of the family's homes.

Although St. John's was a nondenominational institution, the students were required to study the Bible, something that Frankie Key in his first year found a tad intimidating. "I am in the Bible at school," the ten-year-old wrote to his mother. "I am in Kings and I am but three leaves to get into Chronicles. I have got the ten chapters of Nehemiah to get by.... It is hard words, but I hope I shall get it."

In the letter, the boy also talked about a dream he had. "Robinson Crusoe and all the savages danced and Friday was a negro and all night, Mama, they were dancing in my room," he wrote. "Aunt Scott says I dreamt it, but indeed I did not for I see them [and] it was so pretty."[18]

Among the notable events that took place at St. John's during Francis Scott Key's years there was a visit the president of the United States paid to the college on March 25, 1791. George Washington's step-grandson, George Washington Parke Custis, and two of his nephews, Fairfax and Lawrence Washington, were St. John's students. Accompanied by Maryland's governor John Eager Howard and other dignitaries, President Washington spoke highly of the "infant seminary." In a thank-you note to the St. John's faculty following the visit, he said he sincerely hoped "the excellence of your seminary will be manifested in the morals and sciences of the youths who are favored with your care."[19]

Twelve-year-old Frankie Key had another chance to see the father of his country in July that year at Terra Rubra—riding, family stories have it, the seventy-five miles from Annapolis on horseback. Washington, en route from Virginia to Philadelphia, had spent two days in Frederick. On July 2, 1791, George Washington and his party rode through Pipe Creek. In his diary, the president noted that the "Country from Tawny Town to Yorktown [Pennsylvania] is exceedingly pleasant [and] thickly inhabited and well improved. The dwelling Houses, Barns & meadows being good."[20]

The story has been told that Washington stopped at Terra Rubra and made a speech from the front porch to the delight of the Key family, including the impressionable young Frankie. Washington does not mention the incident in his diary, nor is there other credible evidence that a Washington Terra Rubra oration took place.

In May 1794, a year after the college's first commencement, fourteen-year-old Francis Scott Key moved up to the collegiate level at St. John's. He graduated on October 21, 1796, along with five other young men, including his closest friend Daniel Murray of Annapolis. They called themselves the Tenth Legion, after Julius Caesar's famed Roman fighting force.[21]

2

ANNAPOLIS, FREDERICK TOWN, AND GEORGE TOWN

"I have been to George Town and felt [that] ... it is the very dirtiest hole I ever saw for a place of any trade, or respectability of inhabitants."
—*Abigail Adams, November 21, 1800*

Annapolis was the place to be in Maryland—if not in the entire Middle Atlantic section of the country—at the turn of the nineteenth century. Maryland's capital was thriving economically. Scores of affluent families lived good lives in large, stately homes in the city and its environs. Sometimes called the "Athens of America," the small seaport of about 2,200 residents[1] overlooking a serene, scenic harbor stood as a center of culture and the political hub of the state.

In the early 1780s Annapolis played a pivotal role in the shaping of the new nation. The city served as the nation's capital for seven months beginning on November 26, 1783, when it hosted the Second Continental Congress. George Washington entered the Senate Chamber of the Maryland State House in Annapolis on December 23, 1783, to tender his resignation as commander-in-chief of the Continental Army. The Treaty of Paris, which officially ended the American Revolution, was signed in Annapolis on January 17, 1784.

For a few years after finishing college, the fledging lawyer from Pipe Creek felt he didn't fit in among the lively group of people in his age cohort. "The young folks at present really appear to me to be out of their senses," Key wrote to his friend John Leeds Kerr on February 15, 1798, "nothing but frolicking and paying their addresses to their respective favorites."[2]

A year later, though, the about-to-be twenty year old seemed to have shaken off his aversion to the social scene and took great pleasure in the city's many social activities—and in members of the opposite sex. "The ladies and gentlemen of the theater contribute greatly to the amusements of this city," he wrote to Kerr on July 13, 1799, "both making the private parties more agreeable & by their public performances."

In that letter Frank Key mentioned a young woman named Matilda. "Were I to estimate her beauty by the Dutch standard," he told Kerr, "I should say she is handsomer by a good many pounds than when I saw her last." He then quoted the British satirist, Peter Pindar: "As Pindar says, 'Love! When I marry give me not an ox—I hate a woman like a sentry box.'"[3]

Francis Scott Key lived among a good number of other young, afflu- ent, well-connected, well-educated men in Annapolis reading law under the state's top jurists. The "society of the place…was always gay during the session of the General Assembly," one of the young aspiring lawyers wrote of Annapolis in the 1790s, "and highly cultivated and refined."[4]

The man who wrote those words was a gangly, homely nineteen-year- old from a prosperous southern Maryland family of tobacco planters. He arrived in town in 1796, the year after he'd graduated as valedictorian of his class from Dickenson College in Pennsylvania. Roger Brooke Taney (pronounced "TAW-nee"), the second of four sons, was not in line to inherit his father's vast estate, so he turned to the legal profession to make a living. He read law in Annapolis in the offices of Jeremiah Townley Chase, a distinguished jurist who had been a delegate to the Continental Congress. Taney, whose family had converted to Catholicism, was admit- ted to practice law in Maryland in June 1799 but instead turned to poli- tics. A Federalist with powerful family connections, in 1799 he won a seat in the Maryland legislature from Calvert County in southern Maryland. Taney served just one term and then moved west to Frederick in 1801.

His good friend Frank Key had headed back to Frederick in 1800 after officially being admitted into the Maryland legal fraternity. Taney and Key had met when both were reading law in Annapolis and had formed a close friendship, one that would last until Key's death in 1843.

Their friendship was cemented on January 7, 1806, when Roger B. Taney married Anne Arnold Phoebe Charlton Key, Francis Scott Key's only living sibling, at Terra Rubra. "Roger was a tall, gaunt fellow, as lean, they used to say, as a Potomac herring, and as shrewd as the shrewdest. He married bright little Anne," a neighbor recalled many years later. "It was like the union of a hawk with a skylark."[5]

Taney and Anne Key, who had met in Annapolis, had six children who survived infancy, all girls. The Taney and Key families would spend many summer vacations together at Terra Rubra. Over the years Roger B. Taney and Francis Scott Key worked together on legal cases—and several times faced off against each other in courtrooms.

Frederick was no Athens in 1800 when Frank Key came back home to practice law. But standing as a crossroads between the growing cities of the East and the frontier to the West, it had become a comfortably prosperous town. In 1800 Frederick was the second largest city (behind Baltimore) in Maryland, well known for its inns and taverns, catering to stagecoaches and wagon-train passengers, as well as individual travelers. The population of the city and the surrounding Frederick County, as enumerated in the 1800 U.S. Census, was 31,523. That total included 5,045 African Americans, the overwhelming majority of whom were enslaved.

John Thomas Schley, the leader of a group of some one hundred Palatinate Germans, founded the city (then called Frederick Town) in 1745. Schley, historians believe, chose the name in honor of Frederick Calvert, the sixth (and last) Lord Baltimore, who inherited the English province of Maryland in 1751.

Like Annapolis, Frederick has its place in colonial American history. In 1755, during the French and Indian War, British Major General Edward Braddock, the commander in chief of all British forces in North America, met with Benjamin Franklin (then a member of the Pennsylvania Assembly) and Braddock's trusted military aide George Washington in Frederick. They planned what turned out to be a disastrous expedition to try to take the French-held Fort Duquesne in what today is downtown Pittsburgh.

Ten years later, in 1765, Frederick was the scene of a heated protest over the British Stamp Act. Twelve Frederick County judges issued a statement condemning that much reviled legislation. One of the judges, Thomas Johnson, became the state of Maryland's first elected governor; he later served as an associate justice of the U.S. Supreme Court. Johnson was sixty-seven years old in 1800 when on February 22, he delivered a solemn public eulogy to George Washington, who had died on December 14, 1799. There is little doubt that the Key family, including twenty-year-old Frank, showed up to hear the revered Johnson eulogize the revered father of our country.

Francis Scott Key was admitted to the Frederick County Bar in 1800 and received what was, in essence, an honorary master of arts degree on November 12 from his alma mater, St. John's College.[6] Around this time the fledgling lawyer wrote two poems in which he poured out his adolescent love (and lust) to an otherwise unidentified woman he called Delia. In "To Delia," he rhapsodized over the young woman's "witching smile," and pined for the day when the two could spend a "rapturous hour" sitting under a beech tree's "arching shade."[7]

Key's equally love-struck "To a Golden Key" starts with the lines:

> Long had a golden key concealed
> The treasures of my Delia's breast;
> Treasures one half so sweet and rich
> Sure never key before possessed

Who was Delia? There are no clues in any letters of Key's letters. The best guess is that she was Cordelia Harris, who was born in Anne Arundel County a year before Frank Key, and moved with her family to a farm not far from Terra Rubra soon after. Unhappily for besotted Frank Key, Cordelia Harris married another man in 1806.[8] By that time, however, Frank Key was a married man with two children.

Francis Scott Key met Mary Tayloe Lloyd in Annapolis. She was the daughter of one of Maryland's largest and most powerful landholders, Colonel Edward Lloyd IV, the owner of the enormous Wye Plantation in Talbot County, and Elizabeth Tayloe Lloyd. Her father, known as "the Patriot" to distinguish him from several other generations of Edward Lloyds, inherited tens of thousands of acres of property (mostly farmland) when he was born in 1744. He owned 320 slaves when he died at age fifty-one in 1796.

His Wye Plantation on Maryland's Eastern Shore was one of the state's largest and most prosperous. The income that Lloyd derived from his varied farming and business ventures allowed his family to live lavishly.

"The principal products raised [on Wye Plantation] were tobacco, corn, and wheat," wrote the famed abolitionist Frederick Douglass—who was born into slavery on Wye Plantation and lived there for two years as a boy. "These were raised in great abundance; so that, with the products of this and the other farms belonging to [Col. Lloyd] he was able to keep in almost constant employment a large sloop, in carrying them to market at Baltimore."[9]

Colonel Lloyd, Douglass said, "kept from three to four hundred slaves on his home plantation, and owned a large number more on the neighboring farms belonging to him....If a slave was convicted of any high misdemeanor, became unmanageable, or evinced a determination to run away, he was...severely whipped, put on board the sloop, and sold to Austin Woolfolk, or some other slave-trader, as a warning to the slaves remaining."[10]

Colonel Lloyd's wife, Elizabeth Tayloe Lloyd, also came from a huge landowning, upper-crust family. Her father, John Tayloe II of Richmond County, Virginia, headed one of that state's wealthiest families. At the turn of the nineteenth century he owned some forty thousand acres throughout the state of Virginia, as well as at least five hundred slaves.

Mary Tayloe Lloyd and Francis Scott Key met in Annapolis where she and her mother spent part of the year after Col. Lloyd died in 1896. By all accounts, Key fell in love with the young woman the moment they met. In the poem "To Mary," Frank Key (as the young man was called by family and friends) describes how through "toil and pain" he will "win the beam of Mary's gladdened eyes. He goes on to describe her smile as "More sweet, if smile more sweet can be."[11]

Whether or not those less-than-Shakespearean verses helped or hindered the courtship, Francis Scott Key won the hand of Mary Tayloe Lloyd, known to family and friends as Polly. "I must tell you of an event of Annapolis society," the well-connected Maryland plantation owner Rosalie Calvert wrote on December 30, 1801. "Polly Lloyd is to be married next month to Frank Key who has nothing and who has only practiced for two years as an [attorney]. They are going to live near Fredericktown."[12]

Frank Key had more than nothing, but the young lawyer from western Maryland stood well below the Lloyds socially and economically. Did Polly Lloyd bring a dowry to the marriage? No record has surfaced indicating that she did. Polly remained close to her mother (and her family's wealth) in Annapolis, however, and there is little doubt that the newly married couple enjoyed the largesse of the Lloyds.

The wedding took place on January 19, 1802, in Annapolis at the sprawling, three-story Georgian brick townhouse the bride's father had owned on Maryland Avenue in the city's center. Polly was seventeen; Frank, twenty-two. Soon after, the young couple moved to Frederick, most likely into a small brick house on Market Street in the center of town.

He plied his legal trade; she set up housekeeping. She also paid frequent visits to her family in Annapolis. They produced two children in the next three years: Elizabeth Phoebe (called "Lizzie"), born on October 10, 1803, and Maria Lloyd, born on February 13, 1805. Frank Key enjoyed life in his hometown and appears to have intended to raise his family there. One indication: On August 25, 1802, Key rode about thirty-five miles north to Gettysburg, Pennsylvania, and became the fifth lawyer admitted to the bar of newly established Adams County.

As it turned out, Francis Scott Key never did any legal work in Adams County. He and Polly had their eyes on bigger opportunities in the new national capital, Washington, D.C., about fifty miles southeast of Frederick. Either late in 1805 or early in 1806, about a year after the birth of their second daughter, the Keys moved to Georgetown on the west side of Washington. The city had officially succeeded Philadelphia as the nation's capital in 1800. The Keys would live in Georgetown and Washington for nearly four decades.

Washington, D.C., had been born in 1790 during the John Adams administration when the First Federal Congress, meeting in Philadelphia, agreed to acquire a diamond-shaped, one-hundred-square-mile parcel of land along the Potomac River suggested by George Washington as the site for the new national capital. The new federal city would be adjacent to the thriving port towns of Alexandria and Georgetown.

In 1791 the French artist, engineer, and architect Pierre L'Enfant (who had served as an engineer in the Continental Army) came to the fledgling city at George Washington's behest to lay out a plan for the capital's federal buildings and streets. The surveying work was done by two men from Baltimore, Andrew Elliott and Benjamin Banneker, a free African American scientist, astronomer, farmer, and surveyor.

Hired slaves and freed men did much of the physical labor building the new national capital. By 1800 Washington, D.C., including Georgetown, was home to about six thousand people, including more than two thousand slaves and four hundred free blacks.

Wedged between two slave states, Virginia and Maryland, Washington had the feel of a southern city: Slave sales were common, and by the 1820s, more than two dozen slave sellers plied their trade in the heart of town. It was not unusual to see manacled men, women, and children being marched to and from the slave pens that operated on the streets of what is now downtown Washington, D.C.

One of the biggest of these stood on Pennsylvania Avenue, several blocks from the Capitol where the National Archives sits today. Another bustling slave pen, a hidden basement in a three-story building known as the Yellow House, owned by William H. Williams, sat on the National Mall at the corner of Independence Avenue and 7th Street Southwest, the site of the present-day Hirshhorn Museum.[13]

One of the few firsthand descriptions of conditions in the slave pens was written by Solomon Northup, a free black man from upstate New York who was kidnapped in Washington and sold into slavery from the Yellow House. After being taken off the streets of Washington, Northup found himself in a dank underground room "about twelve feet square—the walls of solid masonry," he later wrote. "There was one small window, crossed with great iron bars, with an outside shutter, securely fastened. An iron-bound door led into an adjoining cell, or vault, wholly destitute of windows, or any means of admitting light."

Northup's cell contained a wooden bench and "an old-fashioned, dirty box stove." There was "neither bed, nor blanket, nor any other thing whatever." The vault had "a flight of steps into a yard, surrounded by a brick wall ten or twelve feet high.... In one part of the wall there was a strongly ironed door, opening into a narrow, covered passage.... The top of the wall supported one end of a roof, which ascended inwards, forming a kind of open shed. Underneath the roof there was a crazy loft all round, where slaves, if so disposed, might sleep at night, or in inclement weather seek shelter from the storm."

The Yellow House yard, he said, "was like a farmer's barnyard in most respects, save it was so constructed that the outside world could never see the human cattle that were herded there."[14]

Northup wrote of a strange juxtaposition: "Within plain sight of this same house, looking down from its commanding height upon it, was the Capitol. The voices of patriotic representatives boasting of freedom and equality, and the rattling of the poor slave's chains, almost commingled. A slave pen within the very shadow of the Capitol!"

It was not uncommon for slaves to be auctioned off in the District Court building, several blocks south of the Capitol. Basil Hall, a British Royal Navy captain, described one such sale, on January 15, 1827, of a young, light-skinned enslaved man named George whose fate had just been decided by a lawsuit. Both the man's parents and his brothers and sisters, Hall said, had "been long ago sold into slavery, and sent to the Southern States—Florida or Alabama, he knew not where!"

The man "trembled all the while" the auction took place, Hall wrote. "He looked very ill at ease" because he feared "being purchased by a person of whom I suppose he had some previous knowledge, and whose looks certainly were as little inviting as any thing could well be."[15]

George "was put up for auction," Hall wrote, at the end of a hallway in the courthouse "near which four or five persons had . . . collected. There was a great deal of laughing and talking amongst the buyers, and several jests were sported on the occasion, of which their little victim took no more notice than if he had been a horse of a dog."

A local farmer won the bidding, paying $143 for the man.

Slave traders shipped nearly all of their human chattel to plantations in the South; Solomon Northup, for example, ended up on a cotton plantation in Louisiana. There was no need for large numbers of slaves in the urban environs of Washington. That led to the capital becoming home to increasing numbers of freedmen and freedwomen as some owners manumitted their slaves and others allowed slaves to work some form of manual labor for others and to keep part of their earnings. Many hardworking enslaved people eventually accumulated enough money to buy their own freedom as well as freedom for their spouses and children. Emancipated slaves and runaways also flocked to the nation's capital.

Living conditions in Washington for freed blacks were certainly better than in rural areas. But most of the city's African Americans were forced to live in houses that were "uncomfortable at best, wretched at worst," urban historian Constance McLaughlin Green wrote. Sanitation, Green noted, was primitive; most residents were forced to use cisterns "or the wells and pumps in the public squares. People generally dumped their slops into the streets with the result that seepage into the public wells spread dysentery and cholera from time to time."[16]

Three black freedmen started the first school for African American children in Washington in 1807 in a small house in the northwest section of the city. A white teacher was brought in to run the school. By 1811 the city had three more schools for African American children, one run by an Englishwoman, Mary Billings, in Georgetown.[17] The city also had several African American churches, including Mt. Zion Negro Church in Georgetown (which opened in 1814), Ebenezer Methodist Episcopal Church, and Israel Bethel Church. Some white churches—including St. John's Episcopal Church in Georgetown where Francis Scott Key would worship—had separate areas for black congregants.

Freed blacks were allowed to work (almost exclusively as laborers, servants, barbers, cooks, maids, and other menial jobs), to own property, and to run their own businesses. But "every imaginable form of humiliating restriction upon the personal freedom of the colored people, both bond and free," pervaded the city's laws "almost from the first year of its corporate existence," a government report later found.[18] "It seems to be assumed," the report noted, that freed blacks "were ready for riot, insurrection, and every species of insubordination and wickedness."

One of the first of the city's Black Codes was an 1808 ordinance declaring that "no black person, or person of color, or loose, idle, disorderly person" was permitted "to walk about or assemble at any tippling house or other house after 10 o'clock at night." Another section of that ordinance forbade slaves and freed blacks from going "at large through the streets, or other parts of the city" after ten o'clock from April 1 to October 1 and after nine at night the rest of the year except for slaves with written permission from their masters or employers. The penalty for breaking that law for a slave was whipping, specifically "39 stripes on his or her bare back." For freed blacks or mulattoes the penalty was a fine of no more than twenty dollars and court costs. If that person could not pay the fine, he or she would be sentenced to ninety days of hard labor.[19]

By 1820 all free blacks in the city were required to post a twenty-dollar bond "with one good and responsible free white citizen," and to carry a certificate of freedom signed by three white people attesting that they were "good" and "sober" and exhibited "orderly conduct." If a freed person did not produce the certificate, he or she could be arrested and sold into slavery.

Even for whites, Washington, D.C., was not exactly the most inviting place to live in the early years of the nineteenth century. A relatively sparsely populated backwater, the city had large tracts of untamed woods and cultivated farmland within its borders. Few buildings other than the nearly completed President's House on Pennsylvania Avenue—the largest dwelling in the nation—dotted the unpaved, perpetually muddy streets.

The Capitol, surrounded by dense woods, was still under construction. The area between the Capitol and what soon would be known as the White House featured boarding houses, bawdy houses, and gambling dens catering to the virtually all-male transient population of members of Congress and their staffs.

The summers were long, hot, and extremely humid; sections of the city along the swampy Potomac were known above all for their swarms of mosquitoes. Cattle grazed throughout Washington, including on the centerpiece of the L'Enfant-designed federal city, the National Mall.

First lady Abigail Adams described Washington in 1800 as "a new country with houses scattered over a space of ten miles, and trees & stumps in plenty." The surrounding countryside, she said, "is romantic but a wild, a wilderness at present."[20]

The British diplomat Sir Augustus John Foster also painted a rustic picture of the young federal capital. "Excellent snipe shooting and even partridge shooting was to be had on each side of [Pennsylvania] avenue and even close under the wall of the Capitol," he wrote in 1805. Foster was exaggerating only slightly when he went on to say: "One may take a ride of several hours within the precincts without meeting a single individual to disturb one's meditations."[21]

As for Georgetown, where the Keys moved into a house on Bridge Street, Abigail Adams said: "I have been to George Town and felt [that] . . . it is the very dirtiest hole I ever saw for a place of any trade, or respectability of inhabitants. It is only one mile from me but a quagmire after every rain."

While it had never been incorporated as a separate city, Georgetown had functioned as one with an elected local government run by a mayor, recorder, alderman, and common council since 1789. The town had been created in 1751 by an act of the Maryland Assembly from sixty acres of privately owned land fronting the Potomac River. The city's founders named it George Town in honor of King George II.

George Town's early economy centered on shipping Maryland- and Virginia-grown tobacco from its Potomac River wharves. By the turn of the nineteenth century, the riverfront area also included several flour mills, a textile mill, and a paper factory. After Washington became the nation's capital, Georgetown developed into a largely residential area of brick townhouses and larger, mostly Georgian-style mansions.

Frank and Polly Key moved into a large, brick, two-and-a-half story house on the south side of Georgetown's main street, then known as Bridge Street and today as M Street.[22] The house had been built in 1795 by Thomas Clark, a local merchant and real estate investor.[23] The Keys could not buy the house because it was tied up in a legal dispute among the heirs of a previous owner.[24]

The gable-roofed house surrounded by large trees had two dormers facing Bridge Street and two brick chimneys. A one-story addition sat on the west end of the house. Framed porches in the rear overlooked a terraced lawn and garden that sloped down to the Potomac River. The property also included a coach house, smokehouse, and an outhouse. Up the hill stood the sixty-acre campus of the Jesuit-run Georgetown College, which had opened its doors in 1789.

Francis Scott Key brought his family to Georgetown for one main reason: to again come under the legal tutelage of his uncle, Philip Barton Key. His father's younger brother, the former Loyalist, now was one of the wealthiest and most influential men in the federal city. When his nephew and young family came to town, Philip Barton Key was spending less time running his lucrative law practice in the city and more on his farm in Montgomery County, Maryland, just north of Washington.

In 1805 Philip Barton had played a prominent role in a far-reaching political and constitutional legal event: the Senate impeachment trial of Supreme Court Justice Samuel Chase. The Jeffersonian Republican-controlled House of Representatives impeached Chase, a bombastic, outspoken Federalist, on charges involving his handling of two politically tinged cases. A sterling defense team that included Philip Barton Key won the day for Chase in the Senate, which could not muster the two-thirds majority vote needed to convict. Chase stayed on the bench. The Senate trial marked the last time in American history that Congress dealt with a "problem" Supreme Court justice through the impeachment process.

Philip Barton Key, who owned hundreds of acres of farmland in Montgomery County, decided to run for Congress in 1806. Thomas Jefferson, who had pushed for the Chase impeachment in an effort to rid the bench of Federalists and curb judicial powers, was in the third year of his first term in the White House. Nevertheless, Philip Barton Key won that election and served three terms in the House of Representatives, from March 4, 1807, to March 3, 1813.

Uncle Philip Barton Key had turned over his law practice to his young nephew, who ran it out of one wing of his big house on Bridge Street in Georgetown. It was a lucrative practice and it kept Francis Scott Key very busy. He and Polly also kept busy filling up their Georgetown house with more children. Francis Scott Key Jr. joined the family on October 7, 1806. The Keys would have eight more children in the next sixteen years.

Frank Key argued his first case before the U.S. Supreme Court in January 1807, serving as cocounsel for two young men—Justus Erick Bollman[25] and Samuel Swartwout. They had been charged with treason, arrested in New Orleans, and shipped to Washington, where they were jailed.

The Jefferson administration prosecuted Bollman and Swartwout for being part of an alleged conspiracy led by Aaron Burr, Thomas Jefferson's former bitter political rival who had served as his vice president. Burr allegedly had hatched his conspiracy in 1805 and 1806 as he traveled throughout the Ohio Valley. Reports circulated that he was lobbying the western states to secede from the Union and create a new empire or that he was recruiting men to form an army to attack Mexico or even to make war on the United States. None of the schemes came close to fruition.

Bollman, a medical doctor, and Swartwout, a close associate of Burr, were apprehended after delivering coded, allegedly treasonous messages for Burr. Francis Scott Key and his cocounsels (Charles Lee, a former U.S. attorney general; former Congressman Robert Goodloe Harper; and William H. Dorsey) argued that the young men had not committed treason and were being held illegally.

The court granted the legal team's request for a writ of habeas corpus in February 1807. In the case's next phase Key, Lee, and Harper argued that the government had acted too hastily in arresting their clients. Chief

Justice John Marshall agreed, ruling that the evidence was not sufficient to support a charge of treason.

Key had "addressed the court in the most impressive and eloquent manner," the *Washington Federalist* newspaper said of his Supreme Court performance on January 29.

"Is the executive of the United States gifted with the extraordinary powers of divination?" Key asked rhetorically. "Is his message to be reported to this court as an indisputable document as matter of facts? I hold up my hand against such a use of executive means. The president of the United States has no such right whatsoever.... The Constitution expressly declares that you are to arrest no man unless there be probable cause on oath or affirmation, and surely nothing can be shown in this communication which will appear to your honors as probable cause of treason against these two men."[26]

Francis Scott Key made a name for himself in that trial. A year later he played a pivotal role in another important trial that made national headlines: the expulsion of Senator John Smith of Ohio. Smith had been instrumental in lobbying for statehood for Ohio, and then became one of that state's first two senators when he took office on April 1, 1803.

The expulsion case, in which Key again joined Robert Goodloe Harper as defense cocounsel, had its origins in Smith's support of Aaron Burr's western adventures in 1805 and 1806. Smith, a Democratic-Republican who supported President Jefferson, nevertheless felt the wrath of the president when it came to light that he had provided supplies to Burr.

Smith became the first U.S. senator to be indicted when a court in Richmond, Virginia, brought charges against him in the summer of 1807 for being part of the Burr conspiracy. Those charges were dropped after the Marshall Supreme Court acquitted Burr himself in August. But Smith's legal troubles continued in November when the Senate investigated his conduct. On December 31, 1807, a Senate committee, chaired by future president John Quincy Adams, the Massachusetts Federalist, recommended that Smith be expelled because of his treasonous activities.

Smith hired Key and Harper in January of 1808. The two attorneys stood at Smith's side as the full Senate spent a week debating the charges against him. The moment of decision came on April 1, when the Senate, acting as a court, heard from witnesses and went over depositions. The defense team tried to discredit the witnesses against Smith, and also argued that the Senate did not have the authority to act as a court. The Senate voted nineteen to ten in favor of expelling Smith, falling short of the two-thirds majority needed to do so.

That was another legal victory for Francis Scott Key on the national stage. As for his client, however, John Smith's political stock plummeted in Washington and at home in Ohio, and he resigned his Senate seat on April 25, 1808.

After the Smith case, Francis Scott Key went back to his more mundane but busy legal practice handling primarily civil actions, many dealing with real estate, and to his growing family. Later in 1808, he returned to the Supreme Court, working as cocounsel with the Jefferson administration's attorney general, Caesar Augustus Rodney and William Lewis. The three attorneys represented the administration in *United States v. Peters*, a long-simmering civil action over the fate of the proceeds from the sale of a captured British ship in a case that dated back to 1778, a year before Key was born. Chief Justice Marshall ruled for the plaintiffs in that case.

Frank and Polly celebrated the birth of their fourth child, whom they named John Ross Key after his grandfather, on March 3, 1808. Soon thereafter, Polly Key took the baby and his three young siblings to her sister Maria West's house in The Woodyard, Maryland, just east of Washington.

Frank Key told his sister-in-law that he hoped the visit would "be useful and improving" to his wife. Polly, her husband said, "is too little accustomed to think seriously on any subject, particularly on the most serious of all subjects." Life's most serious subject in Frank Key's eyes: God's omnipotence—or as he put it, "the abundant offerings which Heaven has given us" [and] "the goodness that bestows them."[27]

From him, Key said, "she might think all this [is] preaching," but from Maria, "it would be more persuasive & agreeable & rendered more effectual by your example & the comfort & fascination which she will see you derive from it."

On a more down-to-earth level, Frank Key placed a classified ad in the *Washington Federalist* on May 2, 1809. Under the headline, "A Black & White Cow," the notice advised that the bovine "has been missing for a week. She is used to the common about the city, and most probably has had a Calf. Five dollars will be given to whoever will return her to F.S. Key."

3

NIL DESPERANDUM

Francis Scott Key's "whole life is spent in endeavoring to do good for his unhappy fellow-men."

—*John Randolph of Roanoke, 1821*[1]

Francis Scott Key purchased his first slave sometime in 1800 or 1801. By 1820, he owned five slaves. It was a natural thing to do for a man born into a world in which the ownership of slaves was a given. All of Key's American forebearers, beginning with his great grandfather Philip Key, owned slaves. His wife, Polly, grew up in one of the biggest slave-owning families in Maryland.

Yet, not unlike many other early nineteenth-century slave owners—Thomas Jefferson comes to mind—Francis Scott Key also believed that slavery was an evil institution. He often spoke vehemently against the slave trade, primarily at meetings of the American Colonization Society, which he helped form in 1816.

Like Jefferson—who owned several hundred slaves—Francis Scott Key's record on slavery is mixed. While Key freed a few of his slaves, he did not free them all. Soon after he set up legal shop in Georgetown, Francis Scott Key began representing slaves and freed African Americans in legal disputes, including civil actions in which slaves petitioned for their freedom.

On the other hand, Key also represented slave owners in legal fights to retain their runaway human property. In 1812, for example, Key defended Hezekiah Wood, whose slaves, John Davis and his siblings, had sued

for their freedom because their mother, Susan Davis, had won her freedom because her mother was a free white woman born in England. The
Supreme Court ruled in Key's client's favor.[2]

Still, Francis Scott Key had a deserved reputation as someone who
spoke out against the evils of slavery and offered his legal services gratis to slaves and former slaves. A newspaper editorial published after his
death noted that Key had been an early opponent of slavery: "So actively
hostile was he to the peculiar institution that he was called 'The Nigger
Lawyer.'... because he often volunteered to defend the downtrodden sons
and daughters of Africa. Mr. Key convinced me that slavery was wrong—
radically wrong."[3]

Key's first case on behalf of a slave petitioning for freedom came in
1810. He and cocounsel Thomas Swann represented a slave known in the
court records as Negro Ben. He had successfully filed a petition in the
Washington, D.C., Circuit Court in 1807, claiming his freedom from his
owner, Sabrett Scott, under a 1783 Maryland law that prohibited bringing
slaves into the state.

Scott appealed, and the case went before the Supreme Court in 1810.
Key and Swann lost the case when Chief Justice John Marshall cited a
provision in Maryland law that held that men or women who had been
enslaved for at least three years and brought to Maryland by their owners
with the intention of living in the state were exempt from the law.

In the summer of 1811 Frank Key took steps to free three of his young
enslaved children—although he attached strings to two of the cases. On
June 23, 1811, Key and Alexander McCormick, a Washington merchant,
who jointly owned a six-year-old girl named Kitty, went to the U.S. District
Court and signed a document setting her free. The reason: Kitty was "the
daughter of Henny, a free woman."[4]

On July 16, Key, in the presence of two witnesses, signed a document
manumitting "my Negro boy named James, two years old last April, and
Negro boy named Joe, about six months old." The document, however,
stipulated that James and Joe would not go free until they "attained the
age of 25 years."[5]

No letters have surfaced, nor has any other document, indicating why
Frank Key acted as he did.

It is well documented, however, that the young lawyer represented a
slave named Mima Queen, in a case similar to Negro Ben's. In a case that

went before the Supreme Court in 1813, Queen claimed she was entitled to her freedom because she was descended from a free black woman.[6]

As it did three years earlier, the Marshall court again ruled against Key and his enslaved client. This time the court found that the only evidence Queen offered amounted to inadmissible hearsay. Key argued that slaves had no recourse but to use hearsay evidence because they were not permitted to have access to traditional documents such as birth and death certificates.

Despite that setback, Key's reputation as a first-rate legal mind and as an accomplished and effective courtroom orator continued to rise through the early 1810s. Key "possesses that higher and nobler species of eloquence, which animates and impels the mind just as it pleases," a courtroom observer from Baltimore wrote in October 1811. "His quickness, his address, his powers of retort and insinuation, combined with an irresistible force of solid argumentation render him almost unrivaled, and certainly rank him among the most pleasing, chaste, able and classical speakers of the age in which we live."[7]

The young lawyer took a step toward becoming an engaged citizen of his community. In January 1808 F. S. Key (the appellation he began using around this time) was elected recorder and president of the Georgetown Board of Alderman, a position he would hold for many years.

Frank and Polly Key's fifth child, whom they named Ann Arnold, was born on March 2, 1811. In 1810, when Polly was pregnant, her thirty-one-year-old husband began to take a strong interest in public education, but not for his young children who received lessons at home and from tutors. Frank Key became very interested in bringing elementary school education to the masses in an era when the idea of state-supported education for children had yet to take hold throughout the young United States.

Key became an exponent of a new system of education developed by an eccentric, innovative Englishman named Joseph Lancaster (1778–1838). Lancaster started teaching poor children to read in his father's house in London when he was fifteen years old. The success of that rudimentary all-boys school, in which he and other older students mentored younger ones, led the young man to develop an elaborately detailed schooling plan that became known as the Lancaster system.

The first Lancaster school opened in London in 1803. Under the direction of one adult master, one older boy taught ten younger ones. The boys sat in rows of ten facing their older mentors in one large school room. They learned reading, writing, and arithmetic and received instruction "in the first principles of the Christian Religion."[8]

To cut costs, the students used slate and chalk instead of paper. Prizes went to students who did well. Although it was not unheard of for early nineteenth century schools to use various forms of corporal punishment for unruly students, the Lancaster system took a particularly hard line on discipline and obedience. The school's instruction manual called for badly behaved students to be pilloried, shackled, yoked, or even placed in cages suspended about the classroom, depending on the severity of the infraction.

Local jurisdictions and philanthropic individuals subsidized the low annual tuition costs for the poorest students. By 1810, Britain had ninety-five Lancaster schools with some thirty thousand students.

The Lancaster school movement came to the United States in 1806. That year, New York City Mayor DeWitt Clinton, a strong backer of public education, used city real estate tax revenues to underwrite a series of Lancaster schools open to boys and girls. Other Lancaster schools—or schools modeled on the concept—soon opened in Albany (New York), Boston, and Philadelphia.

In 1810 Francis Scott Key joined a group of other altruistic, civic-minded men in Georgetown to raise money to start a Lancaster school. Key and the other founding members of the Lancaster Society of Georgetown contributed their own funds and solicited support from the community. The fundraising worked. In June 1811 workers laid the cornerstone for the Lancaster School in the heart of Georgetown at 3126 O Street. The school opened on November 18.

It was "a plain, practical, useful, and Christian system of education," Key and the school's other trustees said in their January 1812 report, "offered to all our citizens...to all classes of society, equally beneficial to the wealthy, and accessible to the most indigent."[9]

An experienced Lancaster school teacher, Robert Ould, came from London to run the school. More than two hundred children enrolled that first year; a year later enrollment topped three hundred. Tuition was eight dollars a year, but free to those who couldn't afford it. The trustees decided to open the school to girls (in a separate building), making the Lancaster School of Georgetown the first public school in Washington, D.C., to do so. The school, which was for whites only, set aside times for African American students and their teachers to use the building. That marked the first time blacks were given access to public education in the nation's capital.

When Francis Scott Key believed in an idea, he was not shy about spreading the word. He envisioned a Lancaster school near Terra Rubra and tried to convince an acquaintance to spearhead the effort. "I have seen Mr. Landis & hope he will be able to make a Lancaster Teacher," Key wrote to his mother on April 21, 1813. "I think perhaps it would be best he should settle in Taney Town or Emmitsburg & suppose he could get a school at either of those places for fifty or sixty children. He could live there...cheaper than in Frederick Town & it would not cost so much to procure & prepare a suitable room."[10]

In the spring of 1813, as president of the Lancaster Society of Georgetown, Key gave speeches extolling the school's virtues in Virginia, Maryland, and Pennsylvania. In a November 27, 1813, letter he listed the ways he believed society's ills should be remedied. End political corruption, Key said. Repair "ruined churches," he continued, and "build Lancaster schools in every hundred."[11]

Frank Key met John Randolph of Roanoke—so-called to distinguish him from a string of other John Randolphs of Virginia—soon after the Keys moved to Georgetown in 1806. One of the most mercurial, brilliant, eccentric, and controversial politicians of the early republic, Randolph had been elected to Congress in 1799 at age twenty-five. He was born in Prince George County in Central Virginia, southeast of Petersburg. The appellation "Roanoke" came from the name of the sprawling plantation he owned in Charlotte County in south-central Virginia.

A child prodigy who studied Shakespeare and Greek and Roman classical literature with a private tutor as a boy, Randolph attended Princeton (then known as the College of New Jersey) and Columbia College in New York. He read law under his uncle Edmund Jennings Randolph, a former governor of Virginia who also had served as George Washington's attorney general and secretary of state.

John Randolph, an outspoken Jeffersonian Republican, was an ardent proponent of states' rights. He was known for his flamboyant oratorical powers, his temper (he challenged Daniel Webster to a duel in 1816, and fought a duel with Henry Clay in 1826), his bitter sarcasm delivered in a harsh, shrill voice, and his strange physical appearance. On more than one occasion during his long on-and-off career in the House (and later in the Senate), Randolph would enter the legislative chamber wearing boots and spurs, his hound dogs at his side, and a riding whip in hand.

John Randolph "was the strangest-looking being I ever beheld," the Baltimore novelist F. W. Thomas wrote. He had "long, thin legs, about as thick as a strong walking cane and of much such shape." His shoes "were old fashioned, and fastened with buckles—large ones." His "waist was remarkably slender." He had "long bony fingers."

His "complexion was precisely that of a mummy, withered, saffron, dry and bloodless"; his lips, thin and colorless; his beardless chin was broad for his small face.

Randolph's head also was small; his hair, fine and thin, worn very long and parted "with great care on the top of his head, tied behind with a black ribbon." His eye, "though sunken, was most brilliant and startling in its glance."[12] Randolph suffered from a variety of physical and emotional ailments throughout his life. Among other things, he had insomnia, chronic pain, frequent headaches, and bouts of severe melancholy.

In short, the flamboyant John Randolph, who never married, was an unlikely friend of staid family man Francis Scott Key. But the two men became very close, especially during some of Randolph's darkest days beginning in 1813. In April that year Randolph lost his House seat to John Wayles Eppes, a son-in-law of Thomas Jefferson, mainly because of Randolph's vociferous, intense opposition to American involvement in the war against England.[13]

Randolph, the bachelor, took great pleasure in visiting Frank and Polly Key and their growing brood of children in their Georgetown house. And Randolph often expressed his admiration for the father of the household.[14]

I know no man "more intrinsically estimable than Frank Key," Randolph wrote in a February 8, 1811, letter.[15] "He perseveres in pressing on towards the goal, and his whole life is spent in endeavoring to do good for his unhappy fellow-men," Randolph noted a few years later. "The result is that he enjoys a tranquility of mind, a sunshine of the soul, that all the Alexanders of the earth can neither confer nor take away."[16]

Key "is indeed as near perfection as our poor nature can go," Randolph said in an 1820 letter, "although he would be shocked to hear it said. Severe to himself, considerate and indulgent to others, speaking ill of none."[17]

Key felt a kinship to Randolph as well. They spent many hours together in Washington and Georgetown when Randolph was in town. And when they were apart, the two men exchanged often lengthy letters filled with personal, religious, and political words. In July of 1811, responding to a letter in which Randolph spoke of his latest series of maladies, Key wrote: "I am sorry for what you say about your health and spirits. I hope it is but a temporary depression of both. Do you make no summer excursion? It would most probably benefit you."[18]

John Randolph and Francis Scott Key both adamantly opposed the United States going to war with England. War hawks in Congress—led by Speaker of the House Henry Clay of Kentucky and firebrand John C. Calhoun of South Carolina—began pushing in 1810 to punish Great Britain in response to years of accumulating disputes over the former mother country's refusal to respect American sovereignty on the high seas. The main issue was the impressment of thousands of American sailors. The war hawks' aggressive answer for that perfidy: an American invasion of British-held Canada. It was a popular idea in the South.

"The acquisition of Canada this year, as far as the neighborhood of Quebec," Thomas Jefferson famously said early in August, "will be a mere matter of marching."[19]

Many in the North did not want war. They had relatively few allies among southerners; one of them, however, was John Randolph of Roanoke, who is credited with coining the term "war hawk" to disparage those thirsting for war.

If the United States went to war, Randolph said on the House floor on December 11, 1811, "it will not be for the protection of, or defense of…maritime rights." The acquisition of more farmland—what Randolph called "agrarian cupidity"—he thundered, "not maritime rights urges the war.…We have heard but one word—like the whip-poor-will, but one eternal monotonous tone—Canada! Canada! Canada!"[20]

As the drumbeat for war grew more insistent, Randolph's antiwar rhetoric rose accordingly. In a long May 30, 1812, letter to his constituents he railed against the French, who had been engaged in the Napoleonic Wars against England since 1803. A war with England, he wrote, was "comporting neither with the *interest* nor the *honor* of the American people; but as an idolatrous sacrifice of both on the altar of French *rapacity, perfidy* and *ambition*."

"I beseech you," Randolph implored his constituents, "put it to your own bosoms how far it becomes you as freemen, as Christians, to give your aid and sanction to this impious and bloody war against your brethren of the human family."[21]

Francis Scott Key called the conflict an "affliction" in a letter to Randolph on May 3, 1813. "'Nil desperandum' [never despair] has been my motto for the republic, though the unaccountable madness of these changing times has somewhat staggered me," he wrote. "I still say it is not to be despaired of. I have had as many melancholy forebodings as most people and I still think we must pass through great afflictions."[22]

Key wrote those words eleven months after the day that President James Madison had asked Congress for a declaration of war on June 1, 1812. After a heated, three-day debate, the House voted seventy-nine to forty-nine to ratify the request. On June 17, the Senate voted, nineteen to thirteen, to go to war. Madison signed the Declaration of War the following day, June 18, 1812.

Virtually every Federalist in Congress, including Francis Scott Key's uncle, Rep. Philip Barton Key of Maryland, voted against the war. John Randolph of Roanoke, who was no Federalist, sided with them, casting his vote against the resolution.

Three months earlier, in March 1812, Frank Key—a thirty-two year old father of five—decided he needed to make a will. "I wish to be prepared for death whenever it may please God to order it," Key wrote to his wife, Polly, on March 20.

"My Dear," he said, "you are the only parent of your children. You are called upon by your situation to be doubly a parent to them. If you discharge your duty in so difficult a state, remember it must be not by your own strength, but by God's assistance. You must live frugally and deny yourself many things you have been used to."

He advised his wife to "get a small, cheap place, wherever you prefer living, and bring our children up in honest industry. Do not be ashamed, nor let any of them be ashamed, to labour. Accustom them to none of the follies or vanities of life. Teach them their religious duties. Have prayers night and morning, and let not your Bible be neglected."[23]

We do not know how Polly Key responded to her husband's advice.

In the spring and summer of 1812 feelings about the war ran high on both sides of the issue in many parts of the country. The most visible manifestation of the divisiveness erupted in Baltimore on June 22, when a mob ransacked and destroyed the offices of the *Federal Republican* newspaper to protest the vehemently antiwar editorials by its founder and editor Alexander Contee Hanson Jr. Hanson fled to Georgetown, where he continued to publish his inflammatory anti-Madison-and-Jefferson paper.

Hanson returned to Baltimore on July 26 with a group of supporters that included the famed Revolutionary War general Henry "Lighthorse Harry" Lee and close Key family friend James Lingan, a prominent, prosperous citizen of Georgetown who held the rank of brigadier general in the Maryland State Militia. A mob attacked the newspaper's new offices. The Federalists fired from their barricaded building, killing one protester.

At that point, the local militia escorted Hanson and company to the Baltimore jail for their protection. The next day, July 27, 1812, the mob stormed the jail and attacked the men with clubs, rocks, and knives. Lingan, sixty-one, was beaten to death. Hanson, Lee, and the others— severely beaten—luckily escaped with their lives.

Francis Scott Key joined other prominent citizens at a town meeting at the Union Tavern in Georgetown on August 7 to express their shock about the mob violence. The meeting took place, a newspaper reported, "for the purpose of expressing their sense of the outrage recently committed in Baltimore, and declaring to the world their testimonies to the virtues and worth of General Lingan."[24] When it came time to choose an orator for a planned memorial service for Lingan, the group called upon Georgetown's most accomplished public speaker, Francis Scott Key.[25]

The conflict sometimes known as the Second American Revolution began on July 12, 1812, when American forces under General William Hull invaded Upper Canada. The first casualties came four days later when two British soldiers died in a skirmish at Canard River in Ontario, followed by a series of American reverses. On July 17, British forces, with the help of Native American fighters, overran Fort Mackinac, an island fortress off the coast of northern Michigan, in the first battle of the war fought on American soil.

On August 5, at the Battle of Brownstone south of Detroit, the famed Shawnee Indian chief Tecumseh routed an American force. Ten days later came the Fort Dearborn Massacre, after which American troops abandoned the fort on the Chicago River in the Illinois Territory and a band of Potawatomi Indians burned the fort to the ground. The next day, August 16, 1812, Hull surrendered Detroit without a fight, and the British took control of the entire territory of Michigan. Less than two months later, on October 13, came another stunning defeat when American forces under General Winfield Scott surrendered to the British following a humiliating defeat at the Battle of Queenston Heights in Ontario along the Niagara frontier.

The war cost John Randolph his seat in Congress, albeit only for one term. He departed Washington in April 1813 in a huff. In his rooming house he left behind, as he put it in a letter to Key, "books, letters, papers &c., in (and out of) an open trunk; also a gun, flask, shot-belt, &c."[26] He asked his good friend to take charge of his possessions, which Key did.

In that same letter, Randolph said that of the "few regrets" he had at his "dismissal from public life," none compared with "the reflection that it has separated me—perhaps forever—from some who have a strong hold on my esteem and my affections." He listed Frank Key among that small group.

Back home at his plantation in Charlotte County, Virginia, Randolph wrote a stream of letters to his friends, Frank Key among them, lamenting what he saw as a useless, disastrous war. He told Key that his letters helped him cope with the loss of his House seat. On May 22, 1813, for example, Randolph wrote that he read the "nil desperandum" letter "again and again, and cannot express to you how much pleasure the perusal has given me."[27]

He wrote to Key the next day, ending the letter with: "I fervently hope that we may meet again. I do not wish you so ill as to see you banished to [Roanoke]; and yet to see you here would give me exceeding great pleasure."[28]

As the War of 1812 dragged on through the spring and summer of 1813, the normally even-tempered Francis Scott Key agonized over its impact on his life. That included a close call after a family visit to Annapolis.

"I supposed you have heard very alarming accounts of the safety of Annapolis," Key wrote to his mother from Georgetown on April 21. You "will be glad to find we have made a...retreat, as we were in sight of the enemy."[29]

In a letter on May 14, 1813, not long after American troops burned the city of York (now Toronto) in Canada, Key wrote to Randolph: "We have been in a state of alarm here for the last three or four days, having reason to believe the British were coming up our river. Today we hear they have passed on down the Bay."

Key went on to say that he saw "nothing which promises better times. The Democrats do not wish for peace, & the Federalists (or a great many of them) will not let the administration make peace if they can help it— preferring anything to the adoption of such measures as should give popularity to their opponents."

Key then told Randolph that he was trying to bear up, but was having trouble. "I feel tolerable ease about it, yet…I cannot live without business, there is none here now, and the Courts in Maryland will be closed. I shall probably go into the Country, if this state of things continues, or turn Lancaster school master or whatever may offer.

"I begin to fancy," the thirty-three-year old lawyer said, "I should like retirement or a change of some sort."[30]

Key, who often disparaged the disingenuousness and pettiness of party politics, considered running for office. He wrote to Randolph from Georgetown late in August, saying that he was "half inclined to turn politician." He felt the urge, Key said, "but the fit is over. I shall, I hope, stay quietly here, and mind my business as long as [the war] lasts." Key pondered what, if any, changes he would make if the war lasted much longer.

The young lawyer, two days away from his thirty-fourth birthday, turned philosophical. "I believe," he wrote, "that a man who does not follow his own inclinations, and choose his own ways, but is willing to do whatever may be appointed for him, will have his path of life chosen for him and shown to him."[31]

On September 26, 1813, Polly Key gave birth to her sixth child, a boy they called Edward Lloyd Key. A few days later, the proud father conveyed the news to his bosom buddy in Virginia.

"My dear Sir," Key wrote to John Randolph, "T'was thinking of your gun a few days before I received your letter, and determined to rub off some of your rust, and try if I could kill Mrs. Key a bird or two. She has just given me another son, and of course deserves this piece of courtesy."[32]

4

PIETY AND PATRIOTISM

All the "the vicissitudes of human affairs...are ordered and controlled by the Almighty Governor of the world."
—*Francis Scott Key, February 22, 1814*

Francis Scott Key wrote two letters on November 27, 1813, from his home in Georgetown. One went to John Randolph. In it, Key decried partisan state politics in Maryland and the quality of life in general in the early republic. "I agree exactly with you," Key told Randolph, "that 'the state of society is radically vicious.'"[1]

Key also wrote to his fifty-nine-year-old father, John Ross Key, back home at Terra Rubra. He reported that he and a business partner had just bought thirty-one acres of vacant land a mile from his house in Georgetown for forty cents an acre. Key said he planned to grow timothy hay there and asked his father to supply him with the seed. Key then mused about leaving Washington because of the war's impact on his law practice. "When I think of the trouble the British will most likely give us next Spring, & the consequent stoppage of my business & the expense of my family being here while I am getting nothing to support them, I feel much tempted to get into the Country."

Key told his father that he didn't know what to do. But, the pious lawyer said he would "submit to what Providence may order for us," and would stay at his "present post till I think I can see clearly that it is my duty to change it. I have sometimes thought I might be justified in giving up my prospects here & removing to Pipe Creek till we could see what would grow out of the war; this I should like better than any other change.... Perhaps it is better to wait another year before taking so decided & important a step, but it does not seem to me improbable that by that time the necessity of the times will justify it."[2]

Key went on to tell his father that Polly had taken their six young children (aged ten to two months) to Bladensburg, Maryland, northeast of Washington, to stay with friends while he readied the house on Bridge Street for winter. "We get no coal," he said, "and I fear [the price of] wood will be very high."

The end of the letter contained a matter-of-fact description of a transaction Frank Key had just made in Montgomery County, Maryland, just north of Washington.

"I bought," he told his father, "an old woman and a little girl about 12 or 18 years old. I know but little of them. The girl is used to housework and the old woman chiefly to plantation work. If [Key's mother] will run the risk of trying whether they would be serviceable, I will send them to her by the first wagon after I hear from her. I can send them to [his sister] Anne [in Frederick] almost every day . . . and you could get them from Fred Town."

Key did send the two women to his mother and father. A month later, he hadn't heard anything from Terra Rubra about how things were working out with the new enslaved arrivals. "I long," Key wrote to his mother on December 27, "to hear how you like the old woman and the girl."[3]

As Randolph and others had predicted, the American attempt to invade Canada proved disastrous. American forces suffered two big setbacks in late October and early November of 1813 that ended all thoughts of taking Montreal.

In the Battle of Châteauguay, fought along the river of the same name near Montreal on October 25–26, American General Wade Hampton's three thousand troops could not overcome a much smaller British force. At the November 11, 1813, Battle of Crysler's Farm, along the north bank of the St. Lawrence River in Ontario, the Americans once again lost to a smaller number of British troops, this time aided by Canadians and their Mohawk allies.

Francis Scott Key was not unhappy by that turn of events. "The people of Montreal will enjoy their firesides for this, and I trust, for many a winter," he wrote to John Randolph early in December. "This I suppose is treason,

but, as your Patrick Henry said, 'If it be treason, I glory in the name of traitor.' I have never thought of those poor creatures without being reconciled
to any disgrace or defeat of our arms!"[4]

There was some positive war news for the Americans in the fall of 1813.
On September 10 Commander Oliver Hazard Perry prevailed against the
British at Battle of Lake Erie, after which Perry famously said: "We have
met the enemy and they are ours." And on September 29, General William
Henry Harrison reclaimed Detroit. Less than a week later, on October 5,
1813, Harrison led 3,500 American troops to a victory over the British and
their Shawnee allies at Moraviantown in Ontario, during which Tecumseh
died on the field of battle.

The war effort, however, ended on a sour note for the Americans as
1813 came to a close. On December 10, American troops evacuated Fort
George in Ontario. On December 19, British troops and their Canadian
militia and Indian allies crossed into the United States and captured Fort
Niagara in New York.

That war news did nothing to lift Francis Scott Key's spirits. He once
again considered leaving Washington and staying at Terra Rubra. "I really
think I shall try to purchase a small flock of sheep in the Spring, & if the
war lasts...I can come up to Pipe Creek and be a shepherd," Key wrote to
his mother on January 2, 1814.

Key said that he had not made up his mind, though, and for the time
being would stay in Georgetown, "and mind my business for as long as
I can. I hope whatever change may be necessary I may be ready for it. The
expenses of living here are enormous...."

Some people, Key said, "Expect peace, but I confess I do not."[5]

As it turned out, during the first few months of 1814 things were relatively
quiet on the war front. In Georgetown, Francis Scott Key turned his attention to other matters.

On December 27, 1813, he had played a role in averting a duel between
two members of Congress, the hot-headed John C. Calhoun of South
Carolina and Thomas Peabody Grosvenor, a Federalist from New York.
Grosvenor had challenged Calhoun to a duel and crossed the Potomac
that morning to wait for his rival. But a group of friends "accommodated
the business that morning," a contemporary newspaper account reported,
"so that no blood has been spilled."[6] A newspaper correspondent later

reported that Francis Scott Key "exerted himself with success to prevent" the "contemplated duel between Mr. Calhoun and Mr. Grosvenor."[7]

During the holiday season Key concerned himself a great deal with religious matters. On January 17, 2014 he arrived at a church in Washington for a meeting to help organize the Bible Society for the District of Columbia. The society's goal: to provide Bibles and biblical teachings to all Americans. Before the evening ended, Key was among twenty-one men chosen to be managers of the society; he became a leader of the group for many years.

Two years after the founding of the Bible Society in Washington, a nationwide group dedicated to the same mission set up shop in New York City. The American Bible Society, which began 1816, still exists. Francis Scott Key, not surprisingly, was an early adherent of the larger organization. He served as its vice president and remained a strong supporter of the ABS until the day he died in 1843.

Key's piety and patriotism were next on public display on February 22, 1814, when he gave what one newspaper called "an elegant and very interesting discourse" at the Washington Society of Alexandria's annual birthday tribute to George Washington.[8] He spoke at the Old Presbyterian Meeting House in Old Town Alexandria, Virginia, just down the Potomac River from Washington. The thirty-four-year-old lawyer, sounding at times like a patriotic fundamentalist preacher, offered flowery words of exaltation for George Washington, then went on to offer his prescription for the future of American society.

Calling Washington "your hero, your patriot, the deliverer and the Father of his country," Key marveled that at the "mere utterance" of Washington's name, it is "as if a magic spell had been pronounced," and the "tide of transport rushes from every heart and throbs through every vein of all who hear it."[9]

Key's main theme was the prescience of Washington's famed Farewell Address of 1796. Key hammered away primarily on his interpretation of Washington's belief in the importance of religion and morality and how both should be ingrained into the American brand of democratic government. "In all our national deliverances we see [Washington] ascribing all the glory to their true and Almighty Cause," Key orated, "and calling upon his countrymen to acknowledge and praise the power that defended them."

Key said that piety and patriotism held special importance during the current "dark and evil times" that he characterized as the "gloom of present distress, [and] the still more awful anticipation of approaching calamity."

A few days after delivering that preachy speech, Key wrote one of his many letters to his confidante John Randolph in Virginia. In it, the young lawyer seemed not to be uplifted by his Washington's Birthday speech. In fact, he sounded weary and depressed.

"I am always hurried and yet I do nothing," Key wrote to Randolph. "Besides what is properly called business, I had a thousand other concerns which some people get through without troubles, but which embarrass me because I am a wretched manager of time and everything else. I believe it is in some measure owing to my being always in a hurry and trying to do more than I can."[10]

The war went on. But Frank Key did not leave Washington. He plied his profession when he could, doing legal work on several real estate transactions.

To add to his financial woes, Key went into debt to help bail out his father. John Ross Key—not the best businessman in Frederick County—had mortgaged a hefty portion of Terra Rubra, where Frank and his sister had grown up in carefree splendor. In 1807 the note holder—identified in court documents as Ann Ogle—foreclosed on the property. An auction took place in August 1811.

Frank Key stepped up and bought the 713 acres in question and took control of Terra Rubra. The closing took place on December 17, 1813. The price: $8,500. Key paid $3,500 in cash and took out a mortgage for $5,000 with his rich uncle Philip Barton Key.

That debt proved to be a big burden on the financially struggling lawyer and his family. Although Polly Key's well-off family easily could have afforded to help, there is no evidence that the Lloyds gave or loaned any money to their daughter and son-in-law.

"I have been obliged to contract (not on account of any concern of my own) a very considerable debt," Key wrote in an April 4 letter. "I do not see how I can extricate myself from my engagements."[11]

Key wrote that letter to Reverend Dr. James Kemp, the rector of St. Paul's Protestant Episcopal Church in Baltimore. The young lawyer had begun taking an active role in Episcopal Church affairs after moving to Georgetown. He became a founding member of St. John's Episcopal Church at 32nd and O Streets in Georgetown and seriously considered giving up the law and entering the ministry.

The April 4 letter came in response to an offer that Kemp had made to Key to become his assistant rector at St. Paul's. Key declined, mainly because he felt he couldn't earn enough money to support his family. "When I thought a few years ago of preparing myself for the ministry," he wrote, "it seemed to me...that I was peculiarly situated, & had entered, almost necessarily, into engagements that made such a step impossible."

Years earlier, after deciding not to go into the priesthood the first time, Key said, he left open the possibility "that if the path of duty would lead me to this change of life, I should be enabled to see it, & that my present course should be stopped if I could serve good more acceptably in the ministry." But he did not see himself on that path in the spring of 1814. "That I could support my family upon the terms you have mentioned I think probable," Key said. "But I should find it difficult (if not impossible) to do more; and to do more I seem to be necessarily bound."

That was the end of Francis Scott Key's agonizing over leaving the law behind for the ministry. However, that was by no means the end of his church work. Until the day he died, Key took an active role in a wide range of parish church activities at three Episcopal churches: St. John's and Christ Church in Georgetown and Trinity Church in Washington. He taught Sunday school. He visited the sick in hospitals. He counseled prisoners in jails. On at least one occasion, in 1818, he baptized an infant after the child's parents knocked on his door late one night pleading with him to do so because they believed the child was dying.

He regularly attended Episcopal General Conventions and was one of five lay trustees of the Maryland General Theological Seminary from its founding in 1820 until his death in 1843. He also was a founder of the Virginia Theological Seminary in Alexandria and a strong supporter of the Episcopal Church's Domestic and Foreign Missionary Society.

The War of 1812 took on a new complexion in the spring of 1814 after Napoleon's defeat in Europe, a situation that freed up large numbers of British troops to cross the Atlantic and join the fight against the Americans.

A British maritime squadron under the command of Rear Admiral George Cockburn had arrived in the Chesapeake Bay in February 1813. Cockburn immediately set up a blockade at Virginia Beach to stop the shipment of goods in and out of Virginia, and to muzzle the movements of American naval vessels. For the next eighteen months, the British mounted raiding parties on cities and towns up and down the Chesapeake Bay in Virginia and Maryland, confiscating ships, livestock, and tobacco, and torching houses when they ran into citizen and militia opposition.

Not long after the British ships had arrived in the Chesapeake, in March 1813, enslaved people in Virginia—who knew that the British had abolished slavery in 1805—found their way to the blockade vessels, where Royal Navy officers welcomed them. By the summer of 1814, hundreds of former slaves had joined the British military in the fight against the country of their former masters, serving as guides, soldiers, and sailors.

On April 2, 1814, Vice Admiral Sir Alexander Cochrane, the commander of the English fleet, issued a proclamation officially welcoming fleeing slaves. The proclamation gave notice "that all those who may be disposed to emigrate from the United States, will, with their families, be received on board of his majesty's ships or vessels of war.... Those former slaves, Cochrane said, would be given the choice of joining the British military as sailors or marines, or "being sent as free settlers to the British possessions in North American or the West Indies."[12]

Early in June a New York newspaper reported from the Chesapeake that the British had "about 80 negroes of both sexes on Kent Island. The men are regularly trained to the musket."[13] Thousands of former slaves took advantage of the British offer before the war ended. That situation did not—to say the least—please slave-owning Americans.

The intensifying British raids during the spring and summer of 1814 in their home states caused John Randolph and Francis Scott Key to do an about-face on their feelings about the war. Both men volunteered for the fight and both served in uniformed militias, albeit only for a matter of weeks.

Randolph did not join until after he learned that the British burned Washington on August 24. He promptly rode to Richmond where Virginia Governor James Barbour swore him into the state militia. Randolph never saw action in the war, though. He served for several weeks on mounted guard duty at Camp Fairfield, a temporary Virginia militia encampment about a mile northeast of Richmond.

Francis Scott Key had brief stints with a field artillery militia unit formed by his Georgetown friend and neighbor George Peter, an Army veteran who in 1808 had organized and led the U.S. military's first light artillery battery. In July 1813, with the British wreaking havoc up and down the Chesapeake, Key signed on as an enlisted man, a matross or gunner's mate. The young lawyer lasted just twelve days before he decided that the military life was not for him.[14]

Key rejoined the Georgetown Artillery nine months later, this time as a quartermaster, an officer's rank. On June 15, 1814, Key and the rest of Peter's men marched sixty miles from Georgetown to Benedict at the mouth of the Patuxent River in Southern Maryland. A few days before Key's unit arrived, other American troops had fought off a British raiding party.

Peter's men were ordered "to descend the Patuxent to quiet the fears of the inhabitants, and to check on the incursions of the enemy," one observer wrote.[15] The British, Key wrote to his mother on June 23, "have now gone down the river & nobody seems to think there is any chance of their coming back again...[with] the troops in the neighborhood." The enemy, Key said, "have driven everybody from their homes here and though the houses are not burnt, they might almost well have been. They are torn to pieces inside & out. The Militia here behaved on Monday remarkably well, and stood a very dense cannonade for some time and made their retreat in very good order."[16]

Key told his mother that life in the camp was tolerable. "I have a more comfortable time of it than I expected," he said. "It is a troublesome place, but [being an officer is] better than living in the ranks."

Part of Frank Key's troubles included being knocked off his horse and tumbling into the river. "Of 'moving accidents by flood and field,'" the erudite lawyer wrote to John Randolph, quoting from *Othello*, I have only to tell of being knocked down by a bone of bacon and pitched by my horse over head and ears into the river." That is "quite as much as I wish to know of the wars."[17]

George Peter's artillery unit demobilized soon after Key wrote that letter, and the men marched back to Georgetown. Frank Key's short tour of quartermaster duty ended on July 1. For all of July the Key family—along with the other residents of Georgetown and Washington—anxiously awaited the British military's next move.

The news that came during the third week of August was ominous. Major General Robert Ross had landed in Benedict, Maryland, with some 4,100 battle-hardened British Army regulars and Royal Marines from France by way of Bermuda. The British force also included a fleet of warships under Vice Admiral Cochrane. That small armada had entered the Chesapeake Bay on August 16. Three days later, Ross landed with his troops at Benedict. He then began the sixty-mile march toward the nation's capital.

Sometime early in August, Frank and Polly Key had sent their six young children to Frederick to stay with his parents at Terra Rubra. His father, John Ross Key, also invited his sister Elizabeth Scott Key Maynadier and her family who lived in Annapolis to come to Pike Creek to escape what appeared to an imminent British attack on the Maryland capital. The Maynadiers stayed put in Annapolis, but not without reservations.

There is "great panic here," Elizabeth Maynadier wrote to her sister-in-law Anne Key on August 19. "The inhabitants here are much disturbed & seemed now to be called on to decide whether or not they will stand still & wait the issue or whether they will endeavor to seek more safety."[18]

According to Frank Key's brother-in-law, Roger B. Taney, Polly wanted to stay with her husband in Georgetown. "Mrs. Key," Taney wrote four decades later, "refused to leave home while Mr. Key was thus daily exposed to danger."[19]

Everyone believed "that an attack would probably be made on George Town," Taney said, and "we became very anxious about the situation of his family. For if the attack was made, Mr. Key would be with the troops engaged in the defence; and as it was impossible to foresee what would be the issue of the conflict, his family, by remaining in George Town, might be placed in great and useless peril."

The Keys ultimately agreed on a compromise; Polly would stay with friends in Middlebrook, in present-day Gaithersburg, Maryland, about half way between Frederick and Georgetown. The Keys arrived in Middlebrook on August 22.

"Polly will stay here for a few days till she hears what is likely to take place," Key wrote to his mother that day. He went on to tell her that he had obtained two wagons to take his "papers & other things" from Georgetown to Frederick the next morning.

"We hear a great many different accounts of the operations & force of the enemy," he wrote. "I beg you will mind nothing that you hear, till you hear it two or three times & from known authority."

Frank Key told his mother he believed that the British were after Barney's Flotilla, a small squadron of barges and gunboats that had been harassing them in the Chesapeake Bay since June under the command of Revolutionary War naval hero Joshua Barney. What Key didn't know was that Cochrane had forced Barney and some four hundred of his men to scuttle their entire fleet on the shoals of the Patuxent River just beyond Pig's Point, Maryland, that very day.

It also was possible, Key said, that the British were after Fort Washington (then commonly called Fort Warburton) on the Potomac south of Washington, and that "the city will not be their first object." If "this is the case," Key said, "and they allow us time, they will, I trust, be too late."

Key pinned his hopes on General William Henry Winder, who had been captured by the British earlier in the war and paroled, and who now commanded the American ground forces in Washington. Key had heard that Winder, "expects to have 15,000 [troops] by tomorrow. His present force is stated at 8 or 9,000 but it is probably not so great." The British, he said, "are said to have landed 6,000 but it is mere conjecture."

He ended the letter, as he tended to do, with spiritual words: "May we commit ourselves to our Heavenly Father who never will forsake those who trust in him!"[20]

5

A CITIZEN OF THE HIGHEST RESPECTABILITY

"I hope I may succeed though it is uncertain."
—*Francis Scott Key to his father, September 2, 1814*

The August 24, 1814, Battle of Bladensburg will not go down as one of the American military's finest hours. In fact, the short intense, early afternoon engagement, in which American troops outnumbered their British foe some six thousand to four thousand, soon became a disastrous rout that led to an inglorious episode in American history: the burning and looting of the nation's capital as President James Madison, his Cabinet, and members of Congress fled into Maryland and Virginia.

The fight began at around one o'clock on that extremely hot late August afternoon as thousands of British troops marched six abreast through the Maryland woods, then faced off against the Americans perched on small hills on the west side of what was then known as the Eastern Branch of the Potomac River (now called the Anacostia River) overlooking the small town of Bladensburg.

The heat, bearable in the morning, turned brutal as noontime neared and the temperature and humidity soared. As the British marched into battle, the sun "beat on us full force," Lieutenant George R. Gleig later wrote. The dust rose "in thick masses from under our feet, without a breath of air to disperse it, [flying] directly into our faces, occasioning the greatest inconvenience both to the eyes and respiration."[1]

Earlier that day General William H. Winder had held an emergency council of war with President Madison, Secretary of War John Armstrong, and Secretary of State James Monroe. The four men arrived in the village of Bladensburg just before noon to reconnoiter. In the chaos that soon followed, Madison, Armstrong, and Monroe (who had served with George Washington in the American Revolution) hastily rode the four miles back into Washington and then fled the city. Most historians believe President Madison left before the fighting began.[2]

All but about five hundred of the American troops Winder had at his disposal at Bladensburg were inexperienced militiamen. They were "sufficiently armed, but wretchedly equipped," Gleig reported, "clothed part in black coats, others in blue, others in ordinary shooting-jackets, and some in round frocks." The "motley" American assemblage, Gleig said, "seemed country people, who would have been much more appropriately employed in attending to their agricultural occupations than in standing, with muskets in their hands, on the brow of a bare green hill."[3]

Those militiamen were no match for the veteran, disciplined British troops. Except for Joshua Barney's men who joined the fray at virtually the last minute and fought courageously and well, and a battery or two of artillery, the American force put up scant resistance, and the battle lasted only about an hour. With "the exception of a party of sailors from the gun boats under the command of Commodore Barney," Gleig said, "no troops could behave worse than [the American militiamen] did."

Barney's four hundred sailors and marines had quick-marched some six miles to Bladensburg in the August heat, carrying their cannons and other weapons by hand. The flotilla-men battled the British but succumbed to superior numbers. Barney himself had his horse shot dead from under him and then took a musket ball in the thigh.

"The enemy," his daughter-in-law later wrote, "had nearly surrounded him. His men, who had been marching continually for three days, without regular rest or supply of provisions, were beginning to be exhausted and wearied and he was himself scarcely able to hold up his head."[4] Overwhelmed, Barney ordered a retreat and then collapsed. He later surrendered personally to Major General Robert Ross and Rear Admiral George Cockburn.

As for the other American fighters, Gleig wrote, they "were driven in as soon as attacked, the first line gave way without offering the slightest resistances, and the left of the main body was broken within half an hour after it was seriously engaged."[5]

The British actually had more casualties than the Americans— probably 64 killed in action and 185 wounded, versus not more than 26 Americans killed, about 50 wounded and some 100 captured.[6] The reason for the disparity: Virtually all the American militiamen rapidly fled the field of battle as the tide began to turn—one reason why some later disparagingly referred to the engagement as the Bladensburg Races.

One of the few other American units that performed creditably at Bladensburg was George Peter's Georgetown Artillery. That outfit's former quartermaster, Frank Key, however, did not fight with them on August 24. Key came to Bladensburg this time as a volunteer aide to General Walter Smith, the commander of the First Columbian Brigade, a reserve force made up of militiamen from Georgetown and Washington. Smith most likely had asked his fellow Georgetown resident to accompany him because Key had some knowledge of the terrain at Bladensburg since he and his family had regularly visited friends there.

Key rode through the fog of battle, at one point relaying tactical advice from General Smith to General Winder. "Mr. Francis Key, of Georgetown," Winder later reported, "informed me that he had thought that the troops coming from the city could be most advantageously posted on the right and left of the road."[7]

Another report had it that Key tried to give tactical advice to Major George Peter.[8] The lawyer allegedly told the artilleryman that he should set up his guns on a particular high bluff. But Peter saw that the position was not ideal and ignored Frank Key's advice. Two months later Key wrote to Peter, saying that he acted only because General Smith ordered him to and that he did not recall telling Peter that he should chose one position over another.[9]

That was the extent of Frank Key's involvement in the Battle of Bladensburg. The young lawyer left the battlefield in ignominious defeat along with his fellow Americans. He headed back to Georgetown in shock. For "two or three days after our disgrace I had neither time or mind to do anything," Key wrote to his mother on September 2.[10] The "disgrace" Key mentioned also included what the British did after defeating the Americans at Bladensburg.

General Ross gave his exhausted troops a short break from the intense heat right after the battle. But by midafternoon, he marched them into the undefended and virtually uninhabited nation's capital. That day and night and into the next day the British burned as many federal buildings as they could, including the Capitol, the President's House, the small national library, and the State, War, and Treasury Department buildings.

Just hours before the British troops marched into the city, as cannons boomed in the distance, President Madison's wife Dolley supervised a chaotic packing of her husband's Cabinet papers, along with the household's silverware, china, books, clocks, and other items. She also helped save the famed full-length portrait of George Washington by Gilbert Stuart, which was in a large frame bolted to a wall.

As Paul Jennings, a fifteen-year-old Madison slave, labored to unscrew the frame, White House steward Jean "French John" Sioussat reportedly cut the painting from the frame to save time. Two friends of the Madison family, Jacob Marker and Robert DePeyster, then packed the portrait in their wagon and spirited it out of town.

In the days before the British attack Secretary of State Monroe had ridden out to Benedict to see for himself what the British were up to. When he discovered the extent of the British force, Monroe wrote a note directing his staff to safeguard the nation's most important papers. That task fell to Stephen Pleasanton, a State Department clerk. Pleasanton and several fellow clerks dutifully gathered up international treaties, the papers of George Washington, and other documents, and stowed them inside jerry-rigged linen carrying cases. That took several days.

Then, on August 24, with the British entering the city, Pleasanton thought to add the original Declaration of Independence and the Constitution to the lot. He and his fellow clerks loaded those national treasures onto carts with the other documents and took them into Virginia for safe-keeping. The precious cargo wound up safely stored in a house in Loudoun County, some thirty-five miles west of Washington.

It is believed they were hidden in the basement of Rokeby House outside Leesburg. That privately owned home, which was built around 1765, today includes a shrine in the basement honoring the spot where the Declaration of Independence, the Constitution, and the other documents were safely stored.

Dolley Madison herself escaped just before the British arrived. At around three o'clock, Paul Jennings wrote in his memoir, "James Smith, a free colored man who had accompanied Mr. Madison to Bladensburg, galloped up to the [White] house, waving his hat, and cried out, 'Clear out, clear out! General Armstrong has ordered a retreat!' All then was confusion."[11]

The President's wife described what came next. "And now, dear sister, I must leave this house, or the retreating army will make me a prisoner in it by filling up the road I am directed to take," she wrote to one of her sisters. "When I shall again write to you, or where I shall be tomorrow, I cannot tell!"[12]

Soon after Dolley Madison wrote those words, scores of British troops stormed the house, smashed all the windows, stole everything that wasn't nailed down, and torched the place.

"I had no objection to burn arsenals, dockyards, frigates building, stores, barracks, etc., but well do I recollect that fresh from the Duke [of Wellington's] humane warfare in the South of France, we were horrified at the order to burn the elegant Houses of Parliament [Congress] and the President's house," British Captain Harry Smith, Ross's junior adjutant, later wrote in his autobiography.[13]

He would never forget, Smith said, "the destructive majesty of the flames as the torches were applied to the beds, curtains, etc." The flames of the burning President's house and the other federal buildings flew so high into the sky that they could be seen in Baltimore, some thirty-five miles to the north.

The conflagration ended only when a huge thunderstorm with gale-force winds blew in. It was "a regular hurricane," Smith remembered. "It did not last more than twenty minutes, but it was accompanied by a deluge of rain and such a gale that it blew down all our piles of arms and blew the drums out of camp. I never witnessed such a scene as I saw for a few minutes.... We learnt that even in the river, sheltered by the woods, several of our ships at anchor had been cast on their beam ends."

The British—who never intended to occupy Washington—left town and marched back to Benedict, Maryland. They had been in the city for twenty-six hours. General Robert Ross and Admiral George Cochrane decided their next move would be to destroy the city of Baltimore.

The British did not burn any private residences in Washington, and they did not venture into Georgetown. "Not one Englishman has been in this town," Georgetown resident Francis Dodge wrote to his wife at midnight on August 26. "They have burnt all public property in the city. It was a dreadful sight.... I hope they will not return here again and can't think they will.... The town was very quiet last night and I got a good sleep for the first time."[14]

The quiet after the British departure gave Francis Scott Key the opportunity to recover from his post-Bladensburg funk. He had several things on his mind. First, he wanted to get Polly to Frederick to reunite her with the children. His brother-in-law, Roger B. Taney, arrived the day after the British left Washington and promptly took Polly to Maryland.

Second, Frank Key continued to obsess about his finances. "I owe more money [to the] Bank here now than I ought," Key wrote to his father on September 2, and "in these distressing times I really know not what I shall do to provide for the necessities of my family." He advised his father at Terra Rubra to "sell something even at a Sacrifice to raise what you want, & then avoid incurring on any account any new debt." Key saw "no hope of peace," he told his father, "and as the war lasts [money worries] & every thing else will be getting worse."[15]

Another thing on Francis Scott Key's mind early in September had to do with a delicate mission he had been asked to perform by President James Madison. It involved a longtime Key family friend, Dr. William Beanes, a prominent physician, landowner, and businessman. Beanes "was the leading physician in Upper Marlboro [Maryland], and an accomplished scholar and gentleman," Taney later wrote. "He was highly respected by all who knew him...and the intimate friend of Mr. Key. He occupied one of the handsomest houses in Upper Marlboro, and lived very handsomely."[16]

On August 27, before all the British troops had made their way aboard ships at Benedict bound for Baltimore, a group of them broke off from the main force and raided several farms in Maryland, including one owned by Dr. Beanes, who had served as a surgeon in the American Revolution. Beanes organized a group of local men to go after the renegade British troops. The makeshift posse captured several soldiers and threw them in a local jail.

One of the British troops escaped, and the next night, August 28, 1814, he returned with company and took Beanes and two other

Americans—Dr. William Hill and Philip Weems—prisoner. The British rousted the three men from their beds at midnight and forced them to ride on old wobbly horses thirty-five miles to Benedict. The British, Taney said, scarcely allowed Dr. Beanes time to dress, and he was treated harshly and closely guarded.

Prisoner releases (or paroles) and exchanges were common practice during the War of 1812. General Ross, for example, paroled Joshua Barney on the spot at Bladensburg after the British general had his surgeon tend to Barney's leg wound. At Benedict, the British released Hill and Weems, but not the sixty-five-year-old Beanes. He was put aboard the *Tonnant*, Vice Admiral Cochrane's flagship, as the British sailed toward Baltimore. The British wanted Beanes to be punished.

Friends of the Beanes family, including Richard Williams West—Frank Key's brother-in-law (the husband of Polly Lloyd's sister Maria)—tried to intervene with Ross and Cochrane to no avail. That's when Francis Scott Key fatefully entered the picture.

West took it upon himself to ride to Georgetown to ask the well-spoken lawyer to help. Beanes's friends "were persuaded that something might be hoped from Mr. Key's tact and persuasive manners in getting the doctor released," John Stuart Skinner, who accompanied Key on the mission, later said.[17]

Frank Key agreed to go on the potentially dangerous assignment. He never publicly explained why. Most likely he wanted to assuage the shame and guilt he felt following his—and the American military's—sad performance at Bladensburg.

On September 1, Key secured permission to go on the Beanes mission from President Madison and from General John Mason, the commissioner general of prisons in charge of matters relating to military prisoners.[18] Mason, the son of founding father George Mason, spelled out in a letter dated September 2 what he wanted Key to do. He addressed it both to Key and to Skinner, who was on Mason's staff and had been appointed a colonel by the State Department to deal with prisoner exchanges and other issues. The twenty-five-year old Skinner, an Annapolis lawyer and planter when the war began, had arranged several exchanges with British naval officers.

Mason also had contacted the senior British prisoner held after the Battle of Bladensburg in Washington, Colonel William Thornton.

Mason told Thornton he could arrange to have letters from his fellow British prisoners—many of whom had been wounded and were treated humanely—delivered to Ross and Cochrane. Thornton eagerly accepted the offer; many letters were written. Key collected them before he left.[19]

Mason also gave Key a strongly worded missive to be delivered to General Ross, demanding Beanes's release. In it he called his emissary Francis Scott Key "a citizen of the highest respectability."[20]

On September 2, Key wrote to his mother from Georgetown: "I am going in the morning to Balt to proceed in a flag vessel to Gnrl Ross. Old Dr. Beanes of Marlbro' is taken prisoner by the Enemy, who threaten to carry him off. Some of his friends have urged me to apply for a flag [of truce] and go & try to procure his release."

He was cautiously pessimistic about the mission. "I hope," Key wrote, "to return in about 8 or 10 days, though it is uncertain, as I do not know where to find the fleet."[21]

6

A BEAUTIFUL AND ANIMATING EFFUSION

"Our good Frank's patriotic song is the delight of everybody."
—*Elizabeth Maynadier, October 27, 1814*

The most perplexing unanswered question about the life of Francis Scott Key is why he almost never spoke of the momentous events that transpired beginning on the morning of September 3, 1814, when he left Georgetown on horseback on his way to Baltimore, to the morning of September 14, when in a Baltimore hotel he finished writing what would become "The Star-Spangled Banner."

In the only surviving document in which Francis Scott Key mentions what happened during those fateful eleven days—an October 5 letter to John Randolph—he does not say a word about the battle. Only once during the rest of his life—in a political speech in Frederick, Maryland, on August 6, 1834—did Key refer publicly to the night in question.

The details come to us almost exclusively from two sources: John Skinner's 1849 reminiscences and a long detailed letter that Frank Key's brother-in-law Roger B. Taney wrote in 1856. In it, Taney explained that shortly after the Battle of Baltimore his wife's brother told him what took place before, during, and after the British attack, and Taney felt it his duty to report them for the historical record.

So, except where noted, the following account of how a thirty-five-year-old lawyer from Washington, D.C., came to write what would become the national anthem of the United States is based on Key's own words and on Skinner and Taney's memories set down well after the fact.

Key left for Baltimore on the morning of September 3, 1814, without high hopes. He had conflicting feelings about the vehemently anti-Federalist and pro-war people of Baltimore, about the British, and about the war itself.

Calling the war "a lump of wickedness," in the October 5 letter to John Randolph, Key wrote: "Sometimes when I remembered that it was there [in Baltimore] the declaration of this abominable war was received with public rejoicings, I [hoped] that [the British] would escape." Then again, Key told Randolph, when he realized that "faithful" pious Baltimoreans supported the war, it gave him strength, or as Key put it: "I could hardly feel a fear."[1]

He remained ambivalent about his mission when he met up with John Stuart Skinner in Baltimore on September 4 and handed him the packet of materials from General George Mason. The following day, the two men hitched a ride on an American sixty-foot sloop, a cartel ship sailing under a safe-conduct flag—mostly likely the *President*, under the command of John Ferguson. The sloop sailed out of Baltimore Harbor down the north-west branch of the Patapsco River toward the Chesapeake Bay in search of the British fleet.

They found the *Tonnant* three days later, in the early afternoon on September 7, at the mouth of the Potomac River. General Robert Ross and Admiral George Cockburn—well rested after Bladensburg and Washington and ready to go back on the offensive—welcomed the Americans aboard. They invited Key and Skinner to discuss the prisoner-exchange matter over an early dinner later that afternoon.

Ross and Cockburn, "particularly the latter," Taney wrote, "spoke of Dr. Beanes in very harsh terms and seemed at first not disposed to release him," They held the doctor below decks under conditions Taney described as "harsh and humiliating."

Beanes "had not had a change of clothes from the time he was seized," Taney said. He "was constantly treated with indignity," and "no officer would speak to him. He was treated as a culprit and not as a prisoner."

Frank Key did not take kindly to his hosts. "Never was a man more disappointed in his expectations than I have been as to the character of the

British officers," Key told Randolph in the October 5 letter. "With some exceptions, they appeared to be illiberal, ignorant and vulgar, and seem filled with a spirit of malignity against every thing American."

In the next sentence of the letter, Key, the forgiving Christian, second-guessed himself, writing: "Perhaps, however, I saw them in unfavourable circumstances."

Key and Skinner, Taney said, told the British that Dr. Beanes, a civilian noncombatant, never should have been taken prisoner. Then they turned the letters from the British prisoners over to their hosts.

Those letters, Taney said, "all spoke of the humanity and kindness with which [the British prisoners] had fallen into our hands." After what Taney said was "a good deal of conversation, and strong representations from Mr. Key as to the character and standing of Dr. Beanes, and of the deep interest which the community in which he lived took in his fate," the British agreed to let the doctor go.

Skinner told a different story, one in which he played the starring role. He claimed that Francis Scott Key did not even take part in the negotiations, which happened while Key was still dining with Admiral Cockburn and his officers. Skinner wrote that he and Ross met privately in Admiral Cockburn's cabin while Key remained "with all the residue of the party at the dinner table." Skinner claimed he alone convinced Ross to release Dr. Beanes without "the eloquence of such a pleader as Mr. Key," as Skinner put it many years later.[2]

Which account is correct? Although Skinner's version is patently self-serving, it does contain more specifics than Taney's version and has the likely ring of truth. In either event, the letters from the British prisoners seemed to sway Ross. In his official dispatch to General Mason, Ross said that the "friendly treatment" given to "the wounded officers & men of the British army" after Bladensburg enabled him "to meet your wishes regarding" Dr. Beanes.[3]

The British had one big condition, however. Key, Skinner, and Beanes could not return to Washington until after the attack on Baltimore.

Skinner quoted one British officer explaining why: "After discussing so freely as we have done in your presence our purposes and plans, you could hardly expect us to let you go on shore now in advance of us," Skinner wrote. "You will have to remain with us until all is over, when I promise you there shall be no further delay."

The three Americans were first escorted to the British frigate *Surprize*, under the command of Admiral Cochrane's son, Sir Thomas Cochrane. On September 10, Key, Skinner, and Beanes were allowed to return to the *President*, accompanied by British marine guards. The *Surprize* towed them into Baltimore Harbor, about eight miles from Fort McHenry, behind the fifty-ship British fleet, where they dropped anchor. They spent the next four days there.

Back in the city of Baltimore, American forces under Major General Samuel Smith, smarting from the debacle in the national capital, had been making final preparations to defend the bustling seaport since the day after the British burned Washington. The sixty-two-year-old Smith, who had served in the Revolutionary War and commanded Maryland's militia during the 1794 Whiskey Rebellion, was a Maryland Senator when the 1812 war began. He returned to Baltimore in 1813 to command the state militia and was given the task of defending the city of some fifty thousand inhabitants in the event of a British attack. That effort suddenly had taken on new urgency.

There had been panic on the streets of Baltimore the night of August 24 as people could see the flames and smoke of Washington burning thirty-five miles away. Adding to the fear were anxieties about two thousand Baltimore militiamen who had fought at Bladensburg. As anxious families saw survivors straggle back to Baltimore at night in the rain, rumors spread that the British were right behind them. Some residents loaded their belongings in carts and fled to the countryside.[4]

But many more Baltimoreans rallied around General Smith. Thousands of men from all walks of life—including farmers, laborers, sailors in port, and free blacks—joined in the frantic effort to fend off a British attack.

"Every American heart is bursting with shame and indignation at the catastrophe" in Washington, Baltimore merchant and militia private George Douglas wrote to a friend on August 30. "All hearts and hands have cordially united in the common cause. Every day, almost every hour, bodies of troops are marching in to our assistance." There were about "10,000 men under arms" in the city, Douglas reported. "The whole of the hills and rising grounds to the eastward of the city are covered with horse-foot and artillery exercises and training from morning until night."[5]

By the beginning of September, Smith had some fifteen thousand militiamen under his command. He massed them on the city's eastern end, and equipped them with—among other things—about a dozen artillery pieces. The city defenses also included about a mile of newly dug trenches and formidable earthworks.

Also protecting the city were about 250 artillerymen and some 750 infantry regulars, sailors, and militiamen under Army Major George Armistead in place at Fort McHenry, the five-sided fortress sitting on a spit of land defending Baltimore Harbor. The fort's castlelike, thick brick walls bristled with fifty-seven naval guns and artillery pieces. Armistead had blocked the entrance of the harbor with purposely scuttled old ships.

The British anticipated another big, easy victory in Baltimore. In Washington, Ross and Cockburn did not destroy personal property, only government buildings. But the plan for the rabidly anti-British citizens of Baltimore was different: nothing less than destroying the city.

British animosity for Baltimore stemmed from the work of ships known as Baltimore Clippers. Fast and highly maneuverable, these former light cargo vessels were fitted with armaments and given permission by President James Madison to pursue English merchant ships on the high seas and to run the English naval blockade. By September 1814 these clipper ships had sunk or seized more than five hundred British ships, a loss of some $16 million, earning the enmity of the world's number-one naval power. The British press referred to the city as a "nest of pirates."[6]

Little wonder that the British troops relished the thought of attacking the city. "The bomb-vessels, brigs, and frigates are all pushing up the river with an eagerness which must annoy the enemy, I presume, as much as it delights me," British Navy Captain Edward Codrington wrote to his wife from the *Surprize* on the night of September 10. "The work of destruction is now about to begin, and there will probably be many broken heads to-night....I do not like to contemplate scenes of blood and destruction; but my heart is deeply interested in the coercion of these Baltimore heroes, who are perhaps the most inveterate against us of all the Yankees."[7]

Many Americans feared the worst. The large British force "leads one to suppose that [they] are determined not to be baffled in their attempt on Balt[imore]," Francis Scott Key's aunt Elizabeth Maynadier wrote to his mother on September 12 from Annapolis. "Every moment we expect to hear the dreadful roar of the Cannon. The Lord in his infinite mercy look down upon us & avert the miseries that are impending over our heads."[8]

On Sunday morning, September 11, the people of Baltimore went about their daily routines more or less as usual. Many attended church. A group of militiamen joined worshippers at the Wilkes Street Methodist Church, leaving their muskets stacked outside the door. At around 1:30 that afternoon, three shots rang out from the cannon sitting on the city's courthouse green. Everyone knew what that meant: The British had arrived; an attack was imminent.

"My brethren and friends," the Wilkes Street minister told his congregation, "the alarm guns have just fired. The British are approaching and commending you to God and the word of His grace. I pronounce the benediction, and may the God of battles accompany you."[9]

The massive, fifty-ship British armada had arrived at the mouth of the Patpsco at around noon. The British command decided on a two-pronged attack strategy: an invasion by land and a massive bombardment by sea.

The land portion of the plan to topple Baltimore began in the early morning hours of Monday, September 12. Some 4,800 British soldiers and Royal Marines, including a naval brigade in five ships under the overall command of Admiral Cockburn with Ross in charge of the ground troops, landed at North Point, a long peninsula some fourteen miles south of the city. The Redcoats promptly began marching toward the city on that very hot and humid late summer day.

At noon, Cockburn and Ross—riding in advance of the main force— encountered a small American skirmish line about seven miles north of where they had landed. During the ensuing sharp fight, Ross took a bullet that went through his right arm and lodged in his chest. He fell off his horse and bled to death.

"As soon as the firing began, [Ross] had ridden to the front, that he might ascertain from whence it originated, and, mingling with the skirmishers, was shot in the side," British Lieutenant George R. Gleig later recalled. "He fell into the arms of his aide-de-camp, and lived only long enough to name his wife, and to commend his family to the protection of his country."

An "officer came at full speed towards us, with horror and dismay in his countenance, and calling loudly for a surgeon," Gleig said. The "aide-de-camp had scarcely passed, when the General's horse, without its rider, and with the saddle and housings stained with blood, came plunging onwards. It impossible to conceive the effect which this melancholy spectacle produced throughout the army."[10]

With Ross dead, Lieutenant Colonel Arthur Brooke took over command of the British attack force as the Battle of North Point raged into the early afternoon. As a steady rain began to fall, the British advanced steadily along the North Point Road and made it to all the way to the eastern edge of the city, where they stopped outside the well-dug entrenchments at Hampstead Hill.

Dozens were killed and hundreds wounded on both sides in the sharp fighting, which ended when the British broke off contact and made camp for the night in the rain in nearby woods. "The rain fell in torrents," a British soldier later wrote. "The roaring of the thunder and the tremendous flashing of lightning was truly awful; at the same time being within musket shot of the enemy, made it such as I never had experienced before— it was most dreadful."[11]

Brooke and Cockburn were ready to continue the attack. But the next day they received a message from Admiral Cochrane, saying it was not possible for his ships "to render you any assistance," and warning that the Americans had a force of twenty thousand defending the city.[12] Brooke and Cockburn reluctantly decided that the best course of action would be to leave the scene. They waited another day, then led their troops back to North Point in the early morning hours of Wednesday, September 14.

"Every hour brought in reinforcements to their army, whereas ours had no source from which even to recruit its losses," Gleig remembered, "and it was, therefore, deemed prudent, since we could not fight at once, to lose no time in returning to the shipping."[13]

As events played out at North Point, a flotilla of five British bomb vessels— with the fearsome names Devastation, Terror, Volcano, Aetna, and Meteor— along with eleven frigates and the rocket ship Erebus under the command of Admiral Cochrane, slowly sailed up the Patapsco. Before dawn on Tuesday, September 13, 1814, the attack flotilla set up in two rows about two miles below Fort McHenry. The stubby, low-to-the-ground bomb ships—each featuring two formidable ten- and thirteen-inch mortar guns that had a range of over two miles, although not with great accuracy—weighed anchor in the first row in a semicircle, just out of range of the fort's guns.

At sunrise, around six thirty, the Royal Marine artillerymen aboard the *Volcano* began the Battle of Baltimore by firing a two-hundred-pound-plus mortar, an explosive shell known as a carcass, packed with a lethal mixture of incendiary materials. Cochrane then ordered all the ships to open fire. The waters roiled violently as the cannonading mortars and Congreve rockets flew toward the fort in an "an incessant and well directed bombardment" as Armistead put it in his official account of the battle written on September 24.[14]

"We were like pigeons tied by the legs to be shot at," Judge Joseph Hopper Nicholson, the chief justice of the Baltimore district of the Maryland Court of Appeals who commanded the Maryland Volunteer Artillery's 1st Regiment (the "Baltimore Fencibles") at Fort McHenry, wrote of that fateful day.[15]

The British were confident that Fort McHenry would capitulate. All "on board the advanced ships had little doubt that the British ensign would soon proudly wave in triumph over the embattled fortress," Robert J. Barrett, a teenage British midshipman on the frigate *Hebrus*, later wrote.[16]

"The attack on Fort McHenry, by nearly the whole British fleet was distinctly seen from Federal Hill [in the city of Baltimore], and from the tops of houses which were covered with men, women, and children," one newspaper reported, "the whole awful spectacle of shot and shells, and rockets, shooting and bursting through the air."[17]

The relentless British bombardment—each of the five bomb ships alone could fire as many as fifty gigantic mortars an hour—lasted throughout that entire day and into the night. The cannonballs "flew like hail stones," *Niles' Weekly Register* reported. "Four or five bombs were frequently in the air at a time, and making a double explosion, with the noise of the *foolish* rockets and the firings of the fort" shaking the foundations of the city's houses, "for never, perhaps from the time of the invention of cannon to the present day, were the same number of pieces fired with so rapid succession."[18]

All told, the British war ships fired at least 1,500 mortars, cannon-balls, and rockets in twenty-five hours. When the British ships moved in closer, the guns at Fort McHenry and its nearby batteries opened fire and scored several hits. The American forces "vomited an iron flame" upon the British ships, the *Niles'* article said, "in heated balls, and a storm of heavy bullets flew upon them from the great semi circle of large guns and gallant hearts."

The British ships retreated out of range of the fort's cannon. But they kept up their bombing, raining a nearly constant stream of shells onto the fort. "A large proportion burst over us," Armistead said, "throwing their fragments among us, and threatening destruction. Many passed over, and about four hundred fell within the works." The British scored a least one direct hit on one of Fort McHenry's guns, destroying a twenty-four-pound cannon and killing or maiming its crew. Miraculously, though, only four Americans at Fort McHenry died and just twenty-four were wounded during the British onslaught.

To add to the mayhem, a torrential rainstorm punctuated with loud bursts of thunder drenched the city and harbor. "All this night the bombardment continued with unabated vigor," the British teenager Barrett remembered, "the hissing rockets and the fiery shells glittered in the air, threatening destruction as they fell, whilst to add solemnity to this scene of devastation, the rain fell in torrents—the thunder broke in mighty peals after each successive flash of lightning, that for a moment illuminated the surrounding darkness."[19]

The British attack continued until Cochrane called a halt in the early morning hours of September 14. When the guns went quiet, the British war fleet turned away from the city and sailed back down the Patapsco, into the Chesapeake Bay, and out to sea.

Baltimore was saved. Even more importantly, the American victory in the Battle of Baltimore signaled a turning point in the War of 1812. The British slunk off in defeat, seeming to lose heart for the fight. One last big conflict remained—the January 8, 1815, Battle of New Orleans, in which Major General Andrew Jackson of Tennessee led the Americans to a smashing victory and became the number one American military hero of the War of 1812.[20]

The retreat from Baltimore "was a galling spectacle for British seaman to behold," the teenage Barrett lamented. As the British ships retreated, the Americans at Fort McHenry, he recalled, "hoisted a most superb and splendid ensign on their battery and fired at the same time a gun of defiance."

The "morning gun was fired, the flag hoisted, Yankee Doodle played," an American at Fort McHenry (most likely newspaper editor Isaac Monroe, a private in the Baltimore Fencibles) reported a few days later, "and we all appeared in full view of a formidable and mortified enemy, who calculated upon our surrender 20 minutes after the commencement of the action."[21]

Francis Scott Key had a ringside seat during the entire Battle of Baltimore on the *President*, which sat an anchor in the Patapsco a mile or two behind the British fleet. Key, Skinner, and Beanes saw a large American flag flying over Fort McHenry before the British bomb ships let loose at 6:30 a.m. on September 13. All that day Key paced the deck as the rockets and bombs burst in the air. Peering through the darkness as day turned to night—at "the twilight's last gleaming," as he would later put it—Key could still make out the Stars and Stripes.

None of the men could sleep during their long night of the soul as the relentless British assault continued hour after hour. The air filled with the hissing of rockets and screaming of cannonballs mixed in with enormous rumblings of thunder and the flashing of lightning.

When the British guns tapered off and then went silent around three a.m., the men did not know whether that meant an American victory or defeat. Even as the horizon lightened at around five a.m. Key, Skinner, and Beanes could not tell if Baltimore had survived. Rain clouds obscured the sunrise just before six and a mist hung over the water. Peering through their spyglass, the three men still could not clearly make out the fort or the British ships in what Key would immortalize as "the dawn's early light."

"As they had no communication with any of the enemy's ships, they did not know whether the fort had surrendered or the attack had been abandoned," Taney wrote. Key, Skinner, and Beanes waited "in painful suspense, watching with intense anxiety for the return of day, and looking every few minutes at their watches to see how long they must wait for it."

Just after six a.m., as Key peered into the cloud-obscured dawn light through his glass, he could make out a flag limply hanging. It was impossible to tell if it was the Stars and Stripes or the Union Jack. Then a slight breeze stirred and Francis Scott Key saw that the American flag was still there. He knew that his countrymen had prevailed against overwhelming odds.

As he witnessed the massive bombardment, Key's feelings of antipathy for the British overcame his grudge against the rabid Baltimore supporters of the war. Admiral Cochran, Key told Randolph in his October 5 letter, had told him that "the town must be burned, and I was sure that if taken it would have been given up to plunder.... It was filled with women and children."

Key felt the "warmest gratitude" for the "most merciful deliverance" when the British attack failed. He expressed these high feelings just after dawn on September 14 as his gaze moved from the American flag at Fort McHenry to the British bomb ships and frigates sailing away. He began to compose a poem on the back of a letter he had in his pocket. The words came tumbling out, as Taney put it, "in the fervor of the moment."

Twenty years later Key said: "I saw the flag of my country waving over a city, heard the sound of battle; the noise of the conflict fell upon my listening ear, and told me that 'the brave and the free' had met the invaders." Through "the clouds of war, the stars of that banner still shone in my view," Key said. "Then, at the hour of deliverance and joyful triumph, my heart spoke [and I thought] 'Does such a country—and such defenders of the country—deserve a song?'" With that, "came an inspiration not to be resisted and even though it had been a hanging matter to make a song, I must have written it."[22]

Key worked on the four verses of the poem while sailing back to shore and then wrote out a finished copy the next day at a hotel, most likely the Indian Queen Tavern, on the corner of Hanover and Market Streets in downtown Baltimore. The following day, September 16, 1814, according to Taney, Frank Key presented the verses to his brother-in-law, Judge Joseph Nicholson, the husband of Polly Lloyd's sister Rebecca.

Either Joseph Nicholson, Rebecca Nicholson, Key, or Skinner took the poem to be printed by the offices of the *Baltimore American and Commercial Advertiser* or—more likely—by the print shop on the corner of Baltimore and Gay Street run by Benjamin Edes, who had commanded a militia company at the Battle of North Point.

Edes printed copies of the verses bearing the title "Defence of Fort M'Henry" on handbills and broadsheets and distributed them throughout the city, including to the troops at Fort McHenry. The text of the song appeared in the daily afternoon newspaper, the *Baltimore Patriot and Evening Advertiser*, on September 20—its first issue since the paper had suspended publication ten days earlier.

The newspaper and broadsheet included a short introduction, most likely written by Judge Nicholson. It read: "The following beautiful and animating effusion, which is destined long to outlast the occasion, and outlive the impulse which produced it, has already been extensively circulated. In our first renewal of publication we rejoice in an opportunity to enliven the sketch of an exploit so illustrious, with strains which so fitly celebrate it."

The broadsheet and the newspaper went on to describe the circumstances under which the song came to be. Key was not named but described only as a "gentleman" who "had left Baltimore, in a flag of truce" to secure the release of Dr. Beanes, and had watched the bombshells, and "at the early dawn his eye was again greeted by the proudly waving flag of his country."

The article indicated that the song was to be sung to the tune of "To Anacreon in Heaven," an English song popular in pubs, composed by John Stafford Smith around 1775. Very well known in the United States, the tune was the theme song of the Anacreontic Society of London, a gentlemen's club that met periodically to listen to musical performances, dine, and sing songs. The club took its name from Anacreon, the ancient Greek poet known primarily for his verses in praise of love, wine, and revelry. Several similar organizations had formed in the United States, including the Columbian Anacreontic Society in New York in 1795 and the Anacreontic Society of Baltimore in 1820.

On September 21, 1814, the *Baltimore American and Commercial Daily Advertiser* published the song. The following day "Defence of Fort M'Henry" appeared in the *Federal Republican* of Georgetown, sandwiched between a paid advertisement and a compilation of news items from London. The introduction said: "A friend has obligingly favored us with a copy of the following stanzas, which we offer to our readers as a specimen of native poetry, which will proudly rank among the best efforts of our national muse."

The original introduction and verses appeared under the headline "Poetry" in the Boston *Independent Chronicle* of October 3, as the verses had started to become known, if not popular, throughout the nation. It is believed that the song was first sung publicly on October 19, 1814, in Baltimore at the Holliday Street Theatre, popularly known as "Old Drury," after the performance of a play.

"Our good Frank's patriotic song," his aunt Elizabeth Maynadier wrote to Frank's mother on October 27, "is the delight of everybody."[23] The song became known as "The Star-Spangled Banner" (from a line in the first stanza) after Carr's Music Store of Baltimore published it for the first time in sheet music form in November. The title of the song on the sheet music reads "THE STAR SPANGLED BANNER," below which are the words "A PATRIOTIC SONG" and "Air, Anacreon in Heaven." The song continued to be widely reproduced in newspapers and magazines and soon appeared on sheet music and in songbooks throughout the nation.

In a report about a December 12 testimonial dinner in Washington during which those in attendance sang the song, the *National Intelligencer* identified its author as "a gentleman (F.S. Key) of this District whom circumstances had thrown on board the British fleet during its tremendous attack on Fort. McHenry."[24]

By 1816 word had spread throughout the young nation that Francis Scott Key of Georgetown wrote the stirring, patriotic air, "The Star-Spangled Banner."

Was Frank Key writing a poem when he scribbled the verses down that night and polished them the next morning? Or was he writing the words to a song to be sung to the tune of "To Anacreon in Heaven?" Since Key never addressed the matter publicly, we can only go on supposition, along with a few scraps of concrete evidence.

Key was a life-long amateur poet, not a songwriter; nothing on the untitled verses he wrote in Baltimore indicated they were anything other than a poem; and Key was unmusical at best and possibly tone deaf. Aside from a few religious hymns and possibly one patriotic song, he had not written the words to any song before 1814—or after that, for that matter. And, despite the fact that he twice referred to what he wrote as "a song" in the 1834 speech, he spoke those words long after his untitled poem had morphed into the patriotic song called "The Star-Spangled Banner."

Pennsylvania journalist and author W. U. Hensel investigated the poem-or-song issue in the early 1880s. After interviewing Key's descendants, Hensel wrote that Francis Scott Key had "an ignorance of musical composition" and "could not tell one tune from another." Songs such as "Old Hundred, Yankee Doodle, Hail Columbia and the Star Spangled Banner," Hensel wrote, "were entirely undistinguishable to the ear of Francis Scott Key." For evidence, Hensel pointed to an incident that allegedly took place in Tuscaloosa, Alabama, in 1833 when a local band played

"The Star-Spangled Banner" at a reception given in Key's honor. "To the great astonishment and amusement of the gentlemen about him," Hensel wrote, Key "innocently remarked that 'It was a pretty air,' densely ignorant of the tune they were playing."[25]

The evidence pointing to Key writing a song on the night of September 13–14 also is speculative. There is, above all, the fact that the poem's rhyme and meter almost perfectly match those of "To Anacreon in Heaven," a song whose tune Frank Key, whether musical or not, certainly had heard. It was used in many other popular songs of his day, including "Adams and Liberty," a pro-Federalist political ditty written in 1798 by Robert Treat Paine Jr.[26]

Plus, it is all but certain that nine years earlier Key wrote a patriotic poem that became a song. The occasion was a December 6, 1805, dinner at McLaughlin's Tavern in Georgetown honoring Tripolitan War naval heroes Stephen Decatur and Charles Stewart. The assembled guests that evening sang a lyric "which had been prepared for the occasion about an hour before Dinner, by a gentleman of George-Town," a newspaper reported. Titled "Song," it is sometimes referred to by its first words, "When the Warrior Returns." Foreshadowing its famed successor, "Song" contains the lines: "And pale beam'd the Crescent, it's splendour obscur'd / By the light of the star-spangled flag of our nation." What's more, it was sung that night to the tune of "To Anachreon on Heaven."[27]

A recent study by music historian David Hildebrand that takes into consideration all of the poem-versus-song evidence concludes that Francis Scott Key did, indeed, write a song during the Battle of Baltimore. "I am convinced that this was the melody going through his mind," Hildebrand, the director of the Colonial Music Institute, said in 2012.[28]

One other question hovers over the Star-Spangled Banner episode: Exactly what flag did Frank Key refer to in his poem? Two extra-large flags flew over Fort McHenry during the Battle of Baltimore. Both were commissioned by Major George Armistead in the summer of 1813 and were made by Baltimore flag-maker Mary Young Pickersgill.[29]

Armistead ordered the large flags because he wanted anyone approaching Baltimore from the water to see that Fort McHenry was flying the colors of the United States. The fifteen stars of the larger, thirty-by-forty-two-foot garrison flag were each about two feet long; the fifteen stripes measured just under two feet in width. The stars were made of cotton; the stripes and the blue canton of English woolen bunting. The massive flag weighed about fifty pounds; it took eleven men to raise it onto a ninety-foot flag-pole at the fort.

Historians believe that the smaller Pickersgill flag—a so-called storm flag that measured seventeen-by-twenty-five feet—flew over the fort during the battle. Flying the much heavier, larger flag during the, bomb-filled, stormy night of September 13-14 "would almost certainly have broken the flagpole," historian Walter Lord wrote. "At the very least it would have hung as a soggy mass, not about to wave poetically in the breeze."[30]

What about the larger flag—the one that today resides in the Smithsonian Institution's National Museum of American History in Washington? It's all but certain that that flag replaced the smaller one at Fort McHenry after the battle ended on the morning of September.

That flag was the "splendid ensign" that the English sailor Robert Barrett referred to and the "hoisted" flag that the American militiaman Isaac Monroe mentioned that the Fort McHenry defenders rose on the morning after the battle. It was the flag that Frank Key saw in the dawn's early light—the flag that has come to be known as the Star-Spangled Banner.

7

A USELESS, PERNICIOUS, DANGEROUS PORTION OF THE POPULATION

"No refuge could save the hireling and slave from the terror of flight, or the gloom of the grave."

—*"The Star-Spangled Banner" third verse*

"Black men had nothing to do with the founding of the American Colonization Society. White men organized the Society and established the colony. If the enterprise has been a failure, the failure must be attributed to the distinguished men who were the originators and whose standing character, learning and experience were sufficient to guarantee the integrity and success of the undertaking."

—The Commonwealth *African American newspaper,*
September 4, 1915

Frank Key left Baltimore around September 21, 1814 and rode back to Georgetown. He made the forty-mile trek to Frederick early in October to retrieve Polly and their children. Key remained bitterly conflicted about the ongoing war. He had no use for the deep political divide in the country. More personally, he still resented the fact that his legal business had slowed to a trickle.

The father of six was more worried about his personal situation than the "great alarm" in Washington over the "removal of the Seat of Government," Key told John Randolph in his October 5 letter. "If the war lasts (as I think it will)," he wrote, "I cannot see how I can live in George Town."

He also had spiteful words for the Madison administration, disparaging "the Conquerors of Canada [who could not] defend their own Capital" and lamenting the fact that Madison and company had fled after the disaster at Bladensburg, a situation he called the "disgrace of abandoning the seat of Government." The administration and its war supporters, Key said, were "in the very dust and mire of ignominy."

Key was particularly unhappy with the nation's rabidly political newspapers. Key felt so strongly about the party-controlled newspapers that he spoke seriously with several other men—including Congressman Richard Stanford of North Carolina—about starting a new, nonpartisan newspaper in Washington. Key told Randolph in November that he was working on a "half-formed project of starting a new Paper...an impartial antiparty paper to prevent [the sectarian] evils to which we are exposed."[1]

That newspaper, he said in a letter to his mother, would "introduce to the public a better set of principles in politics & in everything else than are fashionable at present with either party." With the help of "at least five or six able men whose opinions agree with my own," he said, he believed that the proposed newspaper could be the "only way of preventing disunion & civil war" and might help "save the country from being torn to pieces by the factions who have their hands on her."

The nonpartisan newspaper idea turned out to be little more than a pipe dream. Soon after writing about his big plan, Key told his mother he was too busy to devote the time to what he said surely would be "a most disagreeable and difficult project."[2]

Frank Key also was not pleased with the British policy of encouraging escaped slaves to join their cause and win their freedom. Key's close friend John Randolph, among many other slave-owning Americans, also bemoaned the British practice, which had its roots in the American Revolution. Very few slaves during the revolution, Randolph said in one of his fiery pre-War of 1812 congressional speeches, went over to the British because of the slaves' entrenched "habits of subordination."

But things had changed, he warned. The French Revolution had taken the Jeffersonian ideal of inalienable rights and extended it to all men, regardless of race. The abolitionist movement, which had already met with success in Britain with the passage of the 1807 Abolition of the Slave Trade act, had grown in the northern United States, involving some of the North's most prominent intellectuals and political leaders. In the South, slave insurrections had broken out in Virginia and Louisiana, throwing the region "into a state of insecurity," with many slaves questioning "habits of loyalty and obedience to his master." "God forbid, sir," Randolph orated, "that the southern States should ever see an enemy on their shores with these infernal principles."[3]

But the enemy had made it to American shores during the War of 1812, and Francis Scott Key shared Randolph's indignation and insecurities over the impact of British actions on enslaved people in America.

Key expressed those sentiments in two lines in the third verse of "The Star-Spangled Banner."

"No refuge could save the hireling and slave," he wrote, "From the terror of flight or the gloom of the grave." Those are not exactly the sentiments of someone who has warm feelings about slaves and others who rallied to the side of the British.

In the fourth and last verse of the song, Key—expressing a widely held view among white Americans of the era—excluded enslaved individuals from the lofty ideals he espoused in his patriotic verses. "O thus be it ever," the verse begins, "when freemen shall stand / Between their loved home and the war's desolation." Those freemen would be "Blest with vic'try and peace," the song continues, "may the Heav'n rescued land / Praise the Power that hath made and preserved us as a nation!" The "us" did not include more than a million African Americans held in bondage in the land of the free and the home of the brave.

Francis Scott Key's prediction in early October that the War of 1812 would last turned out to be wrong. After the British failure in Baltimore, the fighting wound down significantly. As it did, and as the business of the nation's capital began returning to normal, Frank Key's business prospects picked up considerably. On January 26, 1815, President Madison named Key, along with Thomas Swann and John Law, to a government commission looking into public land disputes in Georgia and Mississippi. Congress confirmed the appointment soon after, and for the next three years Key, Swann, and Law made up the three-man Yazoo Land Claims Commission. A year later he wrote to his wife that he found "this Yazoo business" troublesome as it "interfered greatly with all my other concerns."[4]

Key and the other commissioners had to wade through scores of land claims that had been wending their way through the legal system since 1796. That convoluted legal maneuvering stemmed from the Georgia Legislature's 1795 selling much of what is now Mississippi and Alabama for pennies an acre, and the next year declaring those sales null and void. Buyers with conflicting claims filed countless lawsuits in the intervening years. The Supreme Court in 1810 set up a $5 million fund to compensate claimants. Key and his fellow commissioners looked into and decided the cases, and wound up distributing some $4.3 million.

Being on the Yazoo Land Claims Commission took up only part of the young lawyer's time. By February 1815, Francis Scott Key's legal practice was humming once again. He made several appearances in the Supreme Court that month. In one case, Key represented Jane Burch, who sued Kenzy Gettings for the return of property she alleged that he had in his possession. Said property: "a negro woman and her four children."[5]

In another Supreme Court case, *Pratt and Others v. Thomas Law and William Campbell*, Key joined two other lawyers (including former Madison administration Attorney General William Pinkney) representing the defendants in a complicated, three-part lawsuit dating from 1801 involving the sale of lots in Washington, D.C. One of the two attorneys on the opposing side was Key's uncle and mentor, Philip Barton Key.

In 1815 the nation entered what is sometimes known as the Era of Good Feelings, a time of general peace, prosperity, and political comity. Whether it was the official end of the war—the Senate had unanimously ratified and President Madison had signed the Treaty of Ghent on February 16 ending the fighting—or the fact that his legal business had picked up, Frank Key by the spring of 1815 seemed to embody that good feeling. He wrote ebullient letters to family and friends expressing his new positive outlook—letters that the young lawyer infused with some of the most pious sentiments he ever put to paper.

"Let us now," Key wrote his mother late in 1814, "use this interval of security (which we are blessed with for this purpose) in preparing ourselves by prayer and consideration for giving up ourselves and all our concerns to God's gracious disposal. Let us remove our affections from this perishing world and often think of the treasures laid up for us in heaven."[6]

Evidently Key's fervent prayers paid off. He reported to Randolph that this latest eruption of religious fervor had taken him "through much anxiety and distress, to a state of peace and happiness as far above what I have deserved, as below what I yet hope, even in this life to attain." Key told his friend that he fervently wished Randolph would be similarly delivered and "experience the most delightful of all sensations, that springs from a well grounded hope of reconciliation with God!"[7]

"You," Key told Randolph, "are on the right track. God grant that it may be so! God is leading you. Your sentiments show the divinity that stirs within you."

Key went on to lay out what he called "the true doctrine of our Church and the plain meaning of the Gospel." To wit: Mankind has "ruined ourselves," and we are all sinners "under the sentence of Almighty condemnation." But there is a "Saviour," Key told Randolph, "who gives us all we want—pardon, peace and holiness." All one has to do is "be pardoned for our sins, and cleansed from all our iniquities."

That fundamentalist theological bent did not go over well with Reverend Walter D. Addison, the rector of St. John's Church in Georgetown. Addison, Key said, "is a very good man but does not suit the times." He continues "in the old way of spending more money in weekly cotillion parties that would support in comfort all the poor in town."[8]

That is one reason that Francis Scott Key and a group of other St. John's parishioners started another Episcopal Church in Georgetown. At a meeting held at Semmes Hotel and Tavern on July 19, 1815, Key joined a committee with six other men to draw up the "rules for the government of the Georgetown Episcopal Company," as a newspaper report put it.[9] Two years later, the company founded Christ Episcopal Church of Georgetown in a building just a few blocks from St. John's. Both churches occupy the same buildings today.

On July 28, Frank Key's revered uncle Philip Barton Key died at age fifty-eight at Woodley, his opulent home north of Georgetown. Francis Scott Key, the family versifier, wrote a poetic eulogy. In it, he praised his uncle's "genius, wit, and eloquence." Not surprisingly, Key infused the eulogy with his religious zeal, advising the "mourning survivors" to bring their "troubled soul[s] to Christ." That way they would be rewarded "beyond the grave" with "a life of bliss."[10]

By 1816 Key's law practice was booming. He worked long and hard on the Yazoo Commission. He served as Recorder and President of the Georgetown Board of Alderman. He kept up his active participation in church matters at both Christ Church and St. John's.

In November, after Reverend Addison came down with a serious vision problem, the members of the St. John's vestry appointed Francis Scott Key as Lay Reader. His "Talents and Piety, and soundness in the Faith, render him apt...to exercise the office thus reposed in him," Addison wrote.[11]

On June 9 Polly gave birth to the couple's seventh child. They named him Daniel Murray Key after Frank Key's lifelong friend Daniel Murray— whom Polly Key called "Brother Daniel."[12] I want "to let you know what a fine boy was added to our family & how well Polly was," the proud father wrote to his mother eleven days after Daniel Key's birth. "They both continue well. So much so that Polly dined out in the office with us to-day."[13]

Throughout the year Francis Scott Key involved himself in a good number of legal and other issues dealing with African-Americans, both free and enslaved. At the end of 1815, he and the noted Maryland attorney Luther Martin (a signer of the Declaration of Independence) had represented the executor of the estate of Mary Fishwick, a long-deceased slave owner, in the Maryland Count of Appeals in Annapolis. At issue in *Fishwick's Administrator v. Sewell* was the disposition of a "negro woman named Dinah."[14] Key and Martin argued that since Fishwick died without a will, the estate should be remunerated for Dinah's value and the value of her offspring because the woman had become the property of Fishwick's stepfather. The court agreed with Key's argument that ownership of slaves was analogous to the ownership of merchandise.[15]

On the other hand, Frank Key also worked during this time—and throughout his professional life—on behalf of African Americans, and did so gratis. If he considered it problematic to represent black people in court one day and then white slave owners the next, he never said so.

In 1816 Key helped set up a Sabbath school for freed people of color in the Georgetown Lancaster School building. "The various Protestant churches sent teachers to aid in the humane work," an observer noted. "Francis S. Key not only taught in the school, but often made formal addresses to the scholars."[16]

In February 1816 Key represented a slave, Sally Henry, who sued for her freedom in a case that went to the U.S. Supreme Court. Henry had been brought into Washington from Virginia as a young child and loaned to a woman who did not register her as required by a Maryland law banning slave importation that applied in the District of Columbia. Key lost the case when Chief Justice John Marshall's court ruled that the Maryland law applied only to residents of the city, not "transients" such as Sally Henry.[17]

Key won a slave-related Supreme Court case on March 2, 1816, a reprise of the 1812 *Davis v. Wood* lawsuit. Key again represented slave owner Hezekiah Wood and again the Marshall court ruled in Wood's favor, allowing him to keep his slaves.[18]

Frank Key appeared as a witness in April at hearings of a special congressional committee set up at the behest of John Randolph to look into illegal slave trafficking in Washington. Slavery was legal in the nation's capital, but the slave trade was rife with abuse, including all-too-common instances of freed persons being kidnapped by slave traders, sold into bondage, and shipped across the Potomac River to be delivered to Deep South slave states.

In one of his typically long and passionate speeches on the House floor, on March 1 Randolph called the situation in the nation's capital "a crying sin before God and man." Illegal selling of slaves in Washington, Randolph thundered, was a practice "not surpassed for abomination in any part of the earth; for in no part of it, not even excepting the rivers on the coast of Africa, was there so great and so infamous a slave market as in the metropolis, in the very Seat of Government of this nation."

He called Washington "a depot for a systematic slave market—an assemblage of prisons where the unfortunate beings, reluctant, no doubt, to be torn from their connections, and the affections of their lives, were incarcerated and chained down, and thence driven in fetters like beasts, to be paid for like cattle."[19]

Key, among others, testified before the committee, confirming Randolph's powerfully damning words. Key said that, indeed, "frequent" seizures of free blacks took place, and they were "hurried off in the night, brought to the City, and transported as slaves." He had "no doubt that many are carried away as slaves who are entitled to their freedom."[20]

There is no record that Congress acted on any findings that the committee made. But Frank Key did take action on more than one occasion to try to right a wrong involving freed slaves taken illegally by slave traders. Not long after he testified before the special congressional committee, for example, in the summer of 1816, Key intervened on behalf of three freed African Americans who had been kidnapped in Delaware and sold into slavery in Maryland.

A Philadelphia physician visiting Washington, Jesse Torrey (who also had testified before the special House committee) had discovered the three people—a man, a young widow, and her infant child—held in chains in a Washington building in December 1815. Torrey, an outspoken abolitionist, took up their case, won an injunction preventing the captors from removing the three from Washington, and then brought suit seeking their release in the U.S. Circuit Court.

The court placed the captives in Torrey's custody. He then set about raising money for their defense. Francis Scott Key led the fund-raising effort, which brought in nearly $200, a not insignificant sum in 1816. What's more, Key also "volunteered his own services as attorney, gratis."[21] In June the court set free the illegally captured freed slaves.

The main slavery issue Francis Scott Key concerned himself with in 1816 was colonization: the idea of encouraging former slaves and other African American freed men and women to leave this country and settle in Africa. Colonization was not a new idea. It began as a progressive, enlightened plan in the mid-eighteenth century when free African Americans, abolitionist whites, and even some slave owners in the South (including Thomas Jefferson) seriously contemplated the idea.

The idea gained strong momentum in 1816. Slavery, which never had taken hold in a big way in the North, was dying out there by the second decade of the nineteenth century. With that demise came a steady increase in the number of freed men and women living in the northern states, as well as in Maryland and other border states, and in the northernmost southern state, Virginia. What to do about the growing number of free blacks concerned many white members of society.

Even though the United States had officially banned the importation of slaves beginning on January 1, 1808, the institution still was legal on these shores. In 1804 a slave uprising in Haiti resulted in the start of the independent Black Republic. Many slave owners in the South feared that the success of the Haiti slave revolt would lead to serious unrest among

American slaves and freed blacks. Colonizing the latter group, many believed, would help ward off insurrections.

In addition, the United States at this time experienced its second Great Awakening, an evangelical Protestant revival. Many of those who came to support colonization did so in the belief that it would spread Christianity in Africa.

The earliest important American proponent of colonization who acted on the idea was Paul Cuffe, a mixed-race (black and Indian) Massachusetts freedman and abolitionist. Since the late 1780s, British philanthropists had been trying to set up a settlement for former slaves—many of whom had escaped from their owners in the South during the American Revolution—in Sierra Leone, on Africa's west coast. Cuffe, who made a small fortune in the shipping industry, sailed one of his ships in January 1811 from his home of Westport, Connecticut, to Sierra Leone to try to set up an American colonization movement there. In Africa, Cuffe formed what he called the Friendly Society to encourage African American immigration to Africa.

The War of 1812 interrupted the venture. But in December 1815 Cuffe took thirty-eight free African Americans to resettle in Sierra Leone. When Cuffe returned to the United States he lobbied to end slavery and to send freed slaves to Africa. But that effort ended when he died at age fifty-eight in September 1817.[22]

Charles Fenton Mercer, a prominent Virginia lawyer, took a strong interest in colonization after he was elected to the state House of Delegates in 1810. Mercer learned in Richmond that in 1800, following the abortive slave revolt known as Gabriel's Rebellion, the Virginia General Assembly had held secret meetings to discuss sending rebellious slaves and freed blacks either to the western United States or to the Caribbean.

The General Assembly adopted a secret resolution on December 31, 1800, authorizing Virginia Governor James Monroe to do just that. The measure also asked Monroe to confer with the President of the United States "on the subject of purchasing lands" outside Virginia "wither persons obnoxious to the law or dangerous to the peace of society may be removed." Monroe dutifully asked for help from his friend, President Thomas Jefferson, on June 15, 1801.

In his letter, which remained secret for years, Monroe asked Jefferson about the feasibility of the federal government or the state acquiring "a tract of land in the western territory of the United States" for the purpose of

resettling those who took part in the "conspiracy of slaves." Monroe indicated that the land also could be used to colonize freed blacks.

Jefferson replied to Monroe on November 14, 1801, in another letter
that remained secret for years, that no law prevented Virginia from purchasing lands in the "country north of Ohio" for colonization purposes.
He also suggested that the West Indies offered "a more probable and prac-
ticable retreat for them" as they were inhabited "already by a people of
their own race and color." The Caribbean climate, he said, seemed "conge-
nial with their natural constitution." Nature, Jefferson concluded, "seems
to have formed these islands to become the receptacle of the blacks trans-
planted into this hemisphere."

In January 1802 the Virginia General Assembly responded to Jefferson's
suggestions by passing a resolution officially broadening the scope of those
who would be resettled: namely, "free negroes or mulattoes, and such
negroes or mulattoes as may be emancipated."[23]

Charles Fenton Mercer, a slave owner, reintroduced the colonization
issue to the Virginia General Assembly in 1816. He introduced a resolution
in mid-December that strongly endorsed colonization for freed African
Americans. The measure sailed through the Virginia House and Senate
and became state law on December 21.

Earlier that year, in April, the thirty-nine-year-old Mercer—who lived
in the Loudoun County, Virginia, village of Aldie, forty miles west of
Washington—had paid a visit to the nation's capital. On Capitol Hill, he
ran into two old friends, fellow College of New Jersey (Princeton) class-
mate Elias Caldwell, the clerk of the Supreme Court, and the prominent
D.C. lawyer Francis Scott Key. Mercer told Caldwell and Key about his plan
to introduce colonization legislation into the Virginia General Assembly.
Both men became immediate proponents, and Frank Key would remain
so for the rest of his life.

Caldwell and Key expressed "the deepest interest in my purpose, and
assured me of their zealous co-operation in effecting it," Mercer later said.
Frank Key was so fired up about the idea, Mercer said, that he vowed to
break his long-standing aversion to politics and run for the Maryland
legislature to work on behalf of colonization in that body. As Mercer put
it: "Mr. Key promptly declared that, if I persevered in it, he would return to
Maryland and obtaining if possible, a seat in her legislature, offer a similar
resolution, of the success of which he would have no doubt."[24]

Mercer persevered, but Key never sought political office. He did, however, work closely with Mercer and Caldwell, talking up the colonization idea among their friends and colleagues in the late winter and spring of 1816. A group of prominent men—including John Randolph of Roanoke, Washington lawyer Thomas Swann, Senator Rufus King of New York, New Hampshire Senator Jeremiah Mason, and future Virginia Governor Littleton Tazewell—met informally on April 29 at Key's Georgetown home. Mercer, with Key's strong support, pitched his idea of having more states petition the president to set aside lands in the west for freed blacks.

Later that year Caldwell recruited his brother-in-law, Robert Finley—a member of Mercer's Princeton Class of 1795—to the cause. Finley, a forty-four-year-old Presbyterian minister in Basking Ridge, New Jersey, embraced the idea wholeheartedly. He soon became the nation's leading advocate for colonization.

But Finley, a trustee at Princeton who headed the college's new theological seminary, chose a different path. Rather than encouraging states to petition the president, he decided to form an autonomous national organization with the sole purpose of raising money to send free blacks to a new colony in West Africa. Although Finley spoke out against the evils of slavery, his plan barely touched on that issue, as it called instead for laws allowing slave owners to free their slaves but only if the slaves agreed to be colonized in Africa. Otherwise, the Finley plan applied only to already freed African Americans.

Finley agreed with the other colonization backers that freed blacks did not fit into American society and could thrive only in Africa, living among others of their race. They also believed that colonized blacks should be encouraged to adopt Christianity in Africa. That would have the added benefit of spreading that religion and "civilization" to that continent. And, in concert with the widely held views of other whites of his day, Finley espoused what would be described today as racist ideas about blacks, characterizing them as lazy and immoral.

Writing in his 1816 pamphlet *Thoughts on the Colonization of Free Blacks*, for example, Finley said that slavery "insensibly induces a habit of indolence. Idleness seldom fails to be attended with dissipation. Should the time ever come when slavery shall not exist in these States, yet if the people of color remain among us, the effect of their presence will be unfavorable to our industry and morals."[25]

Robert Finley unveiled his colonization plan in November of 1816 in Princeton. He came to Washington early in December to work with Caldwell and Key to convince the city's (and the nation's) movers and shakers to start a national colonization organization based in the nation's capital. At the same time Mercer lobbied the Virginia General Assembly for colonization.

Let "the representatives of this great and free people," Finley wrote in his pamphlet, "not only feel it to be their interest, but their duty and glory to repair the injuries done to humanity by our ancestors by restoring to independence those who were forced from their native land, and are now found among us...." Africa, he wrote, "stretches forth her hands, panting for the return of her absent sons and daughters."

The pamphlet—in which Finley called slavery a "great violation of the laws of nature"—appealed to many influential people in the nation's capital, most of whom owned slaves. That group included lame-duck President James Madison, Secretary of State (and president-elect) James Monroe, Chief Justice John Marshall, Speaker of the House Henry Clay, U.S. Attorney General Richard Rush, Washington, D.C.'s U.S. Attorney Walter Jones, and Congressmen Daniel Webster of New Hampshire and John Randolph of Virginia.

Frank Key joined with Finley and Caldwell in organizing a large meeting on December 16 to discuss the colonization idea. Supreme Court Justice Bushrod Washington of Virginia, a nephew of George Washington, presided. The speakers included Henry Clay and John Randolph.

Five days later, on December 21, 1816, the founding meeting of the American Society for Colonizing the Free People of Color of the United States—soon to be known as the American Colonization Society—took place at Davis's Hotel in Washington. Henry Clay presided at the all-male, all-white public meeting, at which Caldwell was the featured speaker. The gathering also heard from John Randolph and Francis Scott Key.

In his remarks Clay noted that the meeting would not "touch or agitate, in the slightest degree" on "any question of emancipation" or anything "connected with the abolition of slavery." Because of "the uncon-querable prejudices resulting from their color," Clay said, freed blacks "never could amalgamate with the free whites of this country." Sending free blacks to Africa, he said, would also introduce "the arts, civilization, and Christianity" there.

"Can there be a nobler cause," Clay asked rhetorically, "than that which, while it proposes to rid our own country of a useless and pernicious, if not a dangerous portion of the population, contemplates the spreading of the arts of civilized life, and the possible redemption from ignorance and barbarism on a benighted quarter of the globe!"[26]

The group adopted a set of resolutions and set up a committee of eight to write a document to submit to Congress asking for federal funds to buy land in Africa for colonization. That committee included Francis Scott Key. The group also appointed Key to a committee to prepare the society's constitution. The *National Intelligencer* reported that Key took the floor at the December 21 meeting to suggest that the resolutions include the "disclamation of any intention of the proposed association to touch the question of the abolition of slavery." Clay suggested instead—and Key agreed—that such a clause should be in the group's constitution.

A week later, on December 28, the committee held its third meeting, this time in the hall of the U.S. House of Representatives, and adopted a constitution. That document also stressed that the group's sole objective was colonization of freed blacks, not the emancipation of slaves. Or, in the document's words, "to promote and execute a plan for colonization (with their consent) of the Free People of Colour residing in our country, in Africa, or such other place as Congress shall deem most expedient."[27]

The founding meeting of the American Colonization Society took place on January 1, 1817, back at the Davis Hotel. Bushrod Washington was elected president. Francis Scott Key joined the board of managers, a position he would hold for many years.

8

A CLASS OF VERY
DANGEROUS PEOPLE

"Free blacks [live] by pilfering and corrupt the slaves and [produce] such pernicious consequences."
—*President James Monroe, March 2, 1819*

Robert Finley died at age forty-five on October 3, 1817. But the American Colonization Society did not die with him. Far from it. The organization gained many adherents in the years following Finley's death through the work of a relatively small core of dedicated volunteers.

Francis Scott Key stood among the most dedicated. He used his lawyerly talents, especially his persuasive oratorical skills, to recruit new members, raise money from private individuals, and lobby Congress and state legislatures to fund the colonization effort.

He regularly spoke at meetings of groups large and small, primarily in Washington, Maryland, and Virginia, on behalf of the society. Key gave an impassioned speech, for example, at a public meeting on July 8, 1817, at the First Presbyterian Church in Baltimore. The purpose of the gathering was to set up a Colonization Society branch in that city. Colonel John Eager Howard, a Revolutionary War hero and a former Maryland governor whose son Charles would marry Frank Key's oldest child, Elizabeth, in 1825, helped organize the meeting. Before it ended, the Baltimore Colonization Society adopted a constitution and appointed officers, including John Howard as chairman.

Francis Scott Key gave "a most impressive, animated and pious recital" at the meeting, one newspaper reported.[1] In it, Key made a rare public reference to the "star-spangled banner." He spoke of his vision of a colony of former freed blacks in Africa, "surrounded with all the blessings of civilization." Among those blessings, Key said, would be "the spires of temples glittering in the sun," busy commercial harbors, and the "hum of industry." When the natives would be asked what country was responsible for this utopia, Key said they "would reply—pointing to the emblem of our sovereignty—the nation with the star-spangled banner."[2]

Frank Key made the trip to Baltimore without his family. Polly and the children were at Terra Rubra in Pipe Creek, where they spent virtually every summer to escape the heat of Washington. When he had time, the thirty-eight-year-old father visited his large brood of seven there. The Key children, who ranged in age that summer from thirteen-year-old Elizabeth to one-year-old Daniel—had a summer tutor named W. B. Hodgeson. Their father and other tutors provided academic and religious instruction in Georgetown; Hodgeson followed that secular-and-religious educational model in Pipe Creek.

The day began at five every morning when the young tutor woke the Key children. In an August 1 letter to their father, Hodgeson wrote that at six o'clock "they read to me in their prayer books," observing that they seemed to enjoy getting back to schooling after a short summer vacation. "They did not regret that their holiday was over," he said, "knowing that it was your wish that they should go to school."[3]

The first annual meeting of the American Colonization Society took place on Thursday, January 1, 1818, at two in the afternoon in the hall of the U.S. House of Representatives. In his opening speech Justice Bushrod Washington predicted a rosy future for the society. He reported that auxiliary groups had been formed in New York, Philadelphia, and Baltimore. Washington also said the society had hired Samuel Mills and Ebenezer Burgess to go to Africa by way of England to find a suitable site on the African west coast for a colony. In England, the men were to meet with the Duke of Gloucester, the president of that nation's colonization group, the African Institution.

Elias Caldwell, the society's secretary, also spoke, as did Charles Fenton Mercer, now a member of Congress. Mercer painted a disturbing picture of the impact on white society of the increasing number of freed people of color.

If the large number of freed blacks "has not endangered our peace, [it] has impaired the value of all the private property in a large section of our country," Mercer told the group. He went on to describe the places where freed blacks lived as "a wretched cultivation," filled with a "degraded, idle, and vicious population who sally forth from their coverts, beneath the obscurity of night, and plunder the rich proprietors of the valleys."[4]

At the end of the meeting Frank Key was reappointed to the twelve-man board of managers that ran day-to-day operations of the national society. The managers sent Key and Mercer to Philadelphia, New York, and Boston (at their own expense) on a fundraising trip for the Mills and Burgess mission. They set off in February, but never made it to the northern cities. Key and Mercer stopped in Baltimore, spoke to some of that city's most prominent citizens, and raised $5,000, but Key returned to Washington soon after.[5]

Frank Key had other matters to attend to: primarily his law practice but also his volunteer work with the Georgetown Lancaster School and with his church work. Now the president of the Georgetown Lancaster School, Key wrote a report to the Georgetown Board of Alderman and Board of Common Council that February on the state of the school. Some 1,100 children, Key said, had "left the school for various employments after making progress in the different classes." Of that group of 604 boys and 498 girls, about three-fourths had studied free of charge.

The school stayed open on Saturdays, Key said, when young women volunteers worked with girls "in want of clothing." The girls learned to sew and were given the materials to make their own clothes. "During the last two years," Key reported, "between forty and fifty poor girls have been clothed by this means," and others were given "comfortable clothes, which, with the assistance and direction of these ladies, have been made by themselves."

On Sundays, Key reported, the school hosted the Sunday School Society, at which young people learned "to read and feel the all-important doctrines of the Bible." This helped keep them out of mischief, Key noted, lest they partake "in the idleness or dissipation prevailing around them."[6]

Christ Church, the new Episcopal congregation that Frank Key helped organize in Georgetown, broke ground on its new building on May 8, 1818.

A month later, on June 9, 1818, Key child number eight came along, a boy Frank and Polly named Philip Barton Key in honor of his beloved uncle. The family called him Barton.

Religious matters remained an important part of Frank Key's activities. In June 1818 he helped found the Society for the Education of Pious Men for the Ministry of the Protestant Church in Maryland and Virginia in Alexandria, Virginia. Known as the Education Society, the school changed its name in 1823 to the Virginia Theological Seminary. Frank Key was the only layman on its board of managers and remained a strong supporter of the Episcopal seminary for the rest of his life.[7]

Later that summer, after years of trying, he successfully induced a fundamentalist religious reawakening in his old friend John Randolph. The eccentric Virginian wrote to Key in September that he had "at last reconciled to my God, and have assurances of his pardon, through faith in Christ, against which the very gates of hell cannot prevail."[8] Key couldn't have been happier.

"I do, indeed, my dear friend, rejoice with you," Key wrote to Randolph. "I have long wished...that you would experience what God has now blessed you with....May the grace that has brought you from 'darkness to light' from 'death to life,' keep you forever!"

Key rejoiced "with some trembling," however, given Randolph's mercurial temperament. "The conversion of such a man if he continues to 'walk in the light' is a most important thing, but the profession without a corresponding life is a cause of failing to many," Key told his friend, Reverend William Meade. If Randolph "is indeed a Christian, he will be no ordinary one. His enthusiasm & talents, if rightly used in the service of his Master, if directed and governed by the holy spirit, will do wonders."[9]

Late on a dark and rainy October night, Frank Key performed an emergency baptism in his Georgetown home. As he and Polly were about to go to bed, a woman with an infant in her arms, her husband, and a female friend showed up at their door.

"One of them I recognized to be a pious woman" from St. John's Church, Key said. "She told me [the baby] was dying," and that she was taking the infant to the home of Reverend Addison of St. John's to be baptized. But the group saw candlelight at the Key house and knocked on the door because they thought the baby would die by the time they reached Addison's residence.[10]

The woman asked Frank Key to baptize her infant on the spot. Key advised the woman to take the baby to an ordained clergyman who lived nearby. But the woman "continued to express [her] conviction that the child would most likely expire before they could get there." Key reconsidered and thinking only of the dying child, "according to the forms of the Church, baptized the infant." Polly Key then looked at the baby and gave it "some medicine," her husband said. The child recovered.

For performing that seemingly good deed Key received a castigating letter from James Kemp, the Episcopal bishop in Baltimore. Key chafed at the scolding. "I cannot acknowledge error where I do not see it," he wrote back to Kemp. Key asked Kemp to show him a church "rule or opinion" forbidding his action. If he found one, Key said, "I will candidly own my mistake." No rule or ruling was forthcoming.

Not long after the baptism episode, in late October 1818, Frank Key joined a group of other prominent landowning Georgetown citizens to express their outrage at an outbreak of illegal hunting that recently had taken place. The group gave written warning in the October 26 issue of the *National Messenger* newspaper to the "idle and disorderly persons passing through, hunting and shooting on our lands, and in our enclosures (but particularly on Sundays)." We "are determined," the landowners said, "from this date to prosecute all we find so trespassing."

American Colonization Society (ACS) business continued to occupy significant amounts of Frank Key's time. He attended a special ACS meeting on November 21 at the City Hotel in Washington. On January 8, 1819, at the second annual ACS meeting (held at the F Street Associated Reformed Presbyterian Church, also known as "Dr. Laurie's church"), Francis Scott Key, Elias Caldwell, and Walter Jones were appointed a committee to write a report to Congress outlining the society's mission and accomplishments. The trio's report would also serve as the opening salvo in the society's attempt to get federal funds to further its mission.

The report reached the House of Representatives on January 23. Speaker of the House Henry Clay, a prominent ACS supporter, sent it to a special committee to look into the matter. It was no coincidence that Charles Fenton Mercer of Virginia was one of the three congressmen on that panel.

Mercer had been working assiduously in Congress to gain federal support for the ACS. He tied that support to a bill he sponsored earlier in January that addressed the fate of Africans removed from confiscated illegal slave-trading vessels in the United States—something the 1807 federal law banning the importation of slaves did not address. Virtually all of those men and women wound up being sold into slavery. Mercer's legislation called on federal authorities to arrange for those freed people to be sent back to Africa. Although the ACS was not named, astute observers knew that the organization would be heavily involved in any government-funded colonization effort growing out of the legislation.

The January 23 ACS report said that the "biggest single question" the society faced was whether or not Congress would authorize federal funds. "Adequate aid and sanction from the Government," the report said, would bring "permanent, practical and important benefits" from colonization, benefits "which will be felt equally in our social and domestic relations, as in the advancement of the great object of political and international morality." The report, taking a page from Mercer's book, defined that "great object" as "the suppression of the slave trade."[11]

On March 3, both the House and Senate approved Mercer's bill. Officially named "An Act in Addition to the Acts Prohibiting the Slave Trade," the legislation authorized the government to use U.S. Navy ships to seize any American vessels carrying slaves and to transport those illegally enslaved people "beyond the limits of the United States."[12] The law also appropriated $100,000 in federal funds to carry out the program.

Mercer secured the support of President James Monroe, whose northern Virginia home, Oak Hill, stood a stone's throw from Mercer's home in Aldie. Secretary of the Treasury William Harris Crawford, a vice president of the ACS, also strongly supported the idea. Monroe signed the bill, ignoring strong opposition from several members of his Cabinet, primarily Secretary of State John Quincy Adams of Massachusetts.

Adams believed that the ACS's real goal was to rid the nation of free blacks who would agitate to end slavery and incite slave revolts. Adams once told an ACS member that the "whole project was unlikely to diminish the number of slaves in the United States by a single number." Even if the ACS "did effect the emigration of free persons of color," Adams said, "it was rather a public injury than a benefit."[13]

In a March 12, 1819, meeting with Adams, President Monroe stressed the negative impact of the growing number of freed blacks as he tried to win his skeptical Secretary of State over to the colonization idea. Monroe told

Adams that day that the problem dated back to the end of the American Revolution when many slave owners freed their human property because of the owners' strongly held antislavery feelings, which in turn, Monroe continued, "introduced a class of very dangerous people." Said class was made up of "free blacks, who lived by pilfering, and corrupted the slaves and produced such pernicious consequences" that the Virginia General Assembly was forced to "prohibit their emancipation by law." The "important object now," Monroe told Adams, "was to remove these free blacks and provide a place to which the emancipated slaves might go."[14]

Adams remained unconvinced. He believed that some ACS members were "exceedingly humane" and that the society's goals were "both useful and attainable." But he characterized those men as "weak-minded." Other ACS men were "speculators in official profits and honors, which a colonial establishment would of course produce." Still others were "speculators in political popularity" trying to please the abolitionists and slave-holders. Then there were the "cunning slave-holders, who see that the plan may be carried far enough to produce the effect of raising the market price of their slaves."[15]

Most abolitionists agreed with Adams's assessment. Colonization, the British antislavery advocate George Smith wrote, "originated in the fears of slave-holders, and is the offspring of the Legislature of Virginia." No part of the ACS's mission, Smith said, is "to abolish slavery [or] to suppress the slave trade or to promote civilization or Christianity in Africa." Its "simple design was and is to get rid of the free coloured people, who are regarded in the slave-holding states as the filth and offscouring of all things. Their influence is obviously dreaded, and their increasing numbers looked upon with the greatest horror and alarm."[16]

The "Act in Addition" legislation did not include any details explaining exactly where the freed slaves would be located. That's why Key and his fellow ACS leaders held separate meetings on March 12, 1819, with President Monroe, Secretary of State Adams, and Attorney General William Wirt. The ACS men pressed the three government leaders to use the appropriated funds to buy land in Africa and establish a colony of freed American blacks, and to authorize the ACS to play a pivotal role in this new, government-sponsored colonization effort.

After the meeting, however, President Monroe nixed the idea of the government buying the land, which didn't go over well with Key. "The

President has forgotten his promises," he wrote in a letter to Reverend William Meade.[17] Monroe, however, told the ACS representatives that if the society itself bought land and set up a colony, the government would help "defray all expenses of transporting the captured negroes & making provisions for their reception" in Africa.[18]

Key met for several hours that day with Attorney General William Wirt, who felt the ACS plan was "impracticable," Key said, "but concurred in all our wishes." Key also said that Wirt seemed to fear "some excitement among the slaves" in reaction to the new, growing support for colonization.[19]

Later that day, Key, Walter Jones, and General John Mason (the same John Mason who had sent Key to Baltimore in 1814) met face-to-face with Secretary of State John Quincy Adams. Adams continued to insist that the new law did not give the government the authority to underwrite any type of colonization effort. And he came out strongly against the government buying land in Africa to set up a colony. The March 2 law, Adams pointed out, "had no reference to the settlement of a colony."

Monroe agreed with Adams that the United States should not buy land in Africa for a colony for freed slaves. But the President disagreed completely with his Secretary of State's opinion that the government should not encourage the ACS colonization effort. Later that year Monroe announced that he would allow government funds to be used to send two American agents—with a "small salary" of $1,500 for one and $1,200 to the other—to the coast of Africa to "make the necessary arrangements" to help colonized Africans adapt and adjust to their new homes.[20]

Monroe's announcement paved the way for the first American Colonization Society mission to Africa. On February 20, 1820, the ACS-chartered ship *Elizabeth* set sail from New York harbor with eighty-eight freed black men, women, and children on board, along with two government agents, Reverend Samuel Bacon of Boston and John P. Bankson, and one ACS man, Samuel Crozer. The Monroe Administration provided a Navy sloop of war to shepherd the *Elizabeth* across the Atlantic.

"The three white agents of the ACS shared a generous-sized cabin. The eighty-eight blacks were back in steerage, sleeping on mildewed mattresses made of corn husks," Helene Cooper, a descendant of Elijah Johnson, one of the freed blacks on the ship, wrote. "The passengers spent a lot of their time praying." Before the *Elizabeth* left port, Reverend Bacon gathered the freed blacks together and read the section of the Book of Deuteronomy in which Moses promises that the Ten Commandments would deliver the Jews to the Promised Land.

Bacon told the blacks "they were pilgrims, new explorers, paving the way for other blacks to follow." They were also missionaries, he told them, going forth to the dark continent of Africa to convert the heathen Africans."[21]

The ships landed at Freetown on the coast of Sierra Leone on March 9, 1820. The freed people and the agents moved on to Sherbro Island about seventy miles down the coast. The swampy island was not exactly a hospitable environment. Within six months forty-nine colonists, along with Bacon, Bankson, and Crozer, died after contracting a virulent fever.

A second ACS contingent of thirty-three freed blacks sailed to Sierra Leone on January 21, 1821, accompanied by four ACS agents: Reverend Ephraim Bacon (the recently deceased Samuel Bacon's brother), Jonathan B. Winn, Christian Wiltberger, and Joseph Andrus. When the Sherbro Island chiefs refused to sell the ACS more land, the agents convinced a group of other tribal leaders to part with a 130-square-mile area on Cape Mesurado, on the coast north of Freetown, for the equivalent of about $300. Soon after, Andrus and Winn died of fever.

The new land was named Liberia ("free land") in 1824 and its capital, first known as Christopolis, was christened Monrovia in honor of the American president who paved the way for the colonization effort. Liberia, however, was not a sovereign state; ACS agents governed the colony under a constitution and set of laws that, among other things, banned slavery and the slave trade. In 1847 the nation of Liberia would declare its independence from the ACS. Colonized peoples made up about five percent of the new nation.

A dark shadow fell across the Era of Good Feelings for two years beginning in 1819: the American nation's first significant economic depression, known as the Panic of 1819. As many banks failed, the severe economic downturn hit cities particularly hard in the form of unprecedented, large-scale unemployment, primarily among factory workers, artisans, and mechanics. John Randolph, among many others, took a large financial hit when he lost a big investment in a large mercantile firm in Richmond.

"You have no conception of the gloom and distress that pervade this place," Randolph wrote to Key from Richmond on May 3, 1819. "There has been nothing like it since 1785, when, from the same causes (paper money and a general peace) there was a general depression of every thing."[22]

Frank Key also lost money on at least one investment, Union Bank shares, and his legal business lagged during the severe economic downturn. In a letter to Randolph on July 21, Key enumerated his "cares and pains and troubles," then spoke of how his religious faith helped him ride out the storm.[23] "In the seasons of despondency which I have felt, great relief has been afforded to my mind by the Psalms," Key wrote to Randolph. Only God-fearing Christians "can endure the many troubles of this life."

He ended the letter with: "May you soon experience His ever-made help and have 'all joy and peace in blessings'!"[24]

On July 21, 1819, the same day that Key wrote to Randolph, an epidemic of yellow fever broke out in Baltimore. By the time the scourge ended, in late October, nearly 2,300 people had died. Thousands of Baltimore residents fled the city in the face of the deadly disease. In Washington early in October, Frank Key joined with a group of other concerned citizens to raise money for the refugees. Key volunteered his time to solicit his neighbors in Georgetown to "afford some pecuniary relief" to the "persons driven from their homes by the malignant fever," a local newspaper reported.[25]

The yellow fever epidemic also struck New York City that summer and fall, forcing the cancellation of a planned Colonization Society meeting. In November Frank Key worked with Reverend Meade on a plan to send twelve captured Africans being held in Baltimore back to their homeland, along with a group of freed blacks. They hoped the ACS would send as many as six hundred families to Africa during the winter of 1819-1820. As it turned out, the group managed to convince only about a hundred free black people to leave the United States and settle in Africa. That would not be the last disappointment for the American Colonization Society.

By the end of November of 1819, Key felt frustrated with the ACS's private fundraising. "I hope you will make a zealous effort as soon as possible" to help raise money," Key wrote to one ACS supporter. "The last shipments have emptied our treasury and put us in debt."

Key suggested that the society recruit "intelligent" agents to canvas areas of Maryland and Virginia to ask "every man and woman for a dollar" for the cause.[26]

9

A STORMY TUMULT
OF FEELING

"He is indeed as near perfection as our poor nature can go, although he would be shocked to hear it said."
—*John Randolph on Francis Scott Key, Feb. 24, 1820*

Frank Key, who owned six slaves in 1820, played a prominent role in the third annual meeting of the American Colonization Society, which took place on January 8 that year at Dr. Laurie's church in Washington. Among other things, the men of ACS decided that the society would stress its "humane views," as Bushrod Washington put it, and its "exalted work of benevolence."

In other words, the ACS would emphasize that its mission aimed at ending slavery, rather than shipping freed blacks out of the country. Among the resolutions adopted was one that Frank Key put forward to appoint a committee to draft a paper to be delivered to Congress making a case for more legislation "to ensure the entire abolition of the African Slave Trade."[1]

Key (along with Jones, Caldwell, and Mason) co-wrote the long, wordy, lawyerly "memorial," which John Randolph introduced into the House of Representatives on February 1, 1820, three weeks before the first ACS ship would sail to Africa. In his introductory remarks on the House floor, Randolph said that the ACS was having trouble getting contributions from individuals and looked to Congress for "pecuniary and other aid," as well as to sanction the Society's mission by granting it an official congressional incorporation.[2]

The memorial suggested building on the 1819 law with new legislation that would authorize the federal government to help transport "civilized people of color"—not just freed captured slaves—from the United States to Africa. It mentioned the "rapid increase" in the numbers of freed blacks in the United States and pointed out that this was neither a "useful or happy" situation. The answer, for blacks and whites "should be separation." That "humanitarian" separation effort would be best accomplished by procuring a country for the freed blacks "in the land of their forefathers," an idea that had been accepted by "a vast majority of all classes of our citizens."

The overall message tied colonization to the "disgraceful" slave trade. Key and company said that since the English set up their colonization settlement in Sierra Leone, the slave trade had been "rapidly ceasing in that part of the coast." A new, larger American-led effort, therefore, would bring even more "civilization" to Africa, which would lead to the further "suppression of the slave trade." Colonization, the memorial said, would be the "most powerful and indispensable auxiliary to the means already adopted for the extermination" of the international traffic in human beings.

Not long after the ACS meeting ended, Congress took up the extremely contentious issue of whether or not slavery would be permitted in the two new states about to enter the Union, Maine and Missouri. The Senate hotly debated the question for the better part of two weeks in February. That body finally voted, 24–20, on February 17, 1820, to a compromise in which Missouri would be permitted to be a slave state, but slavery would be prohibited in Maine and—more importantly and portentously—in the rest of the vast Louisiana Territory, which made up most of the Great Plains in the Midwest. The House agreed to the Missouri Compromise on March 2.

Many slaveholders saw that legislation as a grim portent of things to come since this was the first time the federal government had outlawed slavery inside the United States. The law "aroused and filled me with alarm," Thomas Jefferson wrote to a friend in April. "I have been among the most sanguine in believing that our Union would be of long duration. I now doubt it much."[3]

During the second week of February Frank Key had made an emergency trip to Terra Rubra after getting word that his sixty-five-year-old father was seriously ill. It turned out to be a false alarm. "What must it have been to have his bedside attended by such a son!" John Randolph marveled. "He is indeed as near perfection as our poor nature can go, although he would be shocked to hear it said."[4]

Frank Key returned to Washington to find that the owners of the house on Bridge Street in Georgetown where he and Polly had been living since they'd moved to the nation's capital had put the property up for sale. A newspaper advertisement described the house as a "large and commodious two story Brick Dwelling" with a "fine garden, and all the requisite out-buildings...in good repair." The location, the ad said, "is very eligible for a private family or a Hotel."[5] No sale took place.

Key did get some legal work during the two-year Panic of 1819. He continued representing clients, mainly in civil matters, most often in real estate dealings. He also received a small stipend, $60 a year, for his legal work on behalf of the Georgetown Board of Alderman and the Board of Common Council, Georgetown's two governing bodies. At the end of 1820 Key joined the eleven-member Board of Common Council, filling a vacancy.

In one of the many real estate deals he was involved in, Key and another attorney, James Dunlop Jr., made the arrangements for a public property auction on November 6, 1820. On the block: Fruit Hill, a five-hundred-acre farm owned by Martin O'Connor in Montgomery County, Maryland, about five miles from Georgetown. The property included a main house and other buildings. Also auctioned: all of Mr. O'Connor's personal property, consisting of "2 negroes, a woman and a girl, 300 bushels of small grain, corn, hay, tobacco, horses, cows, sheep, hogs, wagon, cart, farming utensils, and household furniture, &c."[6]

Frank Key was a featured speaker at the fourth annual ACS meeting held on January 18, 1821, at Dr. Laurie's church. The group adopted a resolution bemoaning the "calamities" that had "befallen it during the past year." Said calamities included the "untimely" deaths of the three white agents in Africa, Samuel Bacon, John Bankson, and Samuel Crozer.[7]

On August 16, 1821, Polly Key gave birth to her ninth child, a girl the Keys named Ellen Lloyd. On October 13, John Ross Key, "an officer of the revolution and a respectable inhabitant of Frederick county," as the short obituary in the *Washington Gazette* put it, died at age sixty-seven at Terra Rubra.[8] Frank Key's mother Anne, who would outlive her husband by nine years, stayed on at the family estate in the company of her enslaved servants. Her daughter Anne Taney and her family lived nearby; her son Frank and his brood in Georgetown visited often.

In February of 1822 Frank Key associated himself with another do-gooder organization when he joined the board of directors of the newly formed American Society for Promoting the Civilization and General Improvement of the Indian Tribes of the United States. The board included other establishment Washington figures, among them, U.S. Attorney General William Wirt.

Key continued to keep faith with the ACS, attending its fifth annual meeting on March, 7, 1822. At that gathering the society officially mourned the deaths of two more of their agents in Africa, Reverend Joseph R. Andrus, who had died on July 27, 1821, and Jonathan B. Winn, who had succumbed in August.

Meanwhile in Sierra Leone, disease, disorganization, and violent opposition from neighboring African tribes continued to plague the colonization effort. In the summer of 1822, however, things began to change when twenty-eight-year-old Jehudi Ashmun, the editor of a theological journal and a committed colonizationist, arrived in Sierra Leone with his wife and thirty-seven freed blacks.

Sometimes known as "the father of Liberia," Ashmun, who was white, took firm charge of the ACS effort. Working independently—and without full ACS sanction—he helped the colonists fight off the hostile natives. Over the next few years hundreds of Africans died in what one ACS critic characterized as "a murdering war against the natives, in which they were conquered by the superior skill of the emigrants in the use of fire arms."[9]

In one fight in the fall of 1822, Ashmun later wrote, he and his men fired on "eight hundred men [who were] pressed shoulder to shoulder in so compact a form that a child might easily have walked on their heads from one end to another.... Every shot literally spent its force in a mass of living human flesh!"[10] In another skirmish a few weeks later, Ashmun wrote that "the quantities of [native] blood with which the ground was drenched [were] considerable."

Liberia, the staunch abolitionist William Lloyd Garrison noted, "was conceived in blood and its footsteps will be marked with blood down to old age—the blood of the poor natives—unless a special interposition of Divine Providence prevents such a calamity."[11]

Ashmun's wife died of malaria in Liberia, and he became seriously ill but quickly recovered. Ruling with an iron hand, Ashmun continued to lead the settlers in fighting off physical threats from the natives. He also expanded the ACS land holdings in Liberia. Fighting a relapse of malaria, Ashmun left Liberia early in 1828 to try to recover his health in the United States. He died at age thirty-four on August 25.

In June of 1822, still reeling from the implications of the Missouri Compromise, slaveowners north and south were shocked to learn about a long-planned, widespread slave revolt in Charleston, South Carolina, led by a former slave named Denmark Vesey. After authorities learned of the plot—which came to be known as Vesey's Rebellion—the ringleader was arrested and dozens of slaves rounded up. Vesey and three slaves were tried, convicted, and hanged on July 2, 1822. Thirty-two other slaves believed to be part of the plot also were executed.

Six days after Vesey was hung, Frank and Polly Key experienced the worst tragedy of their lives: the death of their eight-year-old son Edward. On Monday, July 8, 1822, the boy did not come home from his tutor's at the regular time, around 4. Frank Key was in Annapolis on business. Polly Key did not worry at first because the boy often played for an extra hour or so at school.

At around 6 p.m., however, one of Edward's schoolmates told fourteen-year-old John Key that he and Edward—whom his siblings called Little Eddy—were playing at the water's edge in the Keys's backyard and that the little boy had disappeared into the Potomac River. John Key "ran to the place and went into the river to dive for" his brother, his father later wrote. "His distress soon brought a crowd to the place, and [Eddy] was found. But life was gone. All efforts to revive him were unavailing, and about 9 o'clock he was brought to his Mother, cold and dead."[12]

Polly Key and their other children experienced the horror of Eddy's death firsthand. Frank Key didn't. "I was spared all that stormy tumult of feeling endured by my poor wife and children who were at the scene of suffering," Key wrote, "all that agony (which I know not how I could have borne) of hearing he was in the water, that they were searching for him, that he was found, that they were attempting to revive him, that it was in vain."

Frank Key's main reaction to the horrific news was a burst of religious feeling imbued with severe self-recrimination—not for not being in Georgetown when the boy died, but for not being a sufficiently devout Christian. Key said that the night before the drowning he had something of a spiritual epiphany that brought him "into a state of mind that greatly softened the shock of my affliction."

After church that day, Key said, he spent the evening and night alone contemplating his "faults and failings." He worried that he hadn't truly "given [himself] to the Lord." He pondered his self-worth and his devotion to Jesus all night and the next day (the day his son drowned), realizing "the folly and ingratitude" of his conduct. Key ultimately decided that the only answer for him would be "a complete submission to the will of God."

That night Francis Scott Key went to bed thinking he had spent the "most spiritual day than I had done for some time." He renewed his "surrender to God, lamented my past failings and prayed for mercy and grace."

Key received word of his young son's death the next morning. "I hurried home," he wrote, "with feelings more composed and subdued than I could have supposed possible."

When he arrived in Georgetown, Frank Key found that his wife had had a similar spiritual experience. "I rejoiced to hear that in the midst of all her terror and distress, she had seen and acknowledged the Hand of God in this chastisement," Key wrote. "She said it was sent for her sins, and that she deserved it all and more, and she seemed earnestly desirous to improve as she ought."

His conclusion: What God "has done is best for us all... [and] is certainly for the improvement of my faith and patience." From then on, Key wrote, he would give himself "and all I have and own, to God."

It's entirely possible that one of the "faults and failings" Frank Key so severely castigated himself for in 1822 was his association with the Delphian Club, a small group of accomplished young professional men (lawyers, historians, editors, and authors) who met monthly in Baltimore to eat, drink, and be frivolous. The club, named after the ancient Greek

Oracle at Delphi, began in August 1816. It had nine permanent members at a time, one for each one of the Greek muses. They met at each others' homes and offices, adopted silly names—Abraham Kenuckkofritz, Orlando Garangula, Jasper Hornblende—and brought original prose and poetry to be read at each gathering.

Frank Key never became a permanent member of the club, which dissolved in 1825. But he did attend meetings periodically. Other nonpermanent Delphians included U.S. Attorney General William Wirt and the acclaimed portrait painter Rembrandt Peale. Those men and the permanent Delphians "indulged in pleasantries, in the manufacture of puns and epigrams and epitaphs and humorous stories," one observer noted, including "many well-written essays and poems."[13]

Frank Key, the inveterate writer of G-rated poetry, very likely contributed a decidedly erotic poem to one of the Delphian Club gatherings. The poem, titled "On a Young Lady's Going into a Shower Bath," does not appear in the posthumously published, Key-family-produced *Poems of the Late Francis S. Key, Esq.* It does appear in Edward Delaplaine's adoring 1937 biography of Key.

It is nothing less than a metaphor-laden ode to the pleasures of a woman's body. To wit:

> O then those charms of which the lighted touch
> Would fire the frozen blood of apathy,
> Each drop of me should touch, should eager run
> Down her fair forehead, down her blushing cheek
> To taste the more inviting sweets beneath,
> Should trickle down her neck, should slowly wind
> In silver circles round those hills of snow....[14]

Francis Scott Key kept up his perfect attendance at the American Colonization Society meetings. In his legal work Key also continued to deal with slavery issues. In April 1823, for example, Key served as cocounsel for a slave, William Jordan, who petitioned for his freedom in the U.S. Circuit Court in Washington.

Jordan had been brought into Washington from Wheeling, Virginia, in January of 1823 by his owner Valentine Peyton, who then sold Jordan to Lemuel Sawyer. Jordan filed suit under a 1796 law which held that slaves brought into the District and sold within three years were entitled to their freedom.

Frank Key convinced the jury that the law applied in Jordan's case, but Chief Judge William Cranch overruled the jury, saying that the evidence did not prove that Jordan was brought to Washington "for sale or to reside." Key then asked the court to suspend its final ruling because the opposing counsel was not in court when the judge made his decision. Cranch granted that request. The parties later settled out of court.[15]

On June 3, 1823, less than a year after the death of young Edward Key, there was cause for a Key family celebration. Eighteen-year-old Maria Lloyd Key married Henry Maynadier Steele, twenty-four, in Annapolis that day. Described by the renowned writer Washington Irving as "pious, intellectual, [and] beautiful," Maria was the second Key daughter, but the first child of Frank and Polly to marry.[16]

In 1823, Frank Key, who had been a trustee of the Maryland General Theological Seminary since 1820, joined with several other pious Episcopalians—including Reverend William Meade, his fellow ACS advocate—to start a seminary in Alexandria to prepare men for the priesthood. The Protestant Episcopal Theological Seminary—today known as the Virginia Theological Seminary—opened its doors that year with two instructors and fourteen students.

Frank Key also continued to work hard to raise money for the ACS. The society had started a nationwide funding drive that summer.

"Want of funds," an ACS report that appeared in many newspapers around the country, said, "has prevented very vigorous and extensive exertions," and "said occurrences have obstructed...operations." The report went on describe the colonization effort's problems with disease and unfriendly African natives.

"Like most uncivilized men," the report said of the Africans, they "are treacherous...they will not hesitate to murder the defenceless."

The report once again emphasized the goal of ending slavery, "an immense evil," and painted the colonization program as the best way to "rescue from present and future ruin a miserable race."[17]

Before 1823 ended, the Keys again celebrated more positive family news: the birth of their tenth child. On November 20, 1823, Polly Key, at age thirty-nine, produced their fifth daughter. They named her Mary Alicia. The family called her Alice.

10

A VIGOROUS AND WELL-CULTIVATED INTELLECT

"By the law of nature all men are free. The presumption that even black men and Africans are slaves is not a universal presumption."
—*Francis Scott Key, February 26, 1825*

In 1825 Francis Scott Key played a starring role in one of the most important Supreme Court cases of the decade. Given the prominence of slavery in Key's life and law career, it was no coincidence that the case involved international slave trafficking.

The overriding issue of the *Antelope* case was whether or not American anti–slave trafficking laws applied in cases involving other countries in which such trafficking was legal.[1]

The long, convoluted *Antelope* case dated to June 29, 1820, when a U.S. Revenue-Marine (the forerunner of the Coast Guard) cutter intercepted the *Antelope* off the coast of Florida, then a Spanish territory. The Americans found 281 African men in chains on the ship. The cutter seized the vessel and took the men to Savannah. The *Antelope*'s captain, John Smith, had taken the African men in raids he had made from his ship, the *Columbia*, on Spanish, Portuguese, and American-owned vessels along the coast of West Africa. In those raids, Smith also had captured the American-owned *Antelope*. The *Columbia* wrecked on its way back across the Atlantic, and the enslaved men were moved onto the seized *Antelope*.

Federal authorities arrested Smith and seized his human cargo under the 1819 law that Charles Fenton Mercer and the American Colonization Society had steered through Congress. The slaves remained in Savannah to await their fate.

The Spanish and Portuguese governments filed claims in the U.S. courts to recover their human cargo. They argued that the slave trade was legal in both countries at the time. The federal government countered that American anti–slave trafficking laws held precedence, and that this country would follow the letter of the 1819 Act in Addition law and send the men back to Africa.

The case wound its way through the courts and came to the Supreme Court on February 26, 1825. Attorney General William Wirt chose Francis Scott Key to be cocounsel because of his long experience before the high court and his well-known ability to sway judges and juries with his astute legal arguing—and because he and Wirt both shared an aversion to international slave trafficking. They maintained that U.S. law trumped international law and that the African men taken off the *Antelope* in chains should be freed and sent back to Africa.

Key and Wirt faced off against John McPherson Berrien, a Georgia lawyer who had just been elected to the U.S. Senate, representing the vice counsel of Spain, and former Congressman John Jared Ingersoll, the U.S. district attorney for the Eastern District of Pennsylvania, who represented the vice counsel of Portugal. Berrien had been active on the case since it began in the Georgia courts in 1820.

The *Antelope* case attracted national attention. The Supreme Court galleries filled with spectators the day oral arguments began. All four lawyers acquitted themselves well, but observers singled out Frank Key for special praise. Henry Stuart Foote, then a twenty-one-year-old Virginia lawyer, wrote in his memoir that he had never "witnessed a more interesting forensic discussion" than what he heard in the *Antelope* case, which, he recalled, drew a large audience "of refined and intelligent persons" of both sexes. "I was very much entertained with the whole argument, but I was particularly charmed with the speech of Mr. Key and that of Mr. Berrien."

Foote, who went on to become a U.S. senator and then governor of Mississippi, described Frank Key as "tall, erect, and of admirable physical proportions" with "handsome and winning features" and "a soft and touching pensiveness of expression." His expression, Foote said, almost bordered "on sadness" but came alive "in moments of special excitement, or when anything occurred to awaken the dormant heroism of his nature." At that point Key exhibited the "the higher powers of his vigorous and well-cultivated intellect," Foote wrote, and his face brightened as he spoke in "a noble audacity of tone and gesture which pleased while it dazzled the beholder."

In the *Antelope* case, Foote said, Key "greatly surpassed the expectations of his most admiring friends," ending his argument with "a thrilling and even electrifying picture of the horrors connected with the African slave trade."[2]

Henry Foote's descriptions of Frank Key in action before the Supreme Court may have been hyperbole, but an objective reading of the forty-four-year-old lawyer's arguments shows that this was among the Francis Scott Key's finest hours in publicly enumerating and denouncing the evils of slavery.

"Slaves are no longer acquired merely by capture in war or by trade," Key argued, but "are seized and carried off by the traders and their agents." Enslaved persons "are clandestinely brought away, under circumstances of extreme cruelty, aggravated by the necessity of concealment, and smuggled into every country where the cupidity of avarice creates a demand for these unhappy victims."

The Spanish and Portuguese owners of the enslaved Africans, he told the packed galleries of the Supreme Court, claimed that the men were their property. The "possessor of goods," Key argued, "is to be presumed the lawful owner." But, he said, "this is true as to *goods*, because they have universally and necessarily an owner. But these are *men*, of whom it cannot be affirmed that they have universally and necessarily an owner."

In some countries, Key said, enslaved people may be considered property, "but by the law of nature, all men are free. The presumption that ... black men and Africans are slaves is not a universal presumption."[3]

Despite Key's and Wirt's best efforts, however, the Marshall Court ruled against them. Chief Justice Marshall was not swayed by issues of morality in human trafficking. In his ruling Marshall said that international law took precedence over American laws. "In examining claims of this momentous importance; claims in which the sacred rights of liberty and of property come in conflict with each other," Marshall said, "this Court must not yield to feelings which might seduce it from the path of duty, but must obey the mandates of the law."[4]

During the five years it took the case to be decided, several of the enslaved Africans had died in captivity. The court ordered that some three dozen of the survivors be sold into slavery in this country and the funds from those sales be used to settle the Spanish and Portuguese claims. The rest, 120 men, were sent to Liberia on the transport ship *Norfolk* in July of 1827—a moral victory for Key and Wirt.

Sixteen years later John Quincy Adams, in arguing the *Amistad* case before the Supreme Court, had these words to say about the *Antelope* case: "For little short of the space of five years, nearly three hundred captured Africans had been kept as prisoners of the United States." He called the imprisonment a denial of the Africans' "inalienable right to liberty" and an act by the United States of "cold blooded apathy to human suffering." Marshall's decision back then, Adams said, was based on "one obnoxious principle" and ignored the fact that the slave trade is "contrary to the laws of nature."[5]

The *Antelope* decision also amounted to another Early Republic governmental sanction of the legality of slavery inside the borders of the United States. It "much relieved the minds of the slavery men of the South, who viewed with apprehension any attempt on the part of the Judiciary to deal with the slavery question in any phase," the constitutional legal scholar Charles Warren wrote.[6]

John Quincy Adams, the sixth President of the United States, took office on March 4, 1825, following an extremely contentious, four-candidate 1824 election. All the candidates were Democratic-Republicans. Two of them—Henry Clay and William H. Crawford—were strong American Colonization Society advocates.

In that watershed election, War of 1812 hero Andrew Jackson of Tennessee won both the popular and electoral votes. But because Jackson didn't receive the majority of the electoral votes, Congress decided that the winner would be determined by a state-by-state vote in the House of Representatives. Clay dropped out of the balloting and threw his support to Adams, who received the votes of thirteen states to Jackson's seven and Crawford's four.

When the vote was announced, "some clapping and exultation took place in the galleries, and some slight hissing," the official congressional record noted. "The House suspended its proceedings until the galleries were cleared."[7] When the House reconvened that day, February 9, 1825, Speaker Clay took the podium and announced that John Quincy Adams, with the majority of the votes, had been duly elected president.

Ten days after the House determined the outcome of the presidential election—and a week before the opening of the *Antelope* case in the Supreme Court—the American Colonization Society had held its eighth annual meeting in the Supreme Court room in the Capitol. Frank Key and the other ACS members welcomed the Marquis de Lafayette, the French nobleman whose service as a volunteer major general in the Continental Army during the Revolutionary War made him the most popular foreigner in the Early Republic.

Lafayette and his late wife, Adrienne, were passionate abolitionists. In the 1780s they had bought land in the French colony of Cayenne (now French Guiana), on the northern coast of South America, to use in an experimental farming program for freed American slaves.[8] That program, however, never came to fruition.

At the ACS meeting, at the suggestion of George Washington Parke Custis, Lafayette was named an honorary vice president for life. The Marquis "then expressed concisely his high gratification at being invited to attend the annual meeting of this Society, for which he had ever felt great respect and affection," the official report of the meeting noted. "To be chosen a member of the Society would be most agreeable to his feelings, and accordant to the principles of all his life."[9]

In one of the many ironies in Frank Key's record in dealing with slavery issues, on June 1—just a few months after he had so eloquently attacked the evils of the enslavement of human beings before the U.S. Supreme Court—Key helped arrange the sale of William Jordan, the slave he had represented in court in 1823. As part of that case's settlement, Key received a power of attorney to sell Jordan (who was being held in a Washington jail) from the attorneys of the two men who claimed they owned the man. He proceeded to pave the way for the sale of Jordan back into slavery by Washington's U.S. marshal. Key took out advertisements in the local newspapers in May and June 1825 headed "Valuable Slave for Sale." The ads stated: "William is a likely fellow, a good coachman, and house servant."[10]

On the family front, the oldest Key child, Elizabeth, known to the family as Lizzie, became Frank and Polly's second daughter to marry. On

November 8, 1825, Lizzie Key, twenty-two, married Charles Howard of the prominent Baltimore Howards, at St. John's Church in Georgetown.

In 1826 the annual ACS meeting for the first time attracted delegates from auxiliary groups around the nation. Attending were men representing the Colonization Society of New Hampshire; local groups from Wilmington, Delaware; Talbot County, Maryland; Hampden County, Massachusetts; Petersburg, Richmond, and Amelia and Greenbrier counties in Virginia.

The society adopted a resolution at the meeting strongly reiterating its opposition to the abolition of slavery while at the same time proclaiming its desire not to "perpetuate" the "peculiar institution." Another resolution reaffirmed that the ACS's "only object" was "the removal to the Coast of Africa, with their own consent... people of color within the United States, as are already free."[11]

By this time the mercurial John Randolph had completely changed his mind about colonization. A founding member of the ACS in 1816, Randolph now spoke bitterly against colonization. "I am more and more set against all new things," he wrote to a friend on January 30, 1826. "I am against all Colonization, &c., societies [and] for the good old plan of making the negroes *work*, and thereby enabling the master to feed and clothe them well, and take care of them in sickness and old age."[12]

Frank Key urged his old friend to reconsider his opposition to colonization. Randolph refused—and also refused to introduce the latest ACS memorial into Congress, convinced that the ACS's aims were "bad and mischievous." A "spirit of morbid sensibility, religious fanaticism, vanity, and the love of display," he wrote, "were the chief moving causes of" the ACS. "True humanity" to the slave, Randolph continued, would be "to make him do a fair day's work, and to treat him with all the kindness compatible with due subordination."

Randolph said he agreed with removing "free negroes" with "their own consent, out of the slave States." But, he said, he could not envision any society in which blacks and whites could live equally. As he put it, from "the institution of the Passover to the latest experience of man, it would be found that no two distinct peoples could occupy the same territory, under one government, but in the relation of master and vassal."

The "Exodus of the Jews," Randolph said "was effected by the visible and miraculous interposition of the hand of God." But without that "same miraculous assistance" the ACS would not be able to send enough freed blacks to Africa to significantly stem their growing number in the United States. What's more, he wrote, the Colonization Society's "proceedings and talks disturbed the rest of the slaves."[13]

Those strong words about an issue that Frank Key felt so ardently about easily could have ended the long friendship between the two men. To Key's credit, however, he didn't let their sharp disagreement on colonization affect their friendly relations. The two men remained close until Randolph's death in 1833.

Randolph was not the only voice speaking out against colonization. But other anti-colonization voices had reasons vastly different than Randolph's. Virtually all abolitionists abhorred the entire idea of uprooting American freed blacks and shipping them to Africa. John Quincy Adams, who opposed colonization from the time he first learned about it in 1817, called colonization an "abortion." As "a system of eventual emancipation of the slaves of this country it was not only impracticable, but" was as "a scheme for relieving the slave states of free negroes, its moral aspect was not comely, and it was equally impracticable."[14]

While some freed blacks embraced the idea of colonization, many more adamantly opposed it. Throughout the 1820s and 1830s at meetings in New York, Boston, Baltimore, Washington, D.C., Pittsburgh, Wilmington, and a dozen other northern cities, African Americans strongly condemned the ACS mission.

A large group of freed blacks in Washington, meeting at the African Methodist Episcopal Church in 1831, for example, resolved that they viewed "with distrust the efforts made by the Colonization Society to cause the free people of color of these United States to emigrate to Liberia on the coast of Africa, or elsewhere." It "is the declared opinion of the members of this meeting," the resolution continued, "that the soil which gave them birth is their only true and veritable home, and that it would be impolitic, unwise and improper for them to leave their home without the benefits of education."[15]

A National Colored Convention held in Philadelphia that same year resolved that colonization amounted to "pursuing the direct road to perpetuate slavery, with all its un-Christian-like concomitants." As "citizens and men whose best blood is sapped to gain popularity for that institution, we would, in the most feeling manner, beg of them to desist: or, if we must be sacrificed to their philanthropy, we would rather die at home.

"Many of our fathers, and some of us, have fought and bled for the liberty, independence and peace which you now enjoy. Surely, it would be ungenerous and unfeeling in you to deny us a humble and quiet grave in that country which gave us birth."[16]

On March 30, 1826, John Randolph delivered one of the most vitriolic speeches ever heard in the Senate. In it, Randolph bitterly and savagely attacked President John Quincy Adams and his secretary of state Henry Clay for sending an American delegation to the Panamanian Congress of Latin American Republics. Randolph ended his long, almost hysterical diatribe by referring to Clay as a "blackleg" (a swindler or cheater). Those words led to a strange duel fought by the hotheaded John Randolph and the usually even-tempered Henry Clay.

The Kentuckian challenged Randolph. The two met at 4 o'clock on Saturday afternoon, April 8, just over the Potomac River in Virginia. Randolph, renowned as an excellent shot, accidentally pulled the trigger on his pistol before the duel began. That could have ended things. But the two men paced off anyway, and each fired. Clay's shot grazed Randolph's coat; Randolph's missed.

Randolph then fired into the air and the duel—and the acrimony— ended. The quixotic Randolph, an eyewitness reported, said to Clay: "I trust in God, my dear sir, you are untouched. After what has occurred, I would not have harmed you for a thousand worlds."[17]

In the fall of 1826 Frank Key and New Englander Ralph Gurley went on the road to promote the American Colonization Society. They paid proselytizing visits to cities from Montpelier, Vermont, to Philadelphia. In his Philadelphia speech Key propounded his oft-stated theme that colonization was the only way to stop international trafficking in slaves. "Before the colony at Sierra Leone was planted, the slave trade raged in that quarter," Key said, claiming that "now it is unknown" for hundreds of miles along the coast. "Before the American settlement was formed," he continued, "ten thousand slaves were annually transported from it; now the trade is unknown, but for one hundred miles south."[18]

Key was exaggerating. It was true that the slave trade had diminished steadily and significantly in recent years along the coast of Upper Guinea, the area that included Sierra Leone. But trafficking did not end there until the early 1840s.[19]

In the spring of 1826, Francis Scott Key Jr. became the first of the Keys's boys to marry. On April 6, Frank Jr., nineteen, took as his bride his first cousin, Elizabeth Lloyd Harwood, known as Betty. She was the daughter of Polly Key's older sister Elizabeth and Henry Hall Harwood, the president of the Farmers Bank of Maryland in Annapolis. Frank Jr., whose family connections had led to his Navy midshipman appointment in 1823, had just returned from patrol on the U.S.S. *John Adams*, a warship that was part of the Navy's West Indies Station, which covered the Caribbean and Gulf of Mexico. His brief naval career ended the next year, in 1827.

Later in 1826, on October 25, Elizabeth and Charles Howard presented Frank and Polly with their first grandchild, a boy they named Francis Key Howard. Less than a year later—on July 30, 1827—the grandparents themselves produced a child, their eleventh and last, a boy they named Charles Henry Key. Polly was forty-three; Frank forty-seven.

Frank Key made one of his frequent trips to Annapolis in February 1827 to attend commencement exercises at St. John's College. Following the February 22 ceremonies, the noted orator was the featured speaker at a gathering of St. John's alumni at St. Anne's Episcopal Church. The meeting convened to discuss the fate of St. John's, which had fallen on hard times. The Maryland Legislature had cut off state funding in 1806 and its founding president, John McDowell, had left. Although the state had restored a minimal amount of funding ($1,000) on January 1, 1812, and in 1821 the Legislature had set aside $20,000 from a special lottery to be used as an endowment, the annual interest fell far short of what the college needed to operate effectively.

Frank Key had those fiscal problems uppermost in his mind when he addressed his fellow alumni. In a long-winded, passionate speech filled with biblical, patriotic, historical, and literary allusions, Key argued for the restoration of a significant stream of state funding to the private institution. St. John's, he said, was now a "dreary ruin," because of the cutback in government funds, and he decried "the madness that had worked this desolation."[20]

Key readily acknowledged that his alma matter educated the affluent—Key used the term "men of leisure"—but argued that it was in society's best interest that such men become well educated. Not educating them, he said, would lead them "to rust in sloth, or to riot in dissipation. This would harm society, Key said, because the wealthy man "has more in his power either for good or evil" than the poor man, and "will be more apt, from his greater temptations, to be depraved himself and the corruptor of others."

Such uneducated men would be tempted, Key said, by the "vain amusements of the world." If that happened, great harm would come to the nation. "This neglect would be peculiarly unwise in a government like ours," Key said. "Luxury is the vice most fatal to republics; and idleness, and want of education in the rich promote it in its disgusting forms."

Key then exhorted his fellow alumni to reach into their pockets to support St. John's, to join their "hearts and hands in a sacred covenant to restore its honors to St. John's, and to swear to its fulfillment by the memory of the dead, the hopes of the living, and the glory of the unborn generations."

11

A FRIEND OF PEACE

"It is beautiful, it is sublime!"
—*Francis Scott Key, at Andrew Jackson's Inauguration,*
March 4, 1829

The election of Andrew Jackson as president in 1828 marked a profound shift in national politics. It also marked a sea change in Francis Scott Key's political, professional, and personal lives. The tepid Federalist who loathed partisan politics morphed into a full-throated Jacksonian Democrat.

At first glance it would seem that the classically educated, pious son of genteel Maryland aristocracy had precious little in common with the rough and tumble populist war hero from Tennessee. Key led a life of the mind; his one military experience was short and disastrous. Jackson was the prototypical unlettered man of the people and a national war hero.

Yet, Francis Scott Key found much to admire in Andrew Jackson, the man and the politician. For one thing, both men were fiercely patriotic. For another, the morally upright Washington lawyer shared Jackson's professed loathing of government corruption and his desire to limit the role of the federal government in individual states' affairs.

Both Key and Jackson owned slaves; Jackson, in fact, brought a large contingent of enslaved household domestic workers with him to Washington to toil without pay at the President's House. Both slave holders shared a strong resentment of the growing abolitionist movement in the United States. And then there was the fact that Key's brother-in-law and close friend Roger B. Taney also had become an ardent Jacksonian, influencing Key's strong support of the pugnacious Jackson's new brand of populist politics.

Or perhaps it was simply opportunism. In Andrew Jackson, Francis Scott Key saw his first good chance to become a presidential confidant.

Jackson did reward Key's devotion by including him in the informal group of his closest advisers, a group that became known as the "kitchen cabinet." The Jackson kitchen cabinet met occasionally in the Key house in Washington, although most likely not in the kitchen. Historians believe that the term "kitchen cabinet" originated in 1829 with the Jackson administration. The then-derogatory term derived from the fact that the Washington establishment believed that Jackson and his advisers were not genteel enough to meet in formal reception rooms.[1]

Although Jackson had decried political corruption and cronyism in the venomously partisan 1828 campaign, soundly defeating John Quincy Adams, once in office he appointed many political supporters, including Francis Scott Key, to plum governmental posts.

When Frank Key boarded the Jackson bandwagon in 1827, his life changed significantly. With Roger B. Taney chairing the Jackson Central Committee of Maryland, Key—the one-time loather of all things political—enthusiastically joined with his brother-in-law in singing Jackson's praises.

Even as Frank Key devoted significant time to helping get Andrew Jackson elected, he still spent many long hours working in his Georgetown law office and in the courts of Maryland and Washington. The hardworking father of ten often did not come home to Polly and the children until late at night, and then typically repaired to his office to do more legal paperwork.

Nor did Key's work for Jackson cut down on his fervent proselytizing for colonization. He faithfully took part in the well-attended eleventh annual American Colonization Society meeting on January 19, 1828, in the hall of the House of Representatives. Colonizationists, he told the group, were acting on "some of the best principles and feelings of the heart."[2]

On May 12, Frank Key was a featured speaker at the annual meeting of the New York-based American Bible Society, for which he had served as a vice president since helping found the organization in 1816. Not long after that meeting, on May 24, 1828, Elizabeth and Charles Howard presented the Keys with their second grandchild, a boy they named John Eager Howard, after his other grandfather.

Frank Key spoke at a November 26, 1828, ACS meeting in Philadelphia, an address that one newspaper called "lucid, eloquent, and very satisfactory."[3] On Christmas Day 1828, Key chaired the founding meeting of the Colonization Society of Georgetown, during which he spoke "in his usual style of impressive eloquence," a Washington newspaper noted.[4]

On February 25, 1829, five days before her eighteenth birthday, Ann Arnold Key, the Keys's fifth child, married Daniel Turner, a thirty-two-year-old congressman from North Carolina. Turner, a West Point graduate who had served in the War of 1812, had decided that one term in Washington was enough. On March 3 the newlyweds moved to his home state where he went on to become the principal of the Warrenton Female Seminary.

On March 4, 1829, just days after Frank and Polly Key celebrated their daughter's wedding, Washington experienced one of the most memorable presidential inaugurations in the nation's history. On that beautiful, sunny late winter's day, Andrew Jackson, the first American president not born in Virginia or Massachusetts, hosted a raucous celebration of his ascendancy to the nation's highest elected office. Thousands of just plain folks—many from Tennessee and the other western fringes of the young United States—flooded into the capital to celebrate the presidency of the white-haired Tennessean. Frank Key stood among the celebrating throngs.

The face of Washington had changed significantly since Frank and Polly Key moved to Georgetown twenty-five years earlier. In the early 1820s the city had reclaimed the swamp not far from the Capitol, and the Capitol itself was rebuilt. Marble floors, staircases, and pillars replaced the old stone and brick ones; Italian marble sculptors were brought in to do the detail work. Lush lawns landscaped with trees and shrubbery were installed on the grounds. Other public buildings sprouted along Pennsylvania Avenue, which soon featured new sidewalks and curbs.

By the time of Jackson's inaugural, nearly all of Washington's main streets had been cleared, graded, and paved with gravel. Soon after, crews paved Pennsylvania Avenue between the Capitol and the White House with macadam, a newly developed road surface made up of tightly compressed layers of small stones. Private companies improved the city's bridges and outlying roads, setting up toll roads on the Washington-Baltimore Road, Seventh Street Pike, and Georgetown Pike.

A visitor to Washington in 1825 said he had been to many cities but not one "whose site is more picturesque and beautiful." The area around the Capitol, he said, "is a delightful resort." In the "immediate neighbor-hood of this beautiful square," instead of being "appropriated by boarding houses, the few [houses] that have been erected" were "occupied by gentle-men of fortune and persons not in business."[5]

"No one who was at Washington at the time of General Jackson's inau-guration is likely to forget that period to the day of his death," journalist Arthur J. Stansbury later remembered.[6] It was evident to all that a momen-tous change in the presidency—and the national government—was about to take place as the populist Jackson, who believed in limited use of the federal powers, supplanted the aloof patrician John Quincy Adams who strongly believed in an activist federal government.

"A monstrous crowd of people is in the city," Senator Daniel Webster wrote to his sister. "I never saw anything like it before. Persons have come five hundred miles to see General Jackson and they really seem to think that the country is rescued from some dreadful danger."[7]

In contrast to the "quiet and orderly period of the Adams administra-tion," Stansbury noted, "it seemed as if half the nation had rushed at once into the capital. It was like the inundation of the northern barbarians into Rome, save that the tumultuous tide came in from a different point of the compass."

On Inauguration Day itself "the vicinity of the Capitol was like a great agitated sea; every avenue to the fateful spot was blocked up with people," Stansbury wrote. He and others especially remembered the electrifying moment when the bare-headed Jackson appeared atop the Capitol steps to take the oath of office. When the crowd "caught sight of the tall and imposing form of their adored leader as he came forth between the col-umns of the portico," Stansbury said, "the peal of shouting that arose rent the air and seemed to shake the very ground."

John Quincy Adams famously did not show up at the Inauguration. Frank Key did, witnessing the spectacle—not with his wife Polly—but with their close friend Margaret Bayard Smith, one of Washington's lead-ing socialites. They joined in the celebration of what Smith called "the People's day and the People's President." She reported that the typically taciturn "Mr. Frank Key, whose arm I had," an "old and frequent witness of great spectacles, often exclaimed" that day: "It is beautiful, it is sublime!"[8]

The first task Andrew Jackson asked Francis Scott Key to perform was to help prosecute Tobias Watkins, the former fourth auditor of the U.S.

Treasury in the John Quincy Adams administration. As such, Watkins had handled all fiscal matters related to the Navy Department.

On March 23, 1829, Jackson had appointed his close friend and adviser Amos Kendall to succeed Watkins at the Treasury Department. The Massachusetts-born Kendall—who would go on to become post-master general and the most influential member of Jackson's kitchen cabinet—soon found evidence that his predecessor had misappropriated some $3,000.

Jackson, still harboring intense dislike for everyone associated with John Quincy Adams, asked Key to join Thomas Swann, the U.S. attorney for Washington, in prosecuting Watkins. Key and Swann presented enough evidence to convince a grand jury to indict Watkins for embezzlement. Federal marshals arrested the former auditor in Philadelphia on May 1 and brought him to Washington to stand trial in the U.S. Circuit Court. Months of legal wrangling ensued. Frank Key spent a good deal of his time on the case, which made headlines in the local newspapers. During one court session, on July 19, the loquacious Key delivered a two-hour speech.[9]

On August 14, the jury found Watkins guilty of improperly obtaining $3,050 in government funds. The judge fined Watkins that amount and sentenced him to nine months in jail. The former auditor did not have enough money to pay the fine and stayed in jail until March 1833.

Frank Key felt that the Jackson Administration did not compensate him enough for the huge chunks of time he put in working on the Watkins case. "Mr. Key," Jackson wrote to his Treasury Secretary Samuel Delucenna Ingham on November 10, "complains of injury & loss by his employment against Watkins [and] thinks he ought to receive more than awarded him." Jackson's advice to Ingham: raise Key's compensation "to the average...and be done with it."[10]

The second legal matter Frank Key attended to for Andrew Jackson involved what became known as the Eaton Affair, an incendiary sex scandal that rocked the nation's capital and bedeviled Andrew Jackson for most of his first two years in office. The scandal (also known as the Petticoat Affair or the Petticoat War) involved the second marriage of President Jackson's close friend and campaign manager, John Henry Eaton. Newly appointed secretary of War, Eaton had served in the Senate since 1817.[11] On the first day of 1829 Eaton, thirty-eight and a widower, married Margaret "Peggy" O'Neale Timberlake, twenty-nine, a recent widow.

To say the least, Peggy Eaton did not fit into the upper-crust Washington social set dominated by former first lady Dolley Madison, Floride Bouneau Calhoun, the wife of Vice President John C. Calhoun, and Margaret Bayard Smith. The daughter of William O'Neale, the proprietor of Franklin House, a Washington saloon and boarding house, Peggy Eaton "has never been admitted into good society, is very handsome and of not an inspiring character and violent temper," Smith wrote. "She is, it is said, irresistible and carries whatever point she sets her mind on."[12]

Smith went on to repeat rumors that Peggy Eaton had had a sexual affair with John Eaton "both before and after her husband's death," a situation that "totally destroyed" her reputation. Rumors also circulated that John Timberlake, Peggy O'Neale's first husband, had slit his own throat after discovering her affair with Eaton; that Peggy O'Neale had had a miscarriage while Timberlake was away at sea; and that she carried on other illicit sexual affairs. Smith called her "one of the most ambitious, violent, malignant, yet silly women you ever heard of."

John Eaton's marriage to Peggy O'Neale scandalized Washington's social elite. Virtually all of the well-connected women in the nation's capital, including all of the wives of Jackson's cabinet members, banded together to shun the saloonkeeper's daughter. "The ladies declare," Smith wrote on the day of the Eaton wedding, "they will not go to the wedding, and if they can help it will not let their husbands go."

The blatant ostracism made Jackson—still in deep mourning over the December 22, 1828, death of his beloved wife, Rachel—furious. Rachel Jackson had been divorced before she married Old Hickory and had been the subject of scurrilous rumors involving her relationship with Jackson before her divorce. The president—who had stayed at the Franklin House when he was in the U.S. Senate and knew all the parties involved—staunchly defended Peggy and John Eaton, whom Smith called Jackson's "bosom friend and almost adopted son."[13]

For his part, Jackson said, he did "not come here by the people's will to make a Cabinet for the fashionable ladies."[14] He went on to blame his arch political enemy Henry Clay and his partisans who exerted themselves to "destroy the character of Mrs. Eaton by the foulest and basest means."[15]

The political ramifications of the Eaton Affair continued for nearly two years. Jackson believed that John C. Calhoun and his wife were also behind the anti-Eaton campaign, and he angrily ended all social contact with the vice president and his wife. Jackson came to trust only one man in his cabinet, Secretary of State Martin Van Buren of New York, a widower who ignored the gossip and made it a point to invite the Eatons to State Department receptions and dinners.

Washington in the 1830s was ripe with both gallantry and gossip. Francis Scott Key, one of the capital's leading citizens, however, did not fit well in that society. Amid the frivolousness and gossip, the "staid and sober-minded Francis Scott Key wrote, in a fine hand, religious hymns for the pleasure of his mother."[16]

His devotion to Andrew Jackson, however, brought the hymn-writing lawyer into the sordid Eaton Affair early in September 1829. That's when Jackson asked him to give legal advice to Reverend John Nicholson Campbell, the thirty-one-year-old minister of the New York Avenue Presbyterian Church in Washington where the president worshipped. Word had reached John and Peggy Eaton that Campbell, former chaplain of the House of Representatives and a manager of the American Colonization Society, had condemned their licentiousness and lobbied the president to separate himself from them. That did not sit well with the Eatons, who confronted Campbell in his church. A scuffle ensued, and Peggy Eaton wound up with a slight head wound.

Fearing a lawsuit, Campbell hired Jackson-insider Frank Key to fend off any litigation. Campbell told Key that if the Eatons sued, he would testify about what he had heard about them in court. But Key, with the Jackson administration's interests uppermost in his mind, advised prudence. Calling Key "the friend of peace," Jackson said that the Georgetown lawyer "entertained great fears of a prosecution as likely to disturb the administration and do infinite injury to the reputation of Mr. Eaton."[17]

Jackson met face-to-face with Campbell at least twice, on September 1 and 3, about the Eaton Affair. The president brusquely challenged him to provide concrete evidence about the allegations he had been spreading. Campbell dug in his heels. Nothing was settled.

A week after the second meeting, Jackson asked Campbell and one of his mentors and confidants, Reverend Ezra Stiles Ely, to meet with him and his entire cabinet to confront the two clergyman about what they knew about the Eatons. Ely—whom John Quincy Adams called a "busybody Presbyterian clergyman" and the "principal mischief-maker in the affairs of Mr. and Mrs. Eaton"—was pastor of the Old Pine Street

Presbyterian Church in Philadelphia and an old friend and strong supporter of Jackson.[18]

Ely had met with Campbell in Washington during Jackson's inauguration, received an earful about Peggy Eaton, and then wrote to Jackson listing a bill of particulars against Peggy Eaton and begging him to disown John Eaton. Peggy Eaton "will do more to injure your peace and your administration than one hundred Henry Clays," Ely wrote to the president.[19] "For your own sake, for your dead wife's sake, for the sake of your administration, for the credit of the government and the country, you should not countenance a woman like this."[20]

John Eaton did not take part in the September 10 meeting during which Jackson angrily challenged Ely, who admitted that he didn't have any first-hand evidence linking Eaton to any misdoings. When Jackson asked Ely about Peggy Eaton, the Philadelphia clergyman said he would not "give an opinion." To which Jackson angrily—if inaccurately—retorted: "She is as chaste as a virgin."[21]

Jackson also got into it with Campbell, who continued to stand by the miscarriage story, claiming he had heard it from reliable sources. Jackson furiously dismissed those claims. Campbell insisted that he was merely trying to save the Jackson administration from scandal, not to tarnish Mrs. Eaton's reputation. The meeting ended when Campbell walked out in a huff.

That same day Frank Key advised Campbell to cease and desist repeating the scurrilous accusations against the Eatons. Campbell relented and said he would keep his mouth shut. No lawsuit materialized. Jackson did not set foot in Campbell's church again and the young minister left Washington two years later.

Still, the Eaton Affair did not go away. Social Washington continued to snub the Eatons. In April 1831 Martin Van Buren came up with a plan. He told Jackson that if he and Eaton resigned their cabinet posts, the president would be free to demand that all the other cabinet members resign. That would give the appearance that he wanted to clean house and put the Eaton Affair behind him.

That is exactly what happened. Eaton stepped down on April 7; Van Buren did so four days later.[22] Jackson then asked his other cabinet heads, with the exception of Postmaster General William T. Barry (an Eaton family friend), to resign. They did. Attorney General John Berrien—a close friend of John C. Calhoun and the man Francis Scott Key had faced off against in the Supreme Court *Antelope* case—did not resign. Berrien had gone to his hometown of Savannah, Georgia, in January and did not plan to return to Washington until June.

Frank Key got involved when he shared a stagecoach with Berrien on the Georgian's way back to Washington. The two men had a chance to discuss the resignation situation in depth. Key reported details of that conversation to Roger B. Taney in a June 14 letter. Taney was living in Baltimore and serving as Maryland's attorney general in addition to running his private law practice and had been mentioned as a likely successor to Berrien.

When Berrien asked Key for the inside story on Jackson's Cabinet machinations, Key told him that it was neither "necessary nor desirable" that Berrien resign. He also said that Taney felt the same way. When Key returned to Washington, he met with two Jackson insiders—newly named Secretary of State Edward Livingston, an old Jackson friend, and the new Navy secretary, former New Hampshire Senator Levi Woodbury—to lobby them to ask Jackson to keep Berrien.

"I told them," Key said, "I thought if Berrien could be retained, it would have a good effect upon the affairs of the party" primarily because of the "Eaton question."[23]

But Key had misread the situation. When he returned home that evening, he found a note from Jackson summoning him to the White House. Key hustled over there, arriving at around 9 p.m. Jackson then told Key he wanted Berrien gone and wanted Taney to be attorney general.

Jackson asked Key if he thought his brother-in-law would take the job. Key said both he and Taney thought it would be best to keep Berrien, "thinking such a thing would be conducive to the success of the administration and gratifying to [Berrien's] friends."

Jackson hit the ceiling, telling Key that keeping Berrien was "entirely out of the question." Key immediately changed his tune. He wrote to Taney that night, encouraging his brother-in-law to say yes if Jackson asked him to succeed Berrien as attorney general.

"I do not think you ought to have any hesitation in accepting," he told Taney, assuring him that the position wouldn't put much of a crimp in Taney's private law practice. "You can be as much in Baltimore as you would find necessary and desirable," he said, "with the understanding that you would come over [to Washington] whenever wanted."

Taking the job might even help business, Key said. "As to the Supreme Court," he wrote, "it would of course suit you entirely, and the increase in your business there would make up well for lesser matters."

Taney accepted the offer. Berrien then resigned. Andrew Jackson appointed Roger B. Taney as U.S. attorney general on June 21, 1831, five days after Frank Key had conveyed Jackson's request.

With Berrien gone, the Eaton Affair ran out of steam. Roger B. Taney became a trusted Jackson insider, and Francis Scott Key solidified his position inside Jackson's kitchen cabinet.[24] Andrew Jackson never forgave Vice President John C. Calhoun for his role in the affair. Martin Van Buren's political stock, on the other hand, skyrocketed. Jackson chose the New Yorker to replace Calhoun as his vice president in the 1832 election. Four years later Jackson paved the way for Van Buren's nomination as the Democratic Party's presidential nominee and his election as the nation's eighth president in 1836.

Francis Scott Key's legal and consulting work on behalf of the Jackson administration did not escape the notice of its political enemies. An article in the rabidly anti-Jackson Washington, D.C., *Daily National Journal* on April 13, 1831, for example, accused Key of being Jackson's "favorite partisan," and claimed that the president had created a "new office in effect, although not in name" for him, that of "Assistant District Attorney" of Washington. The paper said that Key had been "liberally compensated" for the legal work directly from the U.S. Treasury.

"In this way," the accusation continued, "some thousands of dollars have been liberally transferred from the pockets of the populace to those of Mr. Francis Key."

Considering the source and that no other evidence of Frank Key lining his pockets with illegally diverted federal funds has surfaced, it's evident that these bombastic allegations were little more than politically motivated slanders designed to make Jackson and everything he touched look bad.

Francis Scott Key was born at Terra Rubra, his family estate north of Frederick, Maryland, on August 1, 1779. He passed his childhood in idyllic fashion on the prosperous plantation in the company of adoring relatives, tended to by slaves, and passing countless hours playing with his younger sister Anna. (*Library of Congress, Prints & Photographs Division, Detroit Publishing Company*)

In 1784, the Keys sent their only son to Annapolis to attend primary school at St. John's College. He studied Greek and Latin, grammar, mathematics, and the sciences. He graduated from the college on October 21, 1796, along with five other young men, including his closest friend Daniel Murray. (*Library of Congress, Prints & Photographs Division, Historic American Buildings Survey*)

Francis Scott Key and his wife, Mary Tayloe Lloyd (known as Polly), lived in this house on Bridge Street (now M Street) in Georgetown from 1805–1830 when they moved to Capitol Hill after the C&O Canal took a large portion of their backyard. Key kept his law office in the house (seen at the right in photo). (*Library of Congress, Prints & Photographs Division, Historic American Buildings Survey*)

For the seven years he was a student at St. John's, Key lived with his great aunt Elizabeth Ross Scott and her husband, Dr. Upton Scott, in their opulent home, which still stands today on Shipwright Street in downtown Annapolis. (*Library of Congress, Prints & Photographs Division, Historic American Buildings Survey*)

An idealized image of the Key house in Georgetown by Key grandson John Ross Key, Jr., a painter who moved in with Francis and Polly Key as an infant after the sudden death of his father in 1837. (*Photo by Will Brown, Courtesy of the Diplomatic Reception Rooms, U.S. Department of State, Washington, D.C.*)

Woodley, the lavish Washington, D.C., home built by Francis Scott Key's uncle Philip Barton Key, a hugely successful lawyer, businessman, and three-term (1807–1813) U.S. Congressman from Maryland who played an important role in his nephew's professional life. (*Library of Congress, Prints & Photographs Division, Historic American Buildings Survey*)

WASHI NGTON.

Representation of the capture of the CITY of WASHINGTON, by the British Forces under the command of Major Gen.l Ross and Rear Adm.l S.t J.Cockburn, August 24.th 1814; wherein are shewn the Fort and the Flotilla

Francis Scott Key rode out to Bladensburg, Maryland, and was on the field of battle during one of the nation's most catastrophic military defeats there on August 24, 1814. Following the battle the British burned many public buildings in Washington, D.C., including the White House. (*Library of Congress, Prints & Photographs Division*)

Key found himself in Baltimore Harbor on the night of September 13-14 during the fearsome British bombardment of the city. He had just helped arrange the release of an American doctor taken prisoner by the British after the Battle of Bladensburg. In the morning Key was inspired to write the words that would become the National Anthem of the United States. (*Library of Congress, Prints & Photographs Division*)

Although it remained popular from the time Key wrote the song in 1814—as evidenced by the cover of this circa 1860 sheet music—"The Star-Spangled Banner" did not become the official National Anthem until 1931. (*Library of Congress, Prints & Photographs Division*)

When the Keys moved to Washington in 1805 the city was a relatively sparsely populated backwater with large tracts of untamed woods and cultivated farmland within its borders. Few buildings other than the nearly completed President's House on Pennsylvania Avenue—the largest dwelling in the nation—dotted the unpaved, perpetually muddy streets. The Capitol (above, circa 1805), surrounded by dense woods, was still under construction. (*Courtesy of Albert H. Small-George Washington University Collection*)

Key stood among the celebrating throngs on March 4, 1829, at one of the most memorable presidential inaugurations in the nation's history. Andrew Jackson hosted a raucous celebration of his ascendancy to the nation's highest elected office as thousands of just plain folks—many from Tennessee and the other western fringes of the young United States—flooded into the nation's capital to celebrate the presidency of the 61-year-old Tennessean. (*Library of Congress, Prints & Photographs Division*)

ANDREW JACKSON.

Key disdained politics until Andrew Jackson ran for president in 1828. He then became a fervent Jacksonian Democrat. Jackson rewarded Key's devotion by including him in the informal group of his closest advisers—the first presidential "kitchen cabinet." Jackson appointed Key to the post of U.S. Attorney for Washington in 1833, a position he held for more than eight years. (*Library of Congress, Prints & Photographs Division*)

Although the importation of slaves was illegal, the slave trade flourished in Washington, D.C., during Francis Scott Key's life. Slave sales and slave pens were common in the city and its environs, including Alexandria, Virginia. (*Library of Congress, Prints & Photographs Division, Historic American Buildings Survey*)

A Slave-Coffle passing the Capitol.

It was not uncommon to see manacled men, women, and children being marched to and from the slave pens that operated on the streets of what is now downtown Washington, D.C. Although Francis Scott Key owned slaves during this entire adult life, he spoke out against the slave trade and represented slaves and freed blacks gratis in the Washington, D.C., courts. He also was a founder in 1816 of the American Colonization Society, which worked to send freed blacks to Africa. (*Library of Congress, Prints & Photographs Division*)

Key was a close friend of the eccentric Virginia Congressman John Randolph of Roanoke. The two men spent many hours together in Washington and Georgetown when Randolph was in town. When they were apart, they exchanged often lengthy letters filled with personal, religious, and political words. Randolph named Key one of three executors of his will. (*Library of Congress, Prints & Photographs Division*)

As a favor to President Jackson, Key defended Sam Houston in 1832 after he viciously attacked U.S. Congressman William Stanbery in Washington after Stanbery had accused him of fraudulently receiving a government contract. Houston was convicted of assualt, but never served a day in jail. (*Library of Congress, Prints & Photographs Division*)

Francis Scott Key met Roger B. Taney when the two men were young readers of the law in Annapolis at the turn of the nineteenth century. They soon formed a close friendship—one that lasted until January 1843, when Key died. Taney, who later would become Chief Justice of the United States, married Key's only sister in 1806. (*Library of Congress, Prints & Photographs Division, Brady-Handy Collection*)

12

A PARTICULAR FRIEND
OF THE PRESIDENT

The Founding Fathers envisioned "a general government of limited and defined powers... the states to be independent republics in all other respects having exclusive power in whatsoever concerned their separate interests."

—*Francis Scott Key, July 4, 1831*

In mid-October 1829 Francis Scott Key took a trip to New York and Philadelphia on American Colonization Society business. He spoke at an October 14 meeting at the Middle Dutch Church in Lower Manhattan chaired by the city's mayor and urged New York's leading citizens to help raise funds for the ACS. Key, as he tended to do, went on at length when he took to the podium.

At least one member of the audience—most likely the abolitionist African American newspaper editor Samuel Eli Cornish—was singularly unimpressed by what Key had to say. The Washington lawyer's speech "tired every body, and almost emptied the house," an article in Cornish's newspaper, *Rights of All*, reported.[1]

The article went on to say that Key began, as he often did in speeches of this type, by painting a bleak picture of what life was like for freed blacks. They "must always be degraded and oppressed, free only in name," Key said, and it would be "impossible that they can be otherwise." Prejudice, the article said, "dwelt in his little heart, which cannot be bigger than a cherry.... [Is] it not hypocrisy for such men to profess a belief in the Bible? Is not F.S. Key a Pagan."

It's doubtful that Francis Scott Key read that stinging criticism. But he knew very well that most abolitionists had little use for any kind of colonization scheme.

Criticism or no, Key gave what a friendlier newspaper called "an eloquent and instructive address"[2] on October 21, 1829, at a public meeting at the Franklin Institute in Philadelphia. Key hit the same notes he did in most of his proselytizing speeches on behalf of ACS. He claimed that the society knew of large numbers of slaves who wanted to go to Liberia and that their masters would free them, but only if the ACS guaranteed they'd be taken out of the country and shipped to Africa. The problem: ACS didn't have the money to make that guarantee. Key ended with an appeal to the citizens of Philadelphia "for aid in the benevolent project of liberating these slaves and transporting them to the coast of Africa."

On February 3, 1830, Elizabeth Howard gave birth to the third Key grandchild—a boy they named Charles. On February 18, Frank and Polly finally purchased the house in Georgetown in which they had been living since they moved to the nation's capital some twenty-five years earlier; the legal dispute that held up the sale for decades was finally settled.

Ironically, the Keys then moved out of the Bridge Street house and rented a large house on C Street Southeast, three blocks from the Capitol, while Frank kept his law office in one wing of their former home. It appears that the Keys abandoned living in the Georgetown house because a section of the newly built Chesapeake and Ohio (C&O) Canal paralleling the Potomac had taken a significant chunk out of their backyard. On February 18, 1830, the day the Keys officially bought the Georgetown house, Frank Key conveyed part of the lot to the company that owned the canal.

A monumental project designed to connect the Chesapeake Bay with the Ohio River alongside the Potomac, the canal had long been envisioned as a way to ease shipping operations from the Tidewater area to the Ohio Valley, because parts of the Potomac River regular froze over in the winter and because parts became too shallow during droughts and overflowed during floods. The Chesapeake & Ohio Canal Company under Charles Fenton Mercer, its president, formed in the early 1820s to build the mammoth canal. But the effort ran into significant problems—including contentious lawsuits with landowners who did not want give up their property—and was not completed until 1850.

Francis Scott Key got involved in 1822 when he was appointed to a commission representing Georgetown's interests in the construction project. He took part in meetings with other jurisdictions' commissions periodically for the next seven years. In 1829, apparently not feeling any conflict of interest, he served as the C&O Canal Company's cocounsel with his old friend Walter Jones in a lawsuit against the Baltimore & Ohio Railroad over right-of-way issues in Maryland and West Virginia. Oddly enough, that year Key also represented several Washington landowners who contested the amount of money the canal company planned to award them for their property that had been condemned to make way for the waterway. In arguing for "our legal right to a fair compensation," Key made several points, including one dealing with "unhealthiness." The proposed canal, Key said, "would be infested with various winged insects" and "there would be a stagnant atmosphere in its vicinity."[3]

Frank Key kept busy with his legal practice throughout 1830. In a case he argued before the U.S. Circuit Court in Washington on May 14, he represented Harry Quando, a slave seeking his freedom. Quando's owner, a Mrs. Claggett, had decreed in her will that her slaves be "free and manumitted forever." However, the will stipulated that Quando, whom Mrs. Claggett referred to in the document as "my man Harry," serve "one year to any person that will give a fair hire for him." Key filed a petition for Quando's freedom and the court agreed that Mrs. Claggett intended "to emancipate the petitioner."[4]

In *Cushwa v. Forrest,* Key represented a man being sued because he allegedly sold another man a blind horse.

Anne Phoebe Charlton Key, Frank Key's seventy-four-year-old mother, died July 8, 1830, at the Key homestead, Terra Rubra. She was buried in a simple pine coffin in the Key family plot at Mount Olivet Cemetery in Frederick. Her son became the sole proprietor of the Terra Rubra plantation.[5]

Early in February of 1831, Frank Key joined six other prominent Washingtonians named to the board of directors of the Bank of the United States. Known as the Second Bank, this federally chartered private institution opened for business in 1816, five years after the failure of the First

Bank of the United States. Based in Philadelphia, the bank had branches throughout the nation. The federal government owned a twenty percent stake in the bank which—in addition to issuing notes, paying public officials, and regulating state bank notes—also functioned as a private bank, holding deposits and making loans.

Frank Key gave a typically long and animated talk on February 16, 1831, at a meeting of the American Sunday School Union at the First Presbyterian Church in Washington. Key fit right in with this gathering of pious and patriotic Washington power players, which included Daniel Webster and many other members of Congress. The men came together to support this organization, which had been founded in 1824 to set up Sunday schools around the nation.

In May 1831 in the U.S. Circuit Court in Washington, Frank Key argued on behalf of another slave seeking freedom. In *Negro Kitty v. Samuel M'Pherson*, Key represented the plaintiff whose mistress, Mary Brooke, directed in her will that Kitty be freed in 1840. Key claimed that Kitty should be freed immediately because the Brooke estate sold her to Samuel McPherson, and nothing in the will stipulated that Kitty should be sold into bondage. He lost this case.

On July 4, 1831, as the nation celebrated its 55th birthday, James Monroe died at the age of seventy-three in New York City, the third founding father to die on July Fourth.[6] In Washington, "unusual respect" was shown on the holiday, the *National Intelligencer* newspaper reported, "by the closing of stores, shops, and universal suspension of all labors but those of the culinary kind."[7]

The Independence Day celebrations in the nation's capital that year took on a decidedly political tone. The two main political parties held commemorations as they geared up for the 1832 presidential election. Henry Clay's National Republican Party celebration took place at City Hall, followed by a dinner attended by some three hundred at a private home overlooking the Potomac.

Jackson's partisans marked the day with what the *Alexandria Gazette* called "the Jackson celebration" and the *National Intelligencer* dubbed "the Administration celebration" in the Capitol rotunda. Francis Scott Key, described by one newspaper as "a particular friend of the President,"[8] spoke at that event.

In his speech Key laid out his decidedly Jacksonian Democratic vision of how the American government should function. The founding fathers envisioned a "general government of limited and defined powers intended to secure the common interest," he said, with the states functioning as "independent republics [with] exclusive power in whatsoever concerned their separate interests."[9]

Key then issued a warning about two "opposing dangers" facing the nation. The first was that the likelihood—presumably under Clay and the Republicans—that the federal government would grow too powerful, becoming a "vast consolidated dominion, with immense resources and unlimited patronage." That, he said, would be a danger "to the power of the States, and the rights of the people."

Danger number two would come about if the states assumed too many powers, a prospect that would "gradually weaken the powers" of the federal government. That situation, Key presciently observed, could very well "dissolve the Union."[10]

Key gave another passionate pro-Jackson speech two days later at a meeting and Jackson political rally at the Lancaster school in Georgetown. "The Union must be preserved," he said, quoting President Jackson, who, Key continued, "has already done much to maintain it. He has done much also to quiet our apprehensions as to the other source of danger...the accumulation of power in the hands [of] the [federal] government."[11]

Andrew Jackson strongly supported states' rights, but he also was a fervent nationalist who drew the line when extreme states' rights advocates took control of the South Carolina legislature in 1831 and started what became known as the Nullification Crisis of 1832-33. Nullification—the right of a state to declare null and void a federal law it deems unconstitutional—dates from the earliest days of the Republic and the never fully resolved debate between Federalists and Jeffersonian Republicans over the division of federal and state powers.

The 1832-33 crisis stemmed from laws Congress passed in 1828 and 1832 that significantly raised taxes on imported goods. South Carolinians bitterly opposed those higher tariffs, believing they only benefited northern industrial states and hurt agrarian-based southern states whose economies depended heavily on slave labor. Led by the firebrand John C. Calhoun, Jackson's estranged vice president, a South Carolina state convention met in November of 1832 and issued an Ordinance of Nullification declaring the tariffs null and void in the state. The state legislature then enacted a measure preventing the federal government from enforcing the tariffs at the state's ports and threatening to secede from the Union.

President Jackson called the action treasonous and vowed to make good on his pronouncement that the federal union must be preserved.[12] Old Hickory—who easily had won a second term in the November-December 1832 presidential election against Henry Clay—issued a long proclamation on December 10, warning the people of South Carolina that they had no right to nullify a federal law. In it, Jackson said he considered the power to annul a law by a state "incompatible with the existence of the Union, contradicted expressly by the letter of the Constitution, unauthorized by its spirit, inconsistent with every principle on which it was founded, and destructive of the great object for which it was formed."[13]

Jackson then proposed a piece of legislation called the Force Bill that would give him the power to use the military to force South Carolina's compliance with the tariffs.

Henry Clay crafted a compromise in March 1833 that ended the crisis. In it, Congress enacted the Force Bill as well as the Compromise Tariff of 1833, which gradually reduced the tariffs that had been raised in 1828 and 1832. South Carolina then rescinded its nullification ordinance.

"If nothing were done to preserve" the American system of government, Clay wrote, we would "witness its entire destruction or a Civil War. There was a concurrence of favorable circumstances to avert both calamites, and I endeavored to warn the Country of it."[14]

While no other southern states joined South Carolina in the nullification crisis, it nonetheless represented the first serious discussion of secession in the nation. It also offered a hint at what was to come in 1860 when South Carolina became the first of eleven southern states to secede from the Union and form the Confederate States of America.

Frank Key's views on nullification jibed completely with those of Andrew Jackson's. Key expressed them in a letter he wrote in November of 1832 to a relative of his wife's who had asked for his help in getting a presidential appointment. Frank Key told the man that he needed to go through his representatives in Congress.

"I hope you are not a Nullifier," Key warned, "For if you are, I think that will nullify all your hopes."[15]

In the early morning hours of Monday, August 22, 1831, the most extensive, bloodiest, and portentous slave rebellion in the nation's history broke out in Southampton County in Tidewater, Virginia. Six enslaved men led by thirty-one-year-old Nat Turner invaded the home of Turner's master and killed him and his family while they slept. In the next two days Turner and some sixty slaves from surrounding plantations fulfilled a vision he had. Armed with guns, clubs, and axes, the rebellious slaves stabbed, shot, and clubbed to death more than fifty white men, women, and children. Turner had hoped his revolt would lead to a general slave insurrection. It didn't.

The Virginia militia met violence with violence. The militiamen quickly hunted down and killed most of Turner's accomplices, as well as some slaves who had nothing to do with the rebellion. Turner himself eluded capture for ten weeks, hiding in the Great Dismal Swamp. He was discovered on October 30, tried on November 5, and hanged on November 11.

In the aftermath of the bloody rebellion, mobs throughout the South murdered scores of black people. The Virginia General Assembly began debating a measure that would have abolished slavery in the state but instead enacted a series of repressive slavery laws in January of 1832, as did other slave states. The rebellion virtually ended all talk of voluntary manumission of slaves in the border states and the South, but it gave new strength to the abolitionist movement in the North.

The crusading abolitionist William Lloyd Garrison took his post–Turner Rebellion wrath out on the American Colonization Society. In a thick pamphlet titled "Thoughts on African Colonization," Garrison charged that the ACS existed primarily because racist slave owners wanted to rid the nation of freed blacks because they feared the freedmen would foment rebellion among enslaved people.

The society, he said, "is agreeable to slaveholders because it is striving to remove a class of persons who they fear may stir up their slaves to rebellion. All who avow undying hostility to the people of color are in favor of it; all who shrink from acknowledging them as brethren and friends, or who make them a distinct and inferior caste, or who deny the possibility of elevating them in the scale of improvement here, most heartily embrace it."

Garrison also mocked the ACS's oft-stated goal of spreading Christianity and "civilization" to Africa. "The conception of evangelizing

a heathenish country by sending to it an illiterate, degraded and irreli-
gious population belongs exclusively to the advocates of African colonization," he wrote. "For absurdity and inaptitude, it stands, and must for ever
stand, without a parallel. Of all the offspring of prejudice and oppression,
it is the most shapeless and unnatural."[16]

Frank Key's home state of Maryland joined other slave states in enacting laws in the aftermath of Turner's Rebellion that cracked down on the
rights of freed blacks and slaves. Maryland also adopted a statute that all
but mandated that freed blacks be shipped to Liberia. That law, which
went into effect on March 12, 1832, allocated $20,000 in state funds to
the Maryland State Colonization Society—which had declared its independence from the national ACS in order to establish its own settlement
of freed blacks in Liberia.

Turner's Rebellion also had a strong impact on slave owners, many of
whom began to live in fear of violent slave uprisings. Interestingly—and
perhaps not coincidently—Frank Key freed four of his seven slaves not
long after Turner's Rebellion.

Key allowed a forty-year-old slave he owned, described in court documents as a mulatto named Romeo, to buy his freedom in Washington,
charging him a token fee of just one dollar.[17] On September 7, Key let
another of his Washington slaves, William Ridout, who was in his mid-
twenties, purchase his freedom for the not-insignificant figure of $300.[18]

On September 15, Key went to the U.S. District Court in Washington
and signed a Certificate of Freedom for Elizabeth Hicks. It read: "Elizabeth
Hicks is free. She is about 65 years old, a dark mulatto, and is 5′ 8″ tall. She
has lost one of her front teeth."[19] Most likely, Key freed her to rid himself
and his wife of the burden of caring for an aged enslaved woman.

On October 3, Frank Key rode up to Gettysburg, in the free state
of Pennsylvania, with two of his grandsons and Clem Johnson, a longtime Terra Rubra slave. After arriving at the office of Justice of the Peace
Sampson S. King, Key signed papers to free Johnson, whom the family
called Uncle Clem. For five dollars, Key agreed to "manumit and set free
the said Clem Johnson, aged about forty-five years, forthwith. And I do
hereby release and discharge Clem Johnson from all services to me, my
heirs, executors, and administrators."[20]

Clem Johnson "wept, and said he did not care to have the papers and
was unwilling to leave the service of Mr. Key," John H. McClellan, one of

two local witnesses to the transaction, later remembered. "Mr. Key said he wished him to remain with him as a servant and a free man and that he should return to his farm where he should have a home until his death."[21]

As a slave, Clem Johnson had held the position of assistant estate manager at the Key plantation. Following the manumission in Gettysburg, Key, Johnson and the grandsons rode back to Terra Rubra, where the former slave went to work, presumably for a salary, for his former owner, Francis Scott Key. The other slaves owned by Key at the plantation continued in bondage.

Frank and Polly Key faced a traumatic family crisis in May of 1832 when their 25-year-old son Frank Key Jr.—the married father of two young children—was charged with a serious crime in Annapolis where he lived. "We have indeed been almost overwhelmed by this calamity," Frank Key wrote to his son-in-law Charles Howard in Baltimore on May 19.

Frank Sr. went on to relate his son's tale of woe in which a woman who said that he had abducted her and forced himself upon her went to a local magistrate who swore out an arrest warrant. Before the warrant was served, Frank Jr. fled to his parents' house in Washington. "I advised my poor boy when he came to me in shame and wretchedness to acknowledge all his guilt—to repent and return [to Annapolis] and submit to all the consequences of his sin—a Christian parent could not do otherwise," Frank Key wrote. "I would have gone with him."[22]

But Frank Jr. didn't listen to his father's advice. Instead, he left town with his younger brother John. He left a note explaining that he was innocent of the charges but also admitted his "sin and shame," presumably for having an affair with the woman. Frank Jr. wrote that he had proof that he did not rape the woman. Said proof: that a friend had ridden up to the house where he and the woman were having an assignation, and Frank Jr. came out to the yard to speak to his friend, keeping the door to the room unlocked the entire time. The woman, therefore, "could have gone out and escaped" at any time, he told his father, if she had been held against her will.

Frank Sr. sprung into action to defend his son although he told Charles Howard that whatever happened ultimately would be determined by a higher power. He asked his old friend Daniel Murray to go to Annapolis to make the necessary inquiries. He also sent his son Daniel, fifteen, to see what he could find out.

Two days later, on May 21, 1832, Frank Key again wrote to Howard, saying he and Polly were "mercifully relieved." Word had come back from Annapolis that Frank Jr. had been falsely accused. Key said that the woman in question changed her story on a second visit to the local magistrate, and that Murray's investigation found that she was "a vile prostitute of the lowest character" who was trying to blackmail his son. Frank Jr.'s account of the "transaction," he said, "is fully confirmed."

Key added that his son's conduct was "shameful" and that he was "at least equally guilty." But the magistrate ruled that no crime had been committed and agreed not to prosecute.[23]

The following day Frank Sr. wrote to his daughter Elizabeth Howard, saying that her brother had returned to his home and family in Annapolis. "It must have been no little relief to him to find how quickly affairs had changed in his favor."[24]

13

A RANK JACKSON MAN

Francis Scott Key was not "at all happy…to stand at the bar of the House of Representatives to plead the cause of a disgraced, a dying, an impeached administration."

—*United States Gazette, May 1, 1832*

Sam Houston was not a man to be trifled with. The rough-and-tumble Tennessean had run away from home at age sixteen to live among the Cherokee in the mountains of East Tennessee. He spent more than three years with the tribe, wearing buckskin, speaking the native language, and taking the Cherokee name "Colonneh," or Raven. In 1813 at age twenty, he joined the Tennessee Militia under Andrew Jackson to fight in the War of 1812. The young soldier saw plenty of action and was severely wounded at the 1814 Battle of Horseshoe Bend fighting the Creek Indians.

The colorful, controversial Virginia-born Houston left the Tennessee Militia in 1817, went home, read law, and was elected to Congress, and then to the governorship of the Volunteer State. Houston resigned as Tennessee governor in 1829 to live with the Cherokee again, this time in Indian territory in what is now Oklahoma.

He came to Washington in 1830 to ask his old friend Jackson for help in getting a government contract to supply rations to the Indians. This came just prior to Old Hickory's infamous Indian Removal Act that compelled Native Americans to leave their lands east of the Mississippi. The contract never came about, and Houston returned to live among the

Cherokee. In the spring of 1832, he went to Washington, this time to lobby on behalf of Indian rights.

Not long after Houston arrived in town, he read an article in the April 2 edition of the *National Intelligencer* newspaper reporting on a March 31 House floor speech by Ohio Congressman William Stanbery. In it, Stanbery, a staunch Jackson administration opponent, alleged, among other things, that the president had removed Secretary of War Eaton from office "in consequence of his attempt fraudulently to give to Governor Houston the contract for Indian rations."[1]

That allegation did not sit well with the mercurial Sam Houston. He wrote a letter to Stanbery on April 3 to "ascertain whether my name was used by you in debate, and, if so, whether your remarks have been correctly quoted." Stanbery wrote back to Houston the next day, refusing to recognize "the right of Mr. Houston to make this request."[2]

Those were fighting words to Sam Houston. He let it be known that he would shoot Stanbery in the street if he had the opportunity. Word got back to the Ohioan, who armed himself with a pistol for protection. Things came to a head at about eight on the balmy night of April 13, 1832, when the two men crossed paths on Pennsylvania Avenue in downtown Washington, across the street from Mrs. Queen's boarding house where Stanberry lived.

A half hour before, Houston, then thirty-nine, had been chatting amiably in another Washington boarding house with two Jacksonian Democratic senators, Felix Grundy of Tennessee and Alexander Buckner of Missouri, and with Francis Preston Blair, a close Jackson associate from Tennessee who edited the pro-administration *Washington Globe*.[3] Buckner, Blair, and Houston decided to take a stroll. As they stepped onto the street, Houston "took each of us by the arm, one on each side of him, and bore us up the avenue," Buckner later said.[4]

On the way back Houston spotted Stanbery crossing Pennsylvania Avenue across from Mrs. Queen's. Houston walked up to the Ohioan and asked him if he was, indeed, Mr. Stanbery, to which the older man, as Buckner put it, "replied very politely, and bowing at the same time, said, 'Yes, sir.'"

Houston responded, "You are the damned rascal," and began beating Stanberry savagely with his cane.

"I was waylaid in the street," Stanbery later said, "attacked, knocked down by a bludgeon, and severely bruised and wounded."[5]

"Stanbery threw up his hands over his head, and staggered back, his hat fell off, and he exclaimed, 'Oh, don't,'" Buckner said. But Houston continued to hammer away. The congressman tried to run, but Houston "sprung upon him from the rear." A struggle ensued. Stanbery fell to the pavement. Houston continued the onslaught.

The congressman managed to grab his pistol, cock it, and pull the trigger, "aiming at [Houston's] breast," Stanbery later testified.[6] The pistol jammed, Houston grabbed it from Stanbery, and then continued the beating.

"After Houston's giving him several other blows, he lay on his back and put up his feet," Buckner said, "Houston then struck him elsewhere. Mr. Stanbery, after having received several blows, ceased [talking], and lay, as I thought, perfectly still."

Sam Houston finally stopped. A crowd gathered. Houston stalked off, still holding Stanbery's pistol.

The next day, April 14, 1832, Stanbery wrote to Speaker of the House Andrew Stevenson, a Jacksonian Democrat from Virginia, requesting that that body take action against Houston. The House—in which Democrats outnumbered Republicans 126 to 66—took up the question that same day and promptly voted 145–25 to arrest Sam Houston and indict him for contempt.[7] The House as a body would act as judge and jury in a proceeding that would resemble a trial, with attorneys and members questioning witnesses and the House itself rendering a verdict on Houston's guilt or innocence with an up-or-down vote.

Jackson strongly supported his old friend Sam Houston. Never one to shy away from superlatives, he told a friend that the House proceedings were "the greatest act of tyranny and usurpation ever attempted under our government."[8] But that bombastic support did little more than give ammunition to Andrew Jackson's political opponents.

The president "openly bullies all who do not acquiesce in his declarations that the assault upon Stansberry [sic], a member of Congress, by Houston for words spoken in debate is correct," anti-Jackson Virginia Governor John Floyd wrote in his diary on April 13. "He, Jackson, says that he wished there were 'a dozen Houstons' to beat and cudgel the members of Congress."[9]

Sam Houston chose a fellow Jackson associate, the celebrated Washington lawyer Francis Scott Key, to defend him.

The proceedings in the House of Representatives began on April 18 with the arraignment. Houston showed up wearing a buckskin jacket and carrying the same hickory cane he used to attack Stanbery. Frank Key stood at his side as the House sergeant-at-arms escorted Houston to the bar of the House. Speaker Stevenson read the charges and gave Houston the opportunity to respond. Houston handed his written remarks to Key, who read them to the House.

Houston admitted that "he did…assault and beat" Stanbery, the lawyerly statement said, but Houston was "unarmed with any other weapon than a common walking cane, and [he believed] Stanbery to be—as he in fact was—armed with pistols." The statement went on to deny that Houston "intended to commit, or that he believed he was committing any contempt towards the House of Representatives or any breach of its privilege, or of any of its members." Houston, Key said, "is prepared to justify his conduct, as far as the House is concerned, by proof and argument."[10]

And argue Frank Key did. The trail went on for a month, making headlines across the country. Key and Houston, backed by a handful of ardent Jackson allies in the House, unleashed a blizzard of arcane legal arguments and procedural questions that dragged the proceedings out for weeks. At times, the House stopped all business to concentrate on the case. Things were held up in late April and early May when Frank Key was ill and several sessions had to be postponed.

The House galleries were packed to overflowing for many of the trial sessions. Some spectators sat on the House floor to take in the action. Women were given permission to go on the floor "by a special order," one correspondent reported a bit breathlessly, "dazzling the eye of the beholder, and rendering the *coup d'oeil* altogether striking."[11]

Key began his defense with a blunder. He made a motion requesting that any House member who had a preconceived opinion should excuse himself from participating in the trial. Key and Houston left the chamber as the House debated the motion. When they did, Stanbery's supporters objected loudly and indignantly.

The House has "no power to do what the counsel of the accused requested," former president John Quincy Adams (now a Massachusetts congressman) said. "It amounted to a call upon the House to expel one of its members." Tristam Burges, a Rhode Island anti-Jacksonian, said. Key should not have made "a motion which everyone must know would result in nothing, unless it were in giving to the accused a pretext for saying that he had not had a fair trial."

Frank Key promptly withdrew the motion and issued a tepid apology. He blamed his "ignorance of this dark subject, parliamentary law," then backpedaled, saying all he was trying to do was help his client get "a fair and impartial trial."[12]

The trial continued for three more days, breaking on Sunday, April 22, when the House wasn't in session. Then came four more days of testimony and motions. The nadir came on April 26 when Frank Key spoke for more than two hours in Houston's defense.

Houston was plainly guilty, but Frank Key—either under orders from Jackson or because of his unquestioned devotion to the Jackson cause—put on a defense that stands among his least distinguished legal endeavors.

He argued that the House had no right to try his client, even though several times since 1795 the body had tried outsiders for attempting to "corrupt the integrity of the House." He warned direly that putting Houston on trial in Congress constituted a "danger to our free institutions." He blamed opposition newspapers for "doing everything to excite a degree of indignation against" his client, "which should make the fair hearing of his cause impossible."[13] He said Houston did not beat Stanbery because of what he said on the House floor but for those same words that appeared in the newspaper, something over which the House had no jurisdiction.

Most disingenuously, Key argued that Houston—described by one reporter as "portly in his carriage, upwards of six feet high, athletic, and built in proportion, fresh in his appearance, with a good, and at the same time manly countenance"[14]—was "a weak and disabled man." Houston once had "an arm fit to execute the strong impulses of a brave heart," Key orated, "but that arm had been given to his country" in the War of 1812. "On the field of one of her most perilous battles it had been raised in her defense—and on that field it had fallen, crushed and mangled to his side."

One reporter mocked Key, observing that the lawyer "most felicitously inferred that [Stanbery] was flogged with no worse a weapon than a man might legally use for the purpose of chastising his wife" and that Key had said that Stanbery "could have no legitimate cause of complaint that he came off with a dislocated wrist."[15]

Key went on at great length citing English law, English court deci-
sions, English Parliamentary precedents, the Maryland Constitution, U.S.
Supreme Court decisions, the U.S. Constitution, and previous Senate and
House contempt proceedings. He ended his peroration with a paean to
Houston's patriotic selflessness.

Sam Houston, Key said, "in the ardor of youth and devotion to patriotism, heard the call of his country in the day of her danger, and took his
humble, but honorable stand in the lowest rank of her defenders." He "rose
to distinction among the honored and the brave." Yet, Houston took home
"no other spoils than the scars of honest wounds, and the sword which his
valor had won." All Sam Houston had, Key said, was his good name—his
"only earthly treasure." The House, he said, will "therefore pardon me if
I have been unnecessarily solicitous to guard from the breath of its cen-
sure a name that has been thus earned, and is thus valued."

Few people pardoned Frank Key for his rambling, obfuscating defense
of Sam Houston. The anti-Jackson press and politicians pounced on his
performance. The Republican organ, *United States Gazette* of Philadelphia,
questioned whether Key was a "logical and profound orator" and "sound
lawyer." The paper said it was a "known fact" that Key was "a rank Jackson
man," and said that Key was not "at all happy" that his loyalty to Jackson
brought him "to stand at the bar of the House of Representatives to plead
the cause of a disgraced, a dying, an impeached administration."[16]

The *Cincinnati Gazette* brought up the question of how much Frank
Key was paid by the Jackson administration for "for hiring his talents and
lending his character to the present men that control the executive of the
nation." Key "ought to have been well paid," the paper said, "for he has not
escaped some soiling."[17]

"Everybody has become fatigued with the subject," *Niles' Weekly Register*
reported on April 28. But the House would not finish its Sam Houston
business until May 14. On May 7, Houston gave a blustering, two-hour
oration of his own, vigorously protesting his innocence. Near the end, he
followed Key's lead and wrapped himself in the flag, saying that he will-
ingly put his life on the line "to protect the hearths of my fellow-citizens,"
and was always ready "to do and suffer in [my country's] service."

Taking a page from Frank Key's "Defense of Fort M'Henry," Houston
testified that "so long as that proud emblem of my country's liberties, with

its stripes and its stars…shall wave in this Hall of American legislators, so long shall it cast its sacred protection over the personal rights of every American citizen." Convicting him, Houston said, would be tantamount to destroying "the pride of the American character."[18]

The House began debating its verdict the next day, May 8. Future President James K. Polk of Tennessee, a devoted Jackson ally, led the pro-Houston forces. Three additional days of long-winded debate ensued. Pro- and anti-Houston congressmen offered up long, passionate speeches, some of which went on for hours.

At around nine on Friday night, May 11, many legislators were fed up. The House "resounded with cries for the question" to come to a vote, the official congressional record noted.[19] The final tally was 106-88 to convict Sam Houston of contempt of Congress and of violating the privileges of the House.

The congressmen then argued over procedural issues for nearly two more hours. Just before 11 p.m., the House adjourned for the weekend. The marathon proceedings ended on Monday, May 14—exactly a month after the trial had begun. Speaker Stevenson called Houston to the bar and pronounced the judgment of the body: "You have been guilty of a high breach of its privileges and, in obedience to the order of the House, I do reprimand you accordingly."

Stevenson paid flowery tribute to Frank Key, telling Houston he was "ably and eloquently defended by eminent counsel."

Many thought that the entire exercise, especially Houston's beating of Stanbery, was little more than a national fiasco. "From this assault and some things developed in the trial, we should judge that some of our *great* men, so called, are but half civilized, and not Christianized at all," one newspaper editorialized. It was out of the question, the editorial said, that outsiders looking at the trial "should consider us as a nation of barbarians."[20]

Stanbery brought a civil suit against Houston to the U.S. Circuit Court in Washington, in which the unrepentant Tennessean faced assault and battery charges. Key and Houston claimed the defendant could not be punished twice for the same crime. But the court ruled that the conviction of the House was "not a bar to the present prosecution for the assault and battery."[21]

Houston, the court ruled on June 28, "coolly and deliberately meditated the kind of revenge that he took," and "the battery was very severe." Considering "the situation of the parties, their high standing in society, the original provocation, the deliberate revenge, the great outrage upon the public peace, the severity of the battery, and the mitigating circumstances before mentioned," the court found Houston guilty and ordered him to pay a $500 fine, plus court costs, a princely sum in 1832.[22]

The court ruled that Sam Houston did not have to pay the fine until later in the year. As it turned out, Sam Houston never paid a dime, and the court never followed up. Houston left for Texas soon after the trial to continue his work for the Indians—and for Texas's independence from Mexico. On July 4, 1834, President Jackson ordered the federal marshal's office in Washington not to collect the fine.[23]

Sam Houston later told a friend that his conviction in the House actually was a good thing. "I was dying out," Houston said. "Had they taken me before a Justice of the Peace and fined me ten dollars for assault and battery, they would have killed me. But they gave me a national tribunal for a theatre, and that set me up again."[24]

In 1836, Houston led an army of Texans as they defeated Mexican forces at the Battle of San Jacinto to win independence for Texas. Houston then went on to become the first president of the Republic of Texas.

14

THE PROSECUTOR

"There was neither mercy nor justice for colored people in this district."

—Benjamin Lundy, June 1833

Rumors began circulating early in 1833 that Frank Key was about get a plum job as a reward for his loyal legal work for the Jackson administration: U.S. attorney for the District of Columbia. On January 21, President Jackson did, indeed, nominate the fifty-three-year-old lawyer to become the fourth U.S. attorney for Washington, succeeding Thomas Swann.[1] Jackson's secretary, Andrew Jackson Donelson, delivered the nomination to the Senate on January 29, along with a handful of other presidential appointments. The Senate approved Key's nomination unanimously the same day.

Frank Key would hold that position for eight years. During that time he headed a very small office that prosecuted a wide range of criminal cases. That included fraud, perjury, bribery, and forgery, sending and bearing invitations to duels, breaking and entering, disturbing the peace, assault and battery, arson, theft, and the occasional murder. Under his direction, the U.S. Circuit Court of the District of Columbia also handled scores of civil trials, mostly involving debts and other financial issues. His office also dealt with petitions for freedom from slaves.

The court was located in a wing of the old Washington City Hall, just north of Pennsylvania Avenue and five blocks west of the Capitol. In Washington's close-knit legal world, Frank Key had known and worked with the court's judges and clerks for nearly three decades. The chief judge, 53-year-old William Cranch, had been nominated by Thomas Jefferson in 1806 and would hold the position until he died in 1855. The Massachusetts-born Cranch—who served with Key as a manager of the American Colonization Society—was a nephew of President John Adams. James Madison appointees Buckner Thruston, a Virginia-born former Kentucky senator, and James Sewall Morsell of Maryland, a Georgetown lawyer, were the associate judges.

Although the judges received salaries, the U.S. attorney did not; his income depended on the fees his cases earned. Salary or none, Frank Key did not suffer financially during his public service since he continued to earn steady legal fees from his lucrative private law practice.

A bare-bones operation, the U.S. Attorney's Office included twelve magistrates—two in each of Washington's six wards—and just ten constables who were hired by the mayor and aldermen. The constables received only fifty dollars a year for their services to the city.[2] With such low salaries, the constables found other ways to earn money. One was capturing runaway slaves and turning them over to slave traders who did a brisk business in the national capital.

The Circuit Court met periodically throughout the year, usually for month-long terms beginning in March and November. If case loads became heavy, extra terms were added. Francis Scott Key took charge for the first time in the March 1833 term.

Given the fact that more than nine thousand African Americans lived in Washington (about half of whom were slaves) out of a total population of some thirty thousand, a significant portion of the cases Frank Key prosecuted involved freed or enslaved black people.[3] Freed blacks were required to carry certificates of freedom; without them, they could be arrested as runaway slaves, jailed, and sold into slavery. Enslaved blacks, who had no civil rights, nevertheless came under Key's legal jurisdiction when they ran afoul of the law. He also handled cases involving white slave owners and slave traders.

The U.S. attorney's job was to help enforce all of the laws, and Francis Scott Key did not stint in prosecuting freed blacks and slaves. One of his first cases involved the prosecution of a 27-year-old freed black man, John Prout, who had helped a slave named Joseph Dozier escape from his owner, Lucy R. Miller. Dozier had been found and returned to Miller, but Key indicted Prout—who had run schools for black children in Philadelphia and New York and had spoken out against African colonization—for forging a certificate of freedom for Dozier. The government prosecutor asked the court to fine Prout $600 to cover the costs involved in "recovering" Dozier.

The jury found Prout guilty, but ordered that he pay only a $50 fine "because there was no averment of loss of service."[4] Key also prosecuted another freed black man, Abraham Johnson, for helping Prout. He charged Johnson with depriving Miller "of the service of her said slave." The jury convicted Johnson; the judges fined him $50.

A minor revolt took place at the 1833 annual meeting—the sixteenth— of the American Colonization Society in Washington. After the close of mostly routine business on January 20, ACS Secretary Ralph R. Gurley of Connecticut offered a resolution that would have stripped the board of managers of most of its powers. Many members saw this as a move by northern abolitionists to take over the ACS. A raucous debate erupted; things became so contentious that the final vote on the resolution was put off four times.

Finally, at a fifth meeting on February 8, after much discussion, the official meeting minutes noted, the measure failed by only six votes, 63–57.[5] The upshot was that even though Francis Scott Key lost some power in the organization, the ACS mission remained unchanged, and Key stayed a strong supporter until the day he died.

Despite the ACS kerfuffle, Key's professional prospects continued to improve. On March 20, 1833, Francis Scott Key became one of twelve directors of the Bank of Columbia in Georgetown, which had been chartered in 1793. Key joined a group of prominent Washingtonians who had served on the bank's board of directors, including his uncle Philip Barton Key. Among the bank's clients were the famed New York merchant John Jacob Astor, the eminent Washington architect Benjamin Henry Latrobe, and President James Monroe.

Key's close friend John Randolph died on May 24, 1833, in Philadelphia. In his three-part will, Randolph—who never married—all but apologized for owning slaves and granted freedom to the four hundred enslaved individuals he owned at the time of his death.

"I give and bequeath to all my slaves their freedom, heartily regretting that I have ever been the owner of one," he said in his will. "It has a long time been a matter of the deepest regret to me that the circumstances under which I inherited them, and the obstacles thrown in the way by the laws of the land, have prevented my emancipating them in my lifetime, which it is my full intention to do."[6]

To facilitate that humanitarian gesture, Randolph bequeathed much of his estate to three old and trusted friends, to be used to buy at least ten acres of land for each of his slaves over the age of forty "in any of the States or Territories," to "pay the expense of their removal," and to buy them "cabins, clothes, and utensils." The three trustees were William Leigh, a Halifax County, Virginia judge; Reverend William Meade, the American Colonization Society manager who had freed his own slaves and later would become Episcopal bishop of Virginia; and Francis Scott Key.

The will did not go over well with Randolph's other heirs, who filed a lawsuit challenging it. The litigation held up the will's execution for thirteen years—until 1846, three years after Francis Scott Key's death. Judge Leigh eventually fulfilled Randolph's wishes and arranged for his surviving former slaves to go to Ohio, where they permanently settled, although they encountered vicious—and sometimes violent—opposition from white residents of that state.

In June 1833 U.S. Attorney Key prosecuted John Hampden Pleasants, the editor of the *Richmond Whig*, a stridently anti-Jackson newspaper. He did so because Pleasants had decided not to obey a summons from Key to be a witness in a strange case that was to be tried in Alexandria, Virginia. When Pleasants refused the summons, Key had federal marshals arrest him.

In a case that came close to trampling on Pleasants's First Amendment right of freedom of the press, Key sought to question the editor about a letter he had published from "some person in Alexandria to some person in Richmond." Key characterized said letter as "a bill of indictment charging R. B. Randolph and sundry other persons as having conspired to commit an assault upon the President of the United States in the county of Alexandria."

Robert B. Randolph was a former U.S. Navy lieutenant whom Jackson had dismissed from the service on April 21, 1833, because of his large debts.

Randolph had been in the navy for twenty-three years and did not take kindly to the dismissal. He took his revenge on May 6, 1833, in Alexandria, where Jackson had boarded a steamboat on his way to Fredericksburg to dedicate a monument to George Washington's mother.

Randolph wormed his way on board the crowded ship and into the cabin where Jackson, 66, sat reading a newspaper. He came up to the president, took off his gloves, and then—of all things—pulled his nose. Randolph was quickly taken into custody after having the dubious distinction of being the first person to physically assault a sitting American president.

Later that day Jackson "was still highly exasperated at the recent outrage offered him by Lieutenant Randolph," the famed writer Washington Irving, who met Jackson in Fredericksburg that day, later wrote. "It is a brutal transaction, which I cannot think of without indignation, mingled with a feeling of almost despair, that our national character should receive such crippling wounds from the hands of our own citizens."[7]

Irving and others were in high dudgeon about the assault, but Andrew Jackson shrugged off the incident. He declined to have Randolph prosecuted, and instead had Vice President Van Buren pardon the disgraced former naval officer.

Randolph never went before the bar of justice. But Frank Key—no doubt because the *Whig* was so stridently anti-Jackson—pressed the case against Pleasants, the newspaper's editor. Key and Pleasants's attorney, Walter Jones, argued over the case in a Circuit Court hearing on June 18. At the end of session, the judges dismissed Key's argument. They ruled that the government did not have jurisdiction in a case of assault in Virginia, said that that Pleasants was detained "without lawful authority," and ordered that he be "forthwith discharged."[8]

"There was neither mercy nor justice for colored people in this district." Those were the words of the strident abolitionist Benjamin Lundy in the June 1833 edition of his antislavery newspaper, *Genius of Universal Emancipation.*[9] Lundy, a New Jersey-born Quaker who had moved to Washington after being hounded out of Baltimore—went on to describe two troubling incidents that had taken place in the city in May and June 1833.

In the first, a group of freed blacks applied to a city constable for permission to have an elaborate ball; they paid him for a permit and held the party. At eleven o'clock that night, fourteen Washington policemen showed up at the party house "armed with guns, pistols, and clubs," Lundy wrote. The police robbed about forty of the partygoers "of all their watches and money." The next day the freed blacks were hauled before a magistrate. Each one, Lundy wrote, "was fined as much as they could well pay—and then the constables and magistrate made a division of the money between them."

In the second incident, a freed black woman came into Washington from Virginia seeking work. When Washington constable Gilson Dove, "who buys and catches negroes for the traders," Lundy said, confronted the woman, she fled. Dove gave chase, following her so closely, Lundy wrote, that "she had no way to escape but by jumping into the river, where she was drowned." No "fuss or stir was made about it," Lundy reported. "She was got out of the river, and buried—and there the matter ended."

Lundy then castigated the Washington establishment for such "outrages upon unprotected, unoffending people." He singled out the constables, condemning the "depredations of unprincipled men invested with a little brief authority" for not "securing the just and equal administration of the laws."

Lundy did not mention Francis Scott Key by name, but there is little doubt that he had aimed the inflammatory rhetoric directly at the U.S. attorney for allowing law officers under his purview to abuse African Americans so blatantly. It's all but certain that's why Key indicted Lundy and the man who printed his newspaper, William "Billy" Greer, alleging that the article was meant "to injure, oppress, aggrieve & vilify the good name, fame, credit & reputation of the Magistrates & Constables" of Washington.[10]

Learning of his indictment, Lundy left the city and moved his one-man newspaper to Philadelphia. But Billy Greer was not so lucky. A Pennsylvania Quaker who refused to insert advertisements for the arrests of runaway slaves in the newspapers he printed, Greer himself was arrested and put on trial. Gilson Dove and another policeman testified for the prosecution. Greer brought in one witness to the drowning and a fellow Quaker who sold subscriptions to Lundy's paper. The jury found Greer not guilty.

President Jackson shook up his cabinet for a second time in the summer of 1833. This time the issue was the Second Bank of the United States.

Jackson waged what became known as the Bank War against what he perceived as an institution that favored the rich at the expense of his main constituency: ordinary citizens. Jackson, encouraged by Attorney General Roger B. Taney and others, announced that he would withdraw all federal funds from that Second Bank, which was run by wealthy, private, unelected bankers. When newly appointed Treasury Secretary William J. Duane refused to do so because he believed that public funds should not be transferred to state banks, Old Hickory fired him.

Rumors circulated in Washington and around the country that Francis Scott Key or another member of Jackson's kitchen cabinet would replace Duane.[11] Jackson, however, moved Key's brother-in-law, Roger B. Taney, into the job on September 23, the day that Duane left the Treasury Department. Two days later, Taney ordered all federal government funds placed in state banks—not the Second Bank of the United States— beginning October 1.

Some political pundits speculated that Francis Scott Key would replace Taney as Attorney General of the United States.[12] But Jackson instead chose Benjamin Franklin Butler of New York, a former law partner of Vice President Van Buren.

Congress had not been in session when Jackson appointed Taney to the Treasury Department job, and he therefore hadn't been confirmed by the Senate. When Taney's recess appointment expired on June 23, 1834, the president sent the official nomination to the Senate. A majority of the deeply divided Senate loathed Jackson for his actions against the Second Bank, and they took revenge the next day by voting down Taney's appointment, 28-18. That marked the first time in the nation's young history that Congress voted down a president's choice to head a cabinet-level department.

Taney formally resigned as Treasury secretary, left Washington, and went back to practicing law in Baltimore. But his exile from the national political arena did not last long. In 1835 Jackson nominated his former attorney general to a vacancy on the U.S. Supreme Court. The Senate stonewalled the process, voting 24-21 on March 3 to postpone the nomination indefinitely. Frank Key called the action "madness."[13] But Taney and Jackson had the last laugh.

Chief Justice John Marshall died on July 6, 1835. Jackson waited nearly six months, then nominated Taney on December 28 to succeed Marshall.

This time, the Senate went along with Jackson and confirmed Roger Brooke Taney. Francis Scott Key's brother-in-law and close friend became the nation's fifth chief justice on March 15, 1836. He went on to serve in that position for twenty-eight years.

In the fall of 1833 U.S. Attorney Key prosecuted the full gamut of cases in the nation's capital. He convened a special term in September, during which he prosecuted seventy-two cases of assault and twenty-six larceny cases.[14] The morally upright Frank Key also cracked down on two things that he found particularly displeasing: prostitution and gambling.

Washington had a disproportionately large number of houses of prostitution mainly because the city was filled with a disproportionate number of unattached men—members of Congress and their all-male staffs from all over the country, living temporarily in the city.

The city also had a reputation for illegal gambling. "There is not a city in which gambling is carried to greater excess than in [Washington] the metropolis of the country," a visitor from Philadelphia noted in 1833.[15]

That fall Key shut down five gambling dens in Washington and brought seventeen prostitution cases to the court. Nearly all the indictments against the alleged proprietors of houses of ill fame or bawdy houses, as they were then called, contained the same boilerplate language. The complaint against George W. Gray and Cecelia Gray, for example, accused them of keeping "a certain bawdy house for filthy lucre" at which "evil disposed persons" unlawfully "and wickedly did receive and entertain... whores."

Key's indictment went on to accuse the Grays of committing "whoredom and fornications, whereby unlawful assembly, riots, routs, affrays, disturbances and violations of the peace" took place, along with "lewd affairs" in "manifest destruction and corruption of youth and other people in their manners, conversation, morals and estate."[16]

In another typical case Key indicted Harriet and Henriette Jourdine on two counts: for keeping a disorderly house and for keeping a bawdy house. The Jourdine sisters were found guilty, fined $20, and required to post a $200 security bond to ensure their "good behavior for twelve months.[17]

Key's prostitution prosecutions continued into the November term. Most convictions resulted in fines of $266.66. Several of those indicted—including

Ann Johnson and Hannah Contee, Christiana Williams, and Matilda Butler—were African Americans.

Frank Key's crusade against prostitution did not eliminate the world's oldest profession in the nation's capital. Far from it. Prostitution made a big comeback in the 1840s and 1850s. When the Civil War began in 1861, there were some five hundred bawdy houses in Washington in which more than five thousand prostitutes plied their trade.[18]

15

MINISTER TO ALABAMA

"He is very pleasant—intelligent, you at once perceive, and somewhat peculiar in his manners."

—*Sarah Ann Haynsworth Gayle, Dec. 1833*

In November 1833, President Andrew Jackson sent Frank Key on a mission. It involved the second incipient states' rights rebellion of his presidency. This time the issue was whether the federal government or the state of Alabama had jurisdiction over lands that had been left behind by the Creek Indians after Jackson signed the 1830 Indian Removal Act that forced native peoples to move to the Indian Territory west of the Mississippi River, in what is now Oklahoma.

The March 1832 Treaty of Cusseta with the Creek Indians contained a provision that allowed individual Creek families to stay in Alabama on small parcels granted to them by the government if they chose. Some decided to stay, but were not permitted to claim their parcels until the government finished a land survey. Before that long process could be completed, white settlers rapidly moved in and took over virtually all the Creek lands.

"The many ways of defrauding the Indians of their allotments were varied, ingenious, often brazen, and conducted by large speculative consortia as well as individual cheaters," the historian Paul Prucha wrote. "The frauds were spectacular and widespread, making a mockery of the treaty intentions, and the government seemed impotent to stem the speculators' chicanery."[1]

Things got tense in east central Alabama in the summer of 1833 when federal marshals and U.S. troops at Fort Mitchell, located just west of the

Georgia state line, clashed with some of the twenty-five thousand illegal white settlers on Indian lands. In July federal troops killed Hardeman Owens, a local official whom the Creek identified as a particularly egregious taker of Indian lands. Owens was shot in a scuffle as soldiers tried to arrest him. In September soldiers killed a deputy sheriff when he attempted to serve a warrant to arrest the lieutenant in charge at Fort Mitchell after his men had burned a white settlers' village called Irwinton.

Those actions stirred up intense feelings against the federal government throughout the state. Citizen groups formed, pledging to resist all federal actions against settlers. A mass meeting of agitated white citizens in the town of Hayneville on September 28 passed a resolution declaring that "the removal of our citizens by force is unconstitutional, oppressive and utterly subversive of the sovereignty of the States, and *we cannot and will not submit to it.*"[2]

Feelings ran so high that increasing violence between federal troops and white settlers seemed inevitable. If that happened, Jackson would have been faced with another tense states' rights versus federal jurisdiction confrontation like the nullification crisis, one that easily could have spread into the neighboring states.

Alabama Governor John Gayle, a one-time close Jackson friend and ally, turned against Old Hickory and staunchly defended the settlers. In an October 2 letter to Secretary of War Lewis Cass, Gayle—who had just been reelected that year, running unopposed, to a second two-year term—forcefully denounced the federal removal policy, calling it "fatal in its tendency to civil liberty, directly subversive of the acknowledged rights and sovereignty of the state of Alabama," and "an unconstitutional interference with our local and internal affairs."[3]

Attorney General Roger B. Taney—in most matters a states' rights man—weighed in with a letter to Gayle in which he came out squarely in favor of the federal government's right to intervene in the land disputes. "In my opinion the president may lawfully direct the marshal of the district, and employ such military force as he may judge necessary and proper, to remove intruders from the land of Alabama ceded by Creek Indian to the United States," Taney wrote.[4]

On October 7 Gayle—described by one Alabama newspaper as "the wildest and worst of nullifiers"[5]—issued a proclamation denouncing the federal government's removal of the settlers as nothing less than "the suppression of our courts" and "the destruction of the state government throughout these counties." But Gayle then took a conciliatory tone, calling upon Alabama's citizens "to look with abiding and undoubting confidence to the majesty of the law," both state and federal.

He went on, though, to urge state law enforcement officials to "be attentive to the complaints of the people," and do what they could legally to prosecute those "guilty of murder, false imprisonment, house-burning, robbery, forcible entries, and all such like heinous offences."

Gayle also told Alabamans that they were obligated "to yield a ready obedience to any precept or process that may issue from the courts of the United States," another conciliatory gesture. And he paid lip service to the rights of the Creek, admonishing Alabamans to "abstain from all acts of unlawful violence towards the Indians, who being ignorant of our laws, and of their rights, should be taught to look up to their more intelligent neighbors for information and protection."[6]

The governor's directive to Alabama law enforcement authorities to prosecute federal evildoers encouraged a grand jury to indict a group of federal troops for the murder of Hardeman Owens. The commanding officer of Fort Mitchell, though, refused to turn his men over to local authorities. Gayle then ordered the state militia to make what one newspaper called "military preparations ... for the defense of the settlers."[7]

Alabama's congressional delegation in Washington—Senators William Rufus de Vane King and Gabriel Moore, and Congressmen Clement Clay, Samuel Mardis, and Dixon Hall Lewis, all Jacksonian Democrats—met with the president in October and November 1833 to try to defuse the tense situation. Led by Clay, the Alabamans convinced Jackson to call off any federal action against settlers who had obtained their lands legally.

But that left open the question of the ultimate ownership of the former Indian lands and what would happen to the federal troops and marshals accused of crimes by the state of Alabama. Jackson and Secretary of War Cass sent Francis Scott Key to Alabama to negotiate those issues directly with Governor Gayle.

Late in October Frank Key set out from Washington on the eight-hundred-mile trek. He arrived in Tuscaloosa, then the state capital, sometime in the first week of November, and stayed in Alabama for about six weeks. His reputation preceded him. Frank Key played the role of celebrity poet/patriot/lawyer among Tuscaloosa society. A band played "The

Star-Spangled Banner" when he arrived. He was welcomed into the homes of the city's movers and shakers, including that of the governor and his wife.

By the time Key left for home just before Christmas, he had used his lawyerly skills to negotiate a compromise with Governor Gayle that put an end to the crisis. *Niles' Weekly* cheerfully dubbed Francis Scott Key the "minister [ambassador] of the United States to the state of Alabama."[8]

Key went to Alabama with written instructions from Secretary of War Cass, instructions that newspapers across the country published while Key made his way south. Cass stressed that Jackson did not wish to trample on the Alabama civil authorities' legal processes. On the other hand, Cass said, the federal marshals and troops in Alabama "must be defended against vexatious proceedings."[9]

In Tuscaloosa Key met with the leaders of the state legislature. "There are some very clever men among them," Key wrote to Taney on November 6, "and they say they have no doubt a vast majority of the people of the State are decidedly opposed to the course of the Governor." He also met repeatedly with Governor Gayle and found him to be in an "embarrassing" position between states' rights proponents (nullifiers) and those who held strong Federalist leanings (union men).

"If he offends the Nullifiers, he is not sure of appeasing all the Union men," Key wrote to Taney, "and if he says he is satisfied with the U.S., he will be sure to offend the Nullifiers."

Key remained cautiously optimistic that things would be settled without violence. Gayle, he wrote, is "quite disposed to a pacific course." Key warned, though, that he would not be "surprised to see all the South & Virginia committing some folly quite equal to nullification."[10]

The following day, in a letter to his twelve-year-old daughter Ellen, Frank Key reported on the weather—that it had been raining for three or four days—and what life was like for him in Tuscaloosa. "There is nothing strange here to tell you about," he wrote. "There are no Indians, & it is just like one of our towns except that there is no snow or ice or cold. I sit almost all day with my door, opening to the street, wide open, & the flies will not let me take a nap after dinner."[11]

He then told Ellen that he had met Sarah Gayle, the governor's daughter who was about her age, and that the girl had asked him to write some verses for her album. The visiting versifying lawyer could not refuse. He shared the poem he wrote with Ellen in the letter.

"To Miss Sarah Gayle" is a not untypical Frank Key verse, filled with less than graceful rhymes and not a little sentimentality. One need read no more than the first four lines to gauge its style and sentiment:

> Sarah Gayle! thou will't be fair
> So a Thousand youths will swear.
> And beloved thou shall't be
> And be rhymed incessantly.

Frank Key soon left Tuscaloosa for Fort Mitchell. He wrote a long letter to Taney from the fort on November 14, saying he had interviewed the troops and officers who had been subpoenaed. The soldiers, he said, "seem disposed to remain & take their trial," but he wasn't "sure how they will act if they find they are to be marched off to" jail in Montgomery.[12]

Key went on to tell Taney that he also had visited the local authorities who had indicted the soldiers. He disparaged the local justice of the peace as "an obstinate & violent intruder who declares his purpose of resisting any efforts of the government to turn him off [the land he seized]." Describing the courthouse as "a sort of shantee of rough plank," Key said that the grand jury was made up of "intruders & their overseers & the agents of speculators."

The courthouse, clerk's office, judge, sheriff, and jury, Key noted with scorn, "are all here on U.S. land, by the indulgence of the U.S. and they evidently mean to use this indulgence to prevent the U.S. from using the right of ownership of their own lands...." He asked Taney's advice on whether or not the troops could be tried in federal courts and whether state laws or federal statutes took precedence.

Key also met with white settlers and Creek Indians. The Indians, he said in his official report to Cass, were "in a deplorable condition." Most had little food and had sold their land for "any trifle that had been offered to them." Key saw many Creeks "going to Columbus with bundles of fodder on their heads to sell," along with others "in the streets where they exchange everything they carry for whiskey."[13]

It took nearly a month, but Frank Key and John Gayle worked out a compromise that ended what the newspapers called the Creek Controversy.

Gayle convinced local authorities to drop the murder charges against the federal troops in the Owens case. In return, Key secured the Jackson administration's promise to stop removing whites from Indian lands until all the territory was surveyed. What's more, Jackson agreed that once the surveys were complete, settlers would be allowed to buy the Indian lands that they had occupied without interference from the federal government.

As Governor Gayle put it in a special message to the state legislature on December 20: "the settlers [will] remain in the undisturbed possession of their improvements, and the orders of the Secretary of War are to be confined exclusively to the locations which were reserved for the Indians in the treaty."[14]

In that message, Gayle also noted that he had had "several conversations" with Frank Key—whom he called "a gentleman equally distinguished for intelligence and for his frank and honorable character." His conversations with Key, Governor Gayle said, led to the end of the "unpleasant controversy" with the federal government.

The compromise—such as it was—did, indeed, end the antagonism between the state of Alabama and the federal government. It wasn't much of a compromise, though, since the federal government agreed to Gayle's main demand to allow the white settlers to take as much land formerly owned by the Creek as they wished without any interference from federal troops or marshals.

As for the Creek Indians, the compromise did them little good. Tensions between the twenty thousand or so impoverished Creeks who remained in Alabama and the white settlers occupying their former homeland boiled over in May of 1836. Bands of Creeks made a series of bloody attacks on white settlers and their families in Eastern Alabama and Western Georgia. Alabama and Georgia militia forces, along with federal soldiers and marines, soon moved in and crushed the rebellion.

The Creek War of 1836 ended with thousands of Creek men, women, and children being forced on a Trail of Tears march to Indian Territory during which many perished. In the end, only a handful of Creek Indians remained in their ancestral homelands in Alabama.

"*Mr. Francis Scott Key*, the district attorney for the District of Columbia, is here at present for the purpose of assisting to settle the Creek controversy," Sarah Ann Haynsworth Gayle, the twenty-nine-year-old wife of the governor, wrote in her journal in December. "He is very pleasant—intelligent, you at once perceive, and somewhat peculiar in his manners."

Frank Key, she went on to say, "is a little, nay, a good deal, absent in company, not always attending a question, though evidently unconscious of what he has done. His countenance is not remarkable when at rest, but as soon as he lifts his eyes, usually fixed upon some object near the floor, the man of sense, of fancy, and the *poet* is at once seen."

The governor's wife then went on to describe what she called "the crowning trait" of Frank Key's character: "He is a Christian."[15]

Sarah Ann Gayle obviously was quite taken with the poet-lawyer from Washington. And there is little doubt that Frank Key very much enjoyed the company of the vivacious young wife of the Alabama Governor during his extended stay in Tuscaloosa. When he wasn't doing official government business, Key spent a good deal of time at the Gayle home in the company of the governor's wife and her children.

"He has been to see me frequently," Gayle wrote in her journal one day in December, "and sat an hour or two last night chatting to me and the children." The visitor from Washington so impressed her that she was moved to express herself in verse.

The poem she wrote on December 10, "To Mr. F.S. Key," eventually appeared in several newspapers. It begins with the line "Thanks gentle fairy," and goes on to ask Frank Key to write her a poem—"a trifling boon," as she put it, "For me to read and treasure when thou art away!"

Frank Key was happy to fulfill that request. Three days later, on December 13, he wrote a poem to the governor's wife called "To Miss _____." It begins with the lines:

> And is it so? a thousand miles apart
> Has lay of mine e'er touched a gifted heart?
> Brightened the eye of beauty? Won her smile?
> Rich recompense for all the poet's toil!
> ... That fav'ring smile, that brigten'd eye
> That tells the heart's warm ecstasy,
> I have not seen—I may not see—
> But maiden kind! Thy gift shall be
> A more esteemed and cherish'd prize
> Than fairest smiles of brightest eyes.

Key also included one of his rare references to "The Star-Spangled Banner" in a second poem.

> We are not strangers, Well thy lines impart
> The Patriot's feelings in the Poet's heart.
> Not even thy praise can make me vainly deem
> That 'twas the Poet's power, and not his theme
> That woke thy heart's warm rapture, when, from far;
> His song of vict'ry caught thy fav'ring ear.
> That vic'try was thy country's, and his strain
> Was of that starry banner that again
> Had wav'd in triumph, on the battle plain.[16]

Sarah Ann Gayle took pains to point out Key's patriotism and piety in her journal. She described how he read "fine hymns and psalms in the Book of Common Prayer" to her daughter.

But many of the words in the verses Gayle and Key exchanged had little to do with piety and more to do with tenderness and longing. Jefferson Morley, in his book *Snow-Storm in August*, contends that a romance developed between the two. The poems they exchanged, he says, "qualified Mr. Key and Mrs. Gayle as lovers at least in the nineteenth-century sense of the word: as romantic suitors."[17]

Key's devoted 1930s biographer Edward Delaplaine, on the other hand, does not even hint at anything inappropriate in the passionate versifying. Key's poem "To Miss _____," Delaplaine wrote, "shows how he reveled in the natural beauties of Alabama, the leisurely charm of the South, and the generous hospitality of the Southern people."[18]

Whether anything untoward took place between Frank Key and Sarah Ann Gayle is an open question. We do know for certain, though, that they made deep impressions on each other.

"I have often thought of Tuscaloosa and your family circle," Key, back home in Washington in June, wrote to Gayle, "and could I transport myself as easily as my thoughts, I should still be a frequent visitor."[19]

16

AN INCORRUPTIBLE PATRIOT

"I saw the flag of my country waving over a city..."
—*Francis Scott Key, Aug. 6, 1834*

Frank Key threw himself back into his legal work in Washington after his Alabama sojourn. In the March 1834 term at the D.C. Circuit Court, the U.S. attorney renewed his fight against houses of prostitution, bringing six criminal and one civil prostitution prosecutions to the bar of justice. That included at least one that he lost, *U.S. v Sally McDowell*, in which Key charged McDowell with keeping a bawdy house.[1]

That term Key also represented at least five slaves seeking freedom. He argued successfully for the plaintiff in *Negro Robert Thomas v. Elizabeth Magruder*, in which Thomas claimed he had a valid deed of manumission but Magruder said it was not the original. The court ruled for Thomas, and he walked out of the courtroom a free man.[2]

Key lost a case, *Negro Frederick Bowman v. Henry Barron*, in which he represented the plaintiff, a slave suing for his freedom because he had been brought into Washington, and had lived there for more than a year. Barron's attorney argued that Bowman was merely on loan from a widow to her son-in-law and had not legally lived in Washington. The court agreed.[3]

Key won freedom for Joseph Crawford in *Negro Jos. Crawford v. Robert A. Slye* and for Eliza and Kitty Chapman in their lawsuit against

Robert Fenwick. In the latter case, the enslaved women's owner had man-umitted them in her will, but her executors sold them to pay the estate's debts. The court held that the will's instructions for manumission super-seded any transactions that took place.[4]

In the summer of 1834 the Philologian Society, a literary group at the newly opened Bristol College in Bucks County, Pennsylvania, asked Francis Scott Key to give a talk on a topic of his choice. On July 23 Key offered up a long oration "of a deeply pious cast," as a Philadelphia newspaper put it, at the Episcopal college.[5] His topic: "The Power of Literature and Its Connexion with Religion."

He quoted liberally from the Bible to hammer home his main theme: that "a literary education" is a fine thing, but only if it is subservient to an even finer thing, a solid religious education. Religious and literary instruction should be "properly united," Key told the students. If secular education stood "in a station secondary and subordinate to" religious education, he said, "the temptations which are so apt to accompany the acquisition of learning are happily counteracted."

"Literary attainments," Key warned, "are acquired at a hazard and a price which religion can never sanction." Religion, he said, "is the only true and sure foundation for every institution that is to fit man for the duties of life."[6]

A few weeks after that pious oration, on August 6, 1834, Frank Key showed up at a major political event in Frederick in honor of his brother-in-law Roger B. Taney.

That day's events in Frederick had two purposes: as a public show of Democratic Party support for Taney following his June 24 rejection by the Senate as Treasury secretary, and as an 1834 state election campaign event. The festivities began at eleven o'clock that morning when a "small cavalcade of horsemen" met Taney and his party just outside of town.[7] Taney and his small entourage—including Frank Key and Maryland Congressman Francis Thomas—climbed into an elaborate horse-drawn carriage and were escorted to town.

Well wishers joined the cavalcade "until, when he reached the city, his escort amounted to about ninety horsemen," a newspaper reported. The procession moved into the heart of the city and stopped at a tavern where

Thomas offered remarks about the Senate's shabby treatment of Taney. Then the guest of honor made a short speech. Taney said "he cared not a halfpenny for the Senate," and "would rather shake hands in a social way with his old friends of Frederick, than receive all the honors which the Senate could confer."

At two thirty on that hot August day about five hundred people attended a public dinner held outdoors in the Frederick Courthouse yard. The partisan crowd toasted Key, Thomas, and Taney, and each man made "eloquent and soul thrilling speeches," the *Richmond Enquirer* reported.[8] In his speech, Frank Key reflected on his hometown and on the words he wrote in Baltimore Harbor twenty years earlier.[9] Key had never before spoken in public about that fateful night of September 13-14 in Baltimore Harbor.

Key began by saying how much he loved his annual visits to the place of his birth. "Never, even from boyhood," he said, had he "come within the view of these mountains" without having his "warmest affections awakened at the sight."

Then came the political part of his speech. Key said that in writing the "Star-Spangled Banner," it was "peculiarly gratifying to me, to know that, in obeying the impulse of my own feelings, I have awakened yours." The song, he said, "came from the heart, and it has made its way to the hearts of men whose devotion to their country and the great cause of freedom I know so well."

He continued: "I saw the flag of my country waving over a city—the strength and pride of my native state—a city devoted to plunder and desolation by its assailants. I witnessed the preparation for its assaults. I saw the array of its enemies as they advanced to the attack. I heard the sound of battle; the noise of the conflict fell upon my listening ear, and told me that 'the brave and the free' had met the invaders."

Key went on to offer flowery words of praise for the defenders of Baltimore, whom he called "the sons of sires who had left their crimson footprints on the snows of the North and poured out of the blood of patriots like water on the sands of the South." The defenders, he said, were "men who had heard and answered the call of their country—from these mountain sides, from this beautiful valley, and from this fair city of my native country. And though I walked upon a deck surrounded by a hostile fleet, detained as a prisoner, yet was my step firm, and my heart strong, as these recollections came upon me."

Through "the clouds of war," Frank Key orated, "the stars of that banner still shone in my view, and I saw the discomforted host of its assailants driven back in ignominy to their ships. Then, in that hour of deliverance and joyful triumph, my heart spoke; and 'Does not such a country, and such defenders of their country, deserve a song?' was its question.

"With it came an inspiration not to be resisted.... Let the praise, then, if any be due, be given, not to me, who only did what I could not help doing; not to the writer, but to the inspirers of the song!"

Next came the partisan part, in which Key sang the praises of Andrew Jackson and lashed out against his political enemies. He ended by thanking those who fought in the Battle of Baltimore "for the honor you have done me." He was "but the instrument in executing what you have been so pleased to praise," Key said.

The speech went over well with the hundreds of Jacksonians in attendance. At least one newspaper, however, the *Alexandria Gazette*, took the occasion to pillory Frank Key for showing up in Frederick and campaigning for the Democrats.

"Mr. Taney has had a public dinner given to him by the members of his party in Frederick County, Md.," a *Gazette* editorial said. "This is all right and proper.... Among those, however, who figured upon the occasion and accompanied Mr. Taney to the dinner was... Francis S. Key, Esq., the United States Attorney for the District of Columbia, and late Envoy Extraordinary from the 'Government' to the State of Alabama for the settlement of Indian disputes."

For that mission, the paper said, Frank Key "received a large and liberal compensation—quite enough to have induced him to keep away from such a gathering, where his appearance must have caused many unpleasant reflections to his best friends."

Why, the paper asked indignantly, "are the OFFICE-HOLDERS so busy in all *partisan* movements? Are they determined to make good the English minister's assertion 'that every man has his *price*?'"[10]

The Jacksonians put on several other public dinners honoring Taney in Maryland prior to the October 1 state elections. On September 9, for example, Taney addressed a meeting of more than five hundred in Elkton, in rural Cecil County, exhorting the crowd to vote for Jacksonians.

But those events did little good as the opposition Whigs steamrolled the Jacksonian Democrats. When all the votes were counted, the Whigs held a huge 77–18 majority in the Maryland legislature. In Frederick County all four seats went to Whigs.

An opposition newspaper, the *New York American,* gleefully pointed out that the Jacksonians did not win one seat in Frank Key's home territory of Frederick County, in which Taney also had close ties. "Here was thought to be Mr. Taney's strong hold," the paper noted, "it was his former residence, and where he was lately escorted, and feasted, where he made speeches, and was toasted, with an éclat which flattered the party with victory. But what a falling off!"[11]

The Jacksonians did better in the 1835 Maryland congressional election. With stronger candidates, including Francis Thomas, they lost only one of the four seats they had held.[12]

On Christmas Day 1834 Frank Key played a leading role in a religious service at Trinity Church in Washington, though this was no ordinary Christmas service. It included a discussion on how to support the work of the American Tract Society, which Key had strongly supported since its founding in 1816.

The American Tract Society's raison d'être was publishing and distributing Christian literature—not Bibles as the American Bible Society did. The organization, founded in New York, disseminated short, paper-bound, often heavily illustrated tracts, typically telling inspiring stories of nonbelievers being converted to Christianity. The nonbelievers often were nonwhite; their guides to Christian salvation were white people who prevailed on the nonbelievers to accept Jesus as the one true path to eternal salvation and redemption from sin.

Frank Key proposed a resolution that day—and the congregation adopted it—that the word go out that on the second Sunday (Sabbath) in January 1835 Christians around the world should ask their coreligionists to "take a public collection in aid of the Society's operations." The "way is prepared," Key's resolution intoned, "and the Lord Jesus Christ calls on each disciple to do his duty, as a dying man, to a dying world."[13]

"*I am hardly calm enough* yet to write," Frank Key wrote to Roger Taney from Washington on Friday, January 30, 1835.[14]

The cause of Key's lack of calmness: the first assassination attempt on an American president. Earlier that day, as Andrew Jackson was leaving a memorial service for Rep. Warren R. Davis of South Carolina in the Capitol, a deranged, unemployed house painter named Richard Lawrence rushed up to Jackson on the steps just outside the Rotunda and fired a pistol at point-blank range. The gun jammed.

"The explosion of the cap was so loud that many persons thought the pistol had fired," Senator Thomas Hart Benton of Missouri said. "I heard it at the foot of the steps, far from the place, and a great crowd in between."[15]

As the feisty, sixty-seven-year-old Jackson began wailing on his attacker with his cane, Lawrence pointed a second pistol at the president and pulled the trigger. It, too, jammed. It was a "miraculous preservation" of the president, Key told Taney, "from the attack of a ruffian."

One newspaper called it "the most audacious outrage attempted in this country."[16]

Navy Lieutenant Alexander Gedney threw Lawrence to the ground, and a half dozen other men seized him and turned him over to Alexander Hunter, the U.S. marshal for the District of Columbia. Hunter hustled Lawrence away, taking him the few blocks to the District Court Building where he was arraigned before Judge William Cranch.

U.S. Attorney Francis Scott Key was there as Cranch took testimony from eyewitnesses. According to one account, when asked why he tried to shoot the president, Lawrence answered: "The president killed my father."[17]

Cranch set bail at $1,500. Lawrence didn't have a dime and was put behind bars in the city jail to await trial. Frank Key at first believed that Lawrence acted for political reasons. "It seems," Key wrote to Taney, "he has been a furious politician for the opposition party & is represented by some as a very weak man, easily duped or excited, & by others as deranged."

It soon became apparent that the English-born Lawrence was unhinged. It was not apparent to the conspiratorial-minded Andrew Jackson, however. Old Hickory loudly proclaimed that Lawrence acted as the trigger-man in a plot by his political opponents to have him eliminated for his actions against the Second Bank of the United States.

"The attack threw the old soldier into a tremendous passion," Harriet Martineau, an English writer visiting Washington, observed. "He fears nothing, but his temper is not equal to his courage." Martineau said that virtually everyone but the president "had little doubt that the assassin Lawrence was mad," but within hours "the name of almost every eminent politician was mixed up with that of the poor maniac who caused the uproar. The president's misconduct on the occasion was most virulent and protracted."

A few days later, when Martineau used the phrase "insane attempt" while discussing the matter with Jackson, he exploded in anger. The president, she said, "protested, in the presence of many strangers, that there was no insanity in the case," and insisted "there was a plot, and that the man was a tool."[18]

Jackson soon came to believe that Senator George Poindexter of Mississippi, one of his most outspoken opponents, was behind the assassination attempt. "Immediately after Lawrence's two pistols missed fire, the President said it was a Poindexter affair," John Quincy Adams wrote in his memoirs.[19]

Pro-Jackson newspapers followed the president's lead and ran articles and editorials saying that Poindexter masterminded a conspiracy to kill Jackson. Reports surfaced linking Poindexter to Lawrence. One had it that Lawrence had painted Poindexter's house. Another, that Lawrence met with Poindexter the day before the assassination attempt.

Lawrence, one partisan newspaper reported, made daily visits to "the Senate chamber, listening to the impassioned eloquence and wild oratory of men determined to rule or ruin the country, believing as he probably did, what he had so often heard avowed by men in their official station, that Gen. Jackson was a tyrant, a despot, and a traitor to the country's constitution and laws....Is it to be wondered that he should imagine that he was doing the country essential service in ridding it of one whom he had again and again heard denounced as a curse to the land over whose destinies he presides?"[20]

Poindexter vehemently denied the accusations, calling them "a dark and insidious conspiracy to blast my character, and crush me under the weight of Executive denunciations."[21] Then Poindexter called for a Senate investigation into the alleged assassination conspiracy. A special six-member committee held a hearing on February 22. On March 3, the committee submitted its report to the Senate. "It exonerates [Poindexter] from every shade of suspicion," the *Alexandria Gazette* noted, "and was adopted by a unanimous vote of the Senate—forty-one members voting."[22]

The report was "a triumphant vindication of Poindexter's innocence," John Quincy Adams noted. "The public indignation is thus transferred from the assassin of the person to the assassin of character, and Jackson himself bears no small portion of the public odium." The "whole affair," Adams said, "is sickening to me, and looks too much as if we were running into the manners of the Italian republics."[23]

Despite the Senate report, Jackson still believed in a conspiracy and was not shy about letting people know that he did—including the U.S. attorney who would be prosecuting Lawrence.

The day after Lawrence's arraignment, Francis Scott Key began his due diligence by having both pistols examined. The idea was, he said, to see "whether there was any defect in them, or in the charges, or any other way of accounting for the failure to discharge them." A military officer reloaded the pistols with caps taken from Lawrence's shop. He then tested them. "The discharge took effect on every trial," Key noted.[24]

The pious Key attributed the fact that both pistols misfired when Lawrence pulled the trigger to divine intervention. As he put it in his letter to Taney: "We are presented with such a manifestation of the care of Providence over a life destined throughout to be a blessing to the world, that none can fail to see and acknowledge."

On February 4, Key had two doctors, Nathaniel P. Causin and Thomas Sewall, examine the prisoner's mental state. Causin was identified in the newspapers as a Whig and Sewall as a "Jackson Doctor." Both men came to the same conclusion, which they spelled out in their joint report: "This unfortunate man is laboring under extensive mental hallucination on some subjects."[25]

Among other things, Lawrence told the doctors that "no power in the country" would punish him if he had killed Jackson, because prosecuting him "would be resisted by the powers of Europe as well as of this country." Lawrence also stated, the report said, "that he had been long in correspondence with the powers of Europe, and that his family had been wrongfully deprived of the crown of England, and that he should yet live to regain it—and that he considered the President of the United States nothing more than his Clerk."[26]

After reading that report, Key, too, realized that the man was mentally disturbed, and that was how Key prosecuted the case. Although he indicted Lawrence for assault upon the president of the United States with the intent to kill—and although Jackson pushed him to look for conspirators—Key prosecuted Lawrence alone and agreed with the defense that the man was insane and not responsible for his actions.

The trial took place on Saturday, April 11, 1835. Lawrence showed up in court wearing a gray coat, black tie and vest, and brown pantaloons. "His appearance was that of a man perfectly at his ease, and collected," one newspaper reporter wrote, "but there is an appearance about his eyes certainly indicative of mania and an evident assumption of kingly dignity in his demeanor and the expression of his countenance." He took his seat "very quietly by the side of his counsel and conversed smilingly with them."[27]

At 9:30 a.m., before testimony began, Lawrence rose from his seat and addressed the court. "I am under the protection of my father at home," he announced. "The throne of Great Britain and the throne of this country belong to me. I am superior to this tribunal. I ask you to consider whether you are safe in your course."

Later, when the first juror placed his hand on a Bible to be sworn in, Lawrence once again jumped from his seat and said, "Swear on that book, but remember that I am King of England and of this country, and will most assuredly punish you."[28]

Lawrence's lawyer, William L. Brent (cocounsel with his brother James P. Brent), suggested that the defendant be removed from the courtroom, but the judges overruled him. A deputy marshal moved to the defense table to stand next to the prisoner. That didn't prevent Lawrence from repeatedly interrupting the proceedings, which went on until six that evening.

Key opened with an exegesis on the varying degrees of criminal insanity. He told the jury that if they found that Lawrence "was under delusion of mind, and if the delusion originated the act, the whole community would rejoice at his acquittal on that ground."

Key then brought on twenty-seven witnesses, starting with Treasury Secretary Levi Woodbury, Navy Secretary Mahlon Dickerson, and Navy Lt. Gedney, who were with Jackson when Lawrence tried to shoot him. Several times jurors directed questions to the witnesses. U.S. Marshall Alexander Hunter also testified. Frank Key then brought Judge Cranch to the witness stand to testify about Lawrence's demeanor at his arraignment.

"His manners were cool," the judge said, "but he seemed indifferent."[29]

Then came Lawrence's brother-in-law and a string of other witnesses who had known Lawrence for years. Thomas Smith called Lawrence a "deranged man." A relative said that Lawrence's father "was himself deranged and confined in a room frequently in England," and that Lawrence's aunt "died deranged." A physician who had examined Lawrence a year earlier said he "talked so incoherently that I was satisfied that he was deranged," and that Lawrence "might have been able to judge right and wrong," but he "should not like to have trusted his judgment in any amount in either matter."[30]

Key then brought to the stand three doctors who had examined Lawrence. They all concurred with Drs. Sewall and Causin, who also testified that Lawrence was mentally ill and not responsible for his actions.

At around 5:45 in the afternoon, after the brief testimony of the twenty-seventh witness, Lawrence's defense attorney, William Brent, said he would make no comments to the jury, but would let them decide based on the evidence presented by the prosecution. The jury deliberated less than ten minutes. The verdict: not guilty, because when Lawrence acted he had been under the influence of insanity.

Frank Key lost the case, but he won the admiration of all but the most fervent Jacksonians for pushing for an insanity defense in the face of strong pressure from his political patron and hero. As for Richard Lawrence, he spent the rest of his life in mental institutions, winding up in 1855 in Washington's Government Hospital for the Insane, later renamed St. Elizabeth's Hospital. He died there in 1861.

17

AN ALARMING STATE
OF DISORDER

The "great political and moral evil…is supposed to be slavery, but is it not plainly the whole coloured race?"

—*Francis Scott Key, April 1836*

In late May 1835, not long after the Lawrence trial insanity verdict, a frail, twenty-eight-year-old man named Reuben Crandall moved to Washington. A botany teacher who studied medicine at Yale, Crandall came from Peekskill, New York, to work as a botanist, collecting and cataloging plants, and giving lectures. The young bachelor set up a modest office on High Street (now Wisconsin Avenue) in Georgetown. He also received a license to practice medicine in Washington.

Crandall came from a family with strong social convictions. His sister, Prudence Crandall, had faced virulent opposition in 1833 when she opened a school in Connecticut for African American girls. Reuben Crandall himself had been an active member of the Temperance Society in Peekskill and also believed in the abolition of slavery.

Crandall brought a trunk full of copies of antislavery pamphlets, tracts, and newspapers—including the American Anti-Slavery Society's publications *The Emancipator* and *The Anti-Slavery Reporter*—with him to Georgetown. The budding botanist used some of the newspapers to wrap plants in; others he stored in his rooming house room. A few found their way into his office.

The abolitionist movement was gaining momentum in the summer of 1835. Two years earlier, William Lloyd Garrison had started the American Anti-Slavery Society. By 1835, that group had been flooding slave-holding states with pamphlets and tracts filled with inflammatory language pushing for the "immediate and complete" emancipation of slaves. Taking advantage of new advances in printing technology and postal rates as low as a penny, the society mailed the tracts by the hundreds of thousands to clergymen, politicians, public officials, and prominent citizens in all the slave states.

The overwhelming majority of southerners summarily rejected the abolitionists' message. Many postmasters in the South destroyed the literature rather than deliver it, sometimes after being physically threatened by outraged citizens. The Jackson administration sided with the slave-owning states.

"I am not prepared to direct you to forward or deliver the papers of which you speak," U.S. Postmaster General Amos Kendall wrote to the postmaster of Charleston, South Carolina, on August 4, after he had complained about being flooded with abolitionist tracts. "The Post Office Department was created to serve the people of *each* and *all* of the *United States,* and not to be used as the instrument of their *destruction....* By no act or direction of mine, official or private, could I be induced to aid, knowingly, in giving circulation to papers of this description, directly or indirectly."[1]

On December 7, 1835, Jackson, in his annual message to Congress, deemed it "proper" for Congress to "take such measures as will prevent the Post Office Department, which was designed to foster an amicable intercourse and correspondence between all the members of the confederacy, from being used as an instrument of an opposite character." The president went on to ask Congress for a law that would "prohibit, under severe penalties, the circulation in the Southern States, through the mail, of incendiary publications intended to instigate the slaves to insurrection."[2] Congress debated the merits of such a bill but never agreed on any legislation.

Late on Monday afternoon, August 10, 1835, Washington constables Henry R. Robertson and Madison Jeffers arrested Reuben Crandall in his Georgetown office on the charge of possessing, with the intent to distribute, abolitionist tracts.

Weeks earlier a man named Henry King had walked into Crandall's office to look at his botanical specimens and had seen an abolitionist pamphlet on a table with the words "please read and circulate" hand-written on it. King picked up the pamphlet, made a comment to the effect that Washington was a slave-owning jurisdiction—"This latitude is too far south; it won't do here"—and asked if he could keep it.[3] Crandall said he could. King took the pamphlet and showed it to a group of men at the nearby Linthicum's apothecary shop, where he left the publication.

When word of the existence of the pamphlet reached the U.S. attorney's office, Frank Key began an investigation. On the morning of August 10, he impaneled a grand jury that heard from several men who had seen the pamphlet. One witness testified that the words "please read and circulate" were in Crandall's handwriting. Key issued an order that afternoon for Robertson and Jeffers to go to Georgetown to investigate and then bring Crandall in to answer charges of circulating "dangerous and insurrectionary writings and thereby attempting to excite an insurrection."[4]

When the police officers walked into Crandall's shop and saw several copies of *The Emancipator*, they asked the young man if he also had abolitionist pamphlets. Crandall said he did and brought out a box filled with them. The policemen then placed him under arrest. When word spread in the neighborhood that young Crandall was being taken in for possessing antislavery tracts, a decidedly unfriendly crowd formed.

"Carry him across the street and hang him to the tree," one man shouted.[5]

"When we came out" with Crandall, Jeffers later testified in court, "there was a considerable crowd, and we hurried him into the hack for I did [not] know but they might wrest him from us."[6]

Robertson and Jeffers gave Crandall a choice: Go before a magistrate in Georgetown or take a ride to Washington to be arraigned at the U.S. Circuit Court. Crandall chose the latter, fearful of the budding lynch mob that had gathered outside his office.

In the carriage, Robertson asked Crandall: "Don't you think it would be rather dangerous, at the present time, to set the Negroes free?" Crandall replied that he "was for abolition, without regard to consequences."

Jeffers then asked Crandall if he "did not think that abolition would produce amalgamation and also endanger the security of the whites."

The "doctor," Robertson said, "did not object to these consequences; he thought the Negroes ought to be as free as we were."

What about colonization, Jeffers asked, "would it not be better than abolition?" Crandall replied he was in favor of "immediate emancipation."[7]

Jeffers retorted that doing so would "be attended by direful consequences. We should all be murdered and have our throats cut." The "next thing they would be for," he said, would be amalgamation."[8]

At that point, Robertson did the 1830s version of reading Crandall his Miranda rights: "I cautioned him not to say too much or to speak too freely," Robertson later recalled, "that we might be witnesses against him."

Robertson and Jeffers managed to get Crandall safely to the D.C. jail, even though another menacing crowd had gathered outside that building by the time they arrived after dark. Crandall was "greatly agitated," Robertson said as the constables hustled him into a small dank cell.

Crandall went before a magistrate the next day, Tuesday, August 11. U.S. Attorney Francis Scott Key, who had decided that Crandall was an extreme threat to the community, argued that the abolitionist botanist should be held without bail.

"Mr. Francis Scott Key," Crandall later wrote to his father, "the state's attorney, opposed my being admitted to bail. He said that I was an abolition emissary."[9]

Crandall would be held in jail for eight months, until mid-April 1836, when he finally stood trial. His case was the first in the nation in which an individual was charged with encouraging slaves and free blacks to revolt. Frank Key would charge Reuben Crandall with five counts "under the common law of libels, of publishing malicious and wicked libels with the intent to excite sedition and insurrection among the slaves and free colored people" in Washington.[10]

Just after midnight on August 5, five days before Reuben Crandall's arrest, an enslaved nineteen-year-old named Arthur Bowen returned to the place where he lived, a three-story brick townhouse on F Street between 13th and 14th Streets in what is now downtown Washington. The young man, who had been drinking heavily, carried an ax and was babbling when he entered the bedroom of his owner, Anna Maria Thornton, a room in which Bowen's enslaved mother Maria and Anna Thornton's aged mother also slept.

Anna Thornton, fifty-six, was the widow of William Thornton, the first designer of the U.S. Capitol who headed the U.S. Patent Office from 1802 until he died in 1828. The Thorntons, who owned about a dozen slaves, were well acquainted with the Keys, as they moved in the same Washington upper-echelon social circles. William Thornton had been a founding member and strong supporter of the American Colonization Society.

"Arthur entered the room at half after one o'clock with an axe, with the intention we suppose to murder us," Anna Thornton wrote in her diary. "His mother sleeping in the rooms with us & being fortunately awake, seized him & got him out, while I ran next door to alarm Dr. [Henry] Huntt & got help—Oh, what a horrid night."[11]

In her excitement and distress, Thornton told Huntt that Arthur Bowen had killed her mother. A crowd soon gathered outside the townhouse. Constables were called. Huntt and others entered the house to find Ann Brodeau, Anna Thornton's mother, alive and untouched. They found Arthur Bowen in the backyard, pounding on a locked door and screaming drunkenly that he must have his freedom.

At that point Madison Jeffers arrived on the scene. By the time Jeffers made his way into the Thornton house to arrest Bowen, the young man had slipped away into the night.

Anna Thornton offered a $100 reward for his capture in an ad she placed in the *National Intelligencer* on Friday, August 7. It described Bowen as "about five feet nine or ten inches high, straight and well made; one side of his face is scarred by recent blisters, and the mark of a wound on the back of one hand. He has a bushy head of hair, and speaks civilly and softly in general. He went off without shoes, hat, or jacket."

That same day several Washington newspapers ran lurid, inaccurate stories about the incident. The articles said that Arthur Bowen had raised the ax, intending to kill Anna Thornton, and that she was spared only at the last second when his mother awoke and pleaded with him to stop.

The *Intelligencer* saw the murder attempt as "one of the effects of the fanatical spirit of the day, and one of the immediate fruits of the incendiary publications with which this city and the whole slave-holding portion of the country has been lately inundated." The article went on to say that Bowen had shouted "the most ferocious threats," uttering "a tissue of jargon, much of which was a literal repetition of the language addressed to Negroes by the incendiary publications" of abolitionists.

On Saturday, August 8, Arthur Bowen, on his own, returned home to F Street. Soon after, Constables Jeffers and Robinson showed up and took him into custody. On the ride to the jail, the officers asked why he had tried to attack his mistress. Bowen said that he had the right to be free and spoke of bloodshed that would follow if the nation did not emancipate its slaves. Jeffers and Robinson brought Bowen before a magistrate who ruled that he should be tried for attempted murder.

"Oh, this is dreadful," Anna Thornton wrote in her diary. "The people are incensed against him as he is thought to be one of a party instigated by some white friends to raise an insurrection."[12]

Not long after Arthur Bowen was thrown into a cell in the black section of the D.C. jail, an angry crowd gathered outside. Many were roughneck laborers (then called mechanics) from the nearby Washington Navy Yard. The crowd "surrounded the jail and [swore] they would pull the jail down," Michael Shiner, a slave who worked at the Navy Yard and witnessed the event, wrote in his diary. "They said their object was to get Mrs. Thornton's mulatto man out and to hang him without judge or jury."[13]

As the crowd became more agitated, Francis Scott Key, Washington Mayor William A. Bradley, and head U.S. Marshal Harry Ashton showed up and stood between them and the jail. They "made every effort to preserve peace and harmony among these men," Shiner wrote, "but all of it appeared in vain [because] there was not sufficient military force to guard the jail."[14]

As the mob became more agitated, a detachment of Marines from the Navy Yard appeared on the scene. That ended the threat of violence—for the time being.

Two days later, on Monday morning, August 10, Anna Thornton sent a young friend to see U.S. Attorney Key to ask him if she could sell Arthur Bowen to get him out of Washington to avoid a trial. Key's answer: "Nothing can be done but to let him stay and take his trial."[15]

That same afternoon Key issued the order to pick up the young white doctor, Reuben Crandall, for inciting a black insurrection.

Anna Thornton hired one of Washington's most accomplished lawyers, Walter Jones, to defend Arthur Bowen. Jones—the former longtime Washington U.S. attorney who held the rank of major general as the head of the Washington militia—was a friend and colleague of Francis Scott Key. Both prominent members of the Washington legal community were among the founders and strongest proponents of the American Colonization Society.

Walter Jones met with Frank Key on Tuesday, August 11, to see if his friend would reconsider allowing Anna Thornton to sell Arthur Bowen so that he wouldn't have to stand trial. Key response was the same as it was on the previous day: "Nothing can be done at present," he told Jones, and advised him to keep quiet and wait for the trial.

"O my God," Anna Thornton wrote in her diary. "I hope some method may be found... to release him."[16]

The following day, Wednesday, August 12, Washington, D.C., experienced the first race riot in its history. "Popular phrenzy [sic] has broken out at our national capital," one newspaper reported. "The excitement was produced in relation to Reuben Crandall, who was arrested on the charge of distributing incendiary publications.... On Tuesday night [August 11] they were further excited by the report that Beverly Snow, a free mulatto, who kept an eating and drinking house..., had spoken in disrespectful terms of the wives and daughters of mechanics."[17]

"During the past two days," Sarah Gales Seaton, the wife of *National Intelligencer* publisher William Seaton, wrote, "we have been in an alarming state of disorder from a dread of insurrection.... There is great apprehension felt."[18]

The frenzied, alarming state of disorder during which hundreds of white men and boys torched black-owned businesses, houses, churches, and schools in two days and nights of rioting came to be known as the Snow Riot because of the rumors about Beverly Snow that sparked it. Snow was the owner and chef of the Epicurean Eating House, a popular restaurant among the city's white establishment, at the corner of 6th Street and Pennsylvania Avenue.

In the late afternoon an unruly crowd descended on the D.C. jail and cries went up to seize Reuben Crandall and hang him. Frank Key and Washington Mayor Bradley once again physically stood up to the mob. This time Key used his powers of persuasion to convince the men. "Crandall will be punished if you let the trial progress," Key told the throng.[19]

That evening, Mayor Bradley ordered General Jones to call out the Washington militia. Jones rounded up about fifty men armed with "muskets and fixed bayonets," the *Washington Globe* reported.[20] They confronted the mechanics around the city, then retreated to the front of City Hall, leaving the rest of Washington virtually unprotected.

The mob reformed the next day, Thursday, August 13. The men, historian Jefferson Morley wrote, "dispersed across the city streets in squads of tens and twenties in search of new targets and new victims. The constables could not have stopped them if they had wanted to, which they did not."[21]

One group all but destroyed the Asbury Sunday School for blacks run by Reverend John F. Cook Sr., an African American Presbyterian minister, at 14th and H Streets. Another group burst into a boarding house looking for Beverly Snow and found abolitionist newspapers in the room of James Hutton, a free black man who—ironically—ten years earlier had won his freedom with Frank Key's legal help.

"Hutton was immediately seized, and taken before a magistrate," the *Washington Globe* reported. "In a few minutes there were several hundred persons around the magistrate's office, halooing, 'Bring him out! Bring him out!'" At that point Hutton was hustled off to the D.C. jail.

"As soon as he was safely lodged in jail," the newspaper reported, "some persons hallooed 'Now for Snow's house!'"[22]

Snow "will certainly be torn to pieces by the mechanics if he be caught and they are in full pursuit of him," Sarah Gales Seaton wrote. "I tremble for the consequences of any encounter with mistaken, infuriated men who have set the laws at defiance, and must now be put down by force."[23]

Armed with axes and other implements of destruction, the mob headed toward Snow's restaurant just blocks from the jail. Beverly Snow managed, with the help of white friends, to flee just before the angry crowd arrived. The rioters tore down the restaurant's outside lamps and its sign, then "broke and destroyed most, if not all the furniture" in the place, the *Globe* reported. They then drank up Snow's stock of whiskey and champagne.

Another group showed up at the large house where Frank and Polly Key lived at 308 C Street Southeast on Capitol Hill. Polly and the four Key children living at home had gone to Terra Rubra. Frank Key had taken the precaution of bringing in armed guards from Georgetown to protect the house. The mob left without causing any damage.

The following day U.S. Attorney Key indicted twenty-six white men for their parts in the Snow Riot.

"We could not have believed it possible that we should live to see Public Offices garrisoned by clerks, with the United States troops posted at their doors, and their windows [barricaded] to defend them against the citizens of Washington," the *National Intelligencer* editorialized.[24]

About two weeks later, in the last week of August, Key convened a hearing to take testimony in the case of Arthur Bowen. General Jones represented Bowen. The witnesses included Dr. Huntt, the constables Jeffers and Robertson, and Maria Bowen (the accused's mother). Frank Key told Anna Thornton she didn't need to testify.

The trial of Arthur Bowen was set for the November term of the U.S. Circuit Court. Key then rode out to Terra Rubra to join Polly and the children to escape the heat in the city.

Anna Thornton did not want Arthur Bowen prosecuted. She didn't believe he intended to do her harm and greatly feared that his trial would result in a death sentence. She wrote a letter to President Jackson in October, asking him to intervene. The president told her he didn't have the authority to stop the legal proceedings. She then arranged a face-to-face meeting with Judge William Cranch. He told her that "the judges cannot take cognizance of the affair till brought before them judicially," Thornton wrote in her diary, "and then the matter rests entirely with the President to pardon him if he pleases."

At the grand jury held early in December, Frank Key allowed Anna Thornton to testify. She said that Arthur Bowen was guilty of nothing more than drunkenness. But her testimony mattered little. The trial of Arthur Bowen for attempted murder took place on December 10.

Defense attorney Jones told the jury in his opening statement that the evidence would show that Arthur Bowen—whom a newspaper reporter at the trial described as "extremely well dressed"—did not have any "deliberate intent" to do Anna Thornton harm that fateful night and that he was "mad drunk at the time."[25]

In his opening statement, prosecuting attorney Key told the jury that being drunk "was no legal excuse" for attempted murder.[26] Besides, Key said, Bowen "made a deliberate attempt upon the life of his mistress under the influence"—not of alcohol, but—"of excitement of a certain kind that will be described by the witnesses."

That excitement of a certain kind, Key later elicited from Constable Jeffers, was Arthur Bowen's belief that "he had a right to be free, and until the colored people were free, there would be so much confusion and bloodshed as would astonish the whole earth."[27]

Anna Thornton testified that she could not see if Arthur Bowen had "uplifted" the ax, that "he appeared to be very much intoxicated," and that his "behavior was generally good." Dr. Huntt, on the other hand, testified that Arthur Bowen's mother, Maria, told him that her son had come into Anna Thornton's bedroom with an "uplifted axe." Bowen "was quite violent after he got out" of the house, Huntt said. "He struck the door with the axe repeatedly, and cried out, 'I'll have the hearts' blood of you all.'"

Maria Bowen was not called to the witness stand. Two black men, William Costin and Reverend John F. Cook, testified for the defense. Costin, a well-respected leader in the free African American community who worked as a porter at the Bank of Washington, and Cook said that during the night in question Arthur Bowen had been present at a meeting of John Cook's debating society. There's little doubt that issues of slavery and abolition came up at the meeting, but the defense witnesses did not go into specifics about that.

Two witnesses testified that Arthur Bowen was drunk that night, including a neighbor of Anna Thornton, who said she saw him drinking "before sundown." She also said she frequently saw Bowen and "considered him a good character" and "never saw him drunk or disorderly" until the night in question.

In his closing statement Key said that the jury should convict if they believed that Arthur Bowen came into his mistress's bedroom "with the intent to murder her" and was only prevented from doing so by "being seized and forced out of the room." Being drunk, he told the jury, "was no legal excuse for the offense."

In his closing remarks, General Jones again asked the jury to take Bowen's drunken state into consideration, but Judge Cranch overruled him.

The jurors debated just fifteen minutes before they found Arthur Bowen guilty. On January 23, 1836, Judge Cranch pronounced the sentence: Arthur Bowen was to hang by the neck until dead. Cranch fixed the execution date for February 26.

Anna Thornton, an astute woman with widespread connections in Washington, worked assiduously to try to save Arthur Bowen from the gallows. She drew up a petition asking the president to pardon her slave and had it signed by thirty-five influential Washingtonians. When the petition went nowhere, she arranged a meeting with Jackson at the White House on February 19, a week before Bowen's appointment with the gallows. Jackson told Thornton he would consider some type of pardon, but only if U.S. Attorney Key and Judge Cranch agreed to it.[28] There is no indication that either Key or Cranch recommended anything but the death penalty.

Two days later, Anna Thornton wrote a pleading letter to Vice President Martin Van Buren asking him to use his influence with Jackson to pardon Arthur Bowen. Then she wrote an eighteen-page letter to Jackson himself, reiterating her strong belief that Bowen was not a threat to her on the night in question, that he was very drunk, and that he did not raise the ax.

As for Arthur Bowen, he had high hopes that Anna Thornton's work would bear fruit, although he fully realized what would happen if a pardon did not come through. Described in one newspaper as a "very intelligent" young man who "talks well," Bowen wrote a poem in jail expressing his feelings.[29] Several newspapers published the verses. Among the most salient lines:

> At length while drunk I done a crime
> Of a very dreadful sort.
> After being in jail a length of time,
> I was carried before the Court
> The Lawyers argued half the day,
> The jury left the place,
> About two hours they were away,
> When they found me guilty on one case.
> To me was read the awful sentence,
> Oh how dreadful in my ears it rung,
> They gave me time for my repentance,
> And then I must be hung.
> Good bye, good bye, my friends so dear,
> May God Almighty bless you all,
> Do, if you please, but shed a tear
> At Arthur Bowen's unhappy fall.

As workers began putting together a gallows on a vacant lot next to the jail, Jackson conferred with Attorney General Benjamin F. Butler. On February 25—the day before the scheduled hanging—Jackson granted Bowen a stay of execution until June 3.

During the next three months Anna Thornton enlisted the help of a good number of the capital's most influential men with close ties to Andrew Jackson to work on him to pardon Bowen. That included Francis P. Blair, the editor of the pro-Jackson *Washington Globe*; Vice President Van Buren; and Kentucky Congressman Richard Mentor Johnson, an old Jackson friend and former U.S. senator who would be Van Buren's Democratic Party vice presidential candidate in the November election.

On June 2 President Jackson agreed to put the execution off until August 4. Anna Thornton continued to lobby Jackson for a pardon. He acceded on July 4, the very same morning that Anna Thornton's elderly mother died.

Thornton knew that an unspoken part of the deal was that she had to sell Arthur Bowen. She did so for $750 to Jackson's old friend John Eaton. The former secretary of war, then the territorial governor of Florida, in turn sold Bowen to William Stockton, who spirited the young man out of Washington with him as he moved to Florida.

"I never intended to sell him for life, but could not now avoid it," Thornton wrote in her diary. "I hope & pray that he may lead a new life and be happy."[30]

What was Francis Scott Key's reaction to the pardon? No letter or diary entry has surfaced in which he even mentioned the name "Arthur Bowen" before, during, or after the events of 1835-36.

Nor has any letter or other source surfaced in which Key made his feelings known about the arrest and trial of Reuben Crandall. The young man had been languishing in jail since his arrest in August. In late January, Crandall's attorneys Richard S. Coxe and Joseph H. Bradley—two experienced and extremely able Washington lawyers Frank Key knew well—arranged to have Key conduct a bond hearing.

Judge William Cranch suggested bail of $2,000, but Key argued for $15,000, a fortune in 1836. Key did so, Crandall wrote to his father, "saying I was certainly an emissary [of the abolitionist movement] and that he could prove it." By making "this and other false declarations in court," Crandall said, "they were induced to raise the bail to $5,000."[31]

Crandall came to loathe the prosecuting attorney. He "takes very unwarrantable grounds against me for nothing, only to bully people into the belief that he is with them in this affair hook and line," Crandall wrote. "He is very distrustful of people as well as they of him." Key, Crandall told his father, has been called "the Blacks' lawyer, as he took their cases for them when they sued for their freedom, and in this way, has a great many enemies... [and] people are distrustful of his honesty of motive."

Crandall also told his father that Frank Key "has acknowledged to some of his confidential friends that there is no evidence against me that can convict." Key, he said, "is only biting his own nose."[32]

The eleven-day trail of Reuben Crandall began on April 15, 1836. Frank Key called it "one of the most important cases ever tried" in Washington.[33]

Covered heavily by newspapers across the nation, the trial would become Francis Scott Key's last big moment on the national stage. In many respects, Key used Reuben Crandall as a vehicle to lash out against the tenets of abolitionism and to strongly defend the American Colonization Society.

Key may have done so, as Crandall suggested, as a way of gaining credibility among those who distrusted him for his long-standing willingness to represent slaves and freed blacks in court. One newspaper correspondent reported on a rumor that Key "was pledged to the people to procure the conviction of Crandall, for without that assurance they would have torn him to pieces."[34]

It does not appear that Francis Scott Key feared anyone's wrath if he didn't prosecute Crandall. It's much more likely that he prosecuted Reuben Crandall for other reasons. Crandall possessed inflammatory antislavery tracts and had written about his desire to "circulate" them in Washington, which was illegal. In that regard, Key was doing his job enforcing the law. Secondly, the tracts strongly and repeatedly attacked the American Colonization Society, to which Key had been devoted since he helped found the organization nineteen years earlier. In that respect, Key used his judicial powers to further his personal agenda.

Key also could have been reacting to the move made by an antislavery ACS faction in 1833 that ousted him from the society's board of managers.

And then there was politics. A presidential election year was approaching. If he wanted to be reappointed the following year, Key needed to curry favor with Vice President Martin Van Buren, Jackson's chosen Democratic Party successor, who had broad appeal in the slave-owning southern states. Key could not appear to be soft on abolitionism.

Key called slavery "a great moral and political evil amongst us" at the trial, saying that "duty, honor and interest call upon us to prepare the way for its removal." But—as he had done his entire life—the prosecutor tempered those remarks by pointing out that abolition was the wrong way to do it. White people "must act," Key argued, but they must "act discreetly with a just regard to the rights and feelings of others."

That "'great moral and political evil' of which I speak is supposed to be slavery," he said, "but is it not plainly the whole colored race?" Emancipation, he continued, is "a far greater evil."[35]

Whatever his reasons—he never spelled them out other than to say he was enforcing the law—Key charged Reuben Crandall with five counts of "publishing libels tending to excite sedition among the slaves and free colored persons" in Washington.[36]

Much of the trail consisted of tedious legal arguing over evidence. When he wasn't sparring with the defense attorneys Coxe and Bradley over evidentiary matters, Key continually pounded home the point that abolitionists such as Crandall constituted a great danger to society because they fomented insurrection among slaves. Key alluded to the Arthur Bowen trial to make that point.

Crandall, Key said, "was told shortly after his arrival here with these publications that the attempt upon the life of his mistress by Mrs. Thornton's slave [was] instigated by the New York abolition pamphlets, passages from which he had been heard to repeat." Those "incendiary writings," Key warned, were directed against "the safety and happiness" of the "whole slave-owning community."[37]

As the trial wore on, courtroom observers noted that the young defendant appeared to be suffering physically from his long confinement in jail. Crandall is "a young man of respectable appearance," one newspaper correspondent reported, "and of firm though quiet demeanor. His health appears to have been affected by his incarceration of eight months."[38]

Key tried but never could prove that Crandall came to Washington to distribute abolitionist pamphlets. Coxe and Bradley mounted a vigorous defense. Crandall was definitely not guilty of "any injurious or malicious dissemination of" abolitionist pamphlets, Coxe told the jury. If Crandall's actions "had been criminal, Mr. Key had been still more so" for reading lengthy excerpts into the record at the trial, "forcing these same tracts, and particularly the worst passages he could select from them, upon the attention of so many individuals."[39]

Coxe also excoriated Key for trampling on Crandall's First Amendment right of freedom of speech. He told the jury that he had more "feelings of anxiety" mounting his defense of Crandall than he had for any other case during his entire career. That was because the case represented the first time an "indictment for a seditious libel at common law" had been tried in the courts, a situation he characterized as "improper and unconstitutional."

Coxe predicted that a conviction would have serious consequences to the "great principles of constitutional liberty," sowing the seeds "from which will be reaped, for us and for our children, a harvest of woe and disaster."[40]

Key's issuing a warrant against Crandall, Coxe said, meant that "any individual in this community might be arrested, his papers seized and examined, his most private correspondence exhibited to the public gaze." If, "upon testimony thus illegally obtained from him, without having been guilty of any overt act against the peace of the community," Coxe said, Crandall "could be indicted for sedition, incarcerated for eight months preparatory to a trial, and then be told that for having such publications as [he] had in his private custody..., or for loaning one to an intelligent friend for his single perusal, he should be exposed to conviction and punishment for sedition, then he [Coxe] would, to escape such tyranny, expatriate himself, abandoning a land no longer free."[41]

Coxe went on to say that Key had a vendetta against Crandall because he was a northerner. As he put it: "Have we then lived to see the day when in a court of justice, in the federal city, under the very eyes of Congress, and of the National Government, it can be urged against an individual arraigned at the criminal bar, as a circumstance of aggravation, or as a just ground for suspicion, that the individual comes from the North or the South, from the East or the West?"[42]

Bradley—who made Key look foolish early in the trial by reading some strong anti–slave trafficking comments Key made at the 1828 annual ACS meeting—hammered home the fact that Reuben Crandall had done anything more than give one abolitionist tract to one man. "No man who has witnessed this trial can doubt that...there was not another one distributed," Bradley told the jury, "that no other human being within the reach of the prosecution has seen one, be he white or black."

Key, Bradley argued, "has had eight months to find them. He has searched the premises; he has ransacked the jails; he has hunted through society; and if there had been one other paper in this District, though it had been sunk ten fathoms deep in the filthiest well, or burned to impalpable power, it would have been fished up, or its ashes inurned."[43]

In his closing remarks to the jury, Key "stuck to the scare tactics that he used from the [trial's] outset,"[44] demonizing abolitionists, calling them "a set of men of most horrid principles, whose means of attack upon us are insurrection, tumult, and violence."

He railed against immediate emancipation, which, Key told the jury, would open "the floodgates of...extensive wickedness and mischief." If that took place, Key said, he would take his family and "seek refuge in other parts of the United States."[45]

"Are you willing, gentlemen," he rhetorically asked the all-male, all-white jury, "to abandon your country, to permit it to be taken from you, and occupied by the abolitionist, according to whose taste it is to associate and amalgamate with the negro?" Key said that reading abolitionist pamphlets made his "blood boil," that their sole purpose was to inspire violence and insurrection.

His last words to the jury were: "Hear [Crandall's] prevarications in the jail and elsewhere, and if he is an innocent man, cruelly imprisoned under an illegal warrant, and these vile, calumniatory libels, are actually this innocent, persecuted gentlemen's property, stolen from him, then, gentlemen, return him his property and let him go free."[46]

The jury debated about three hours and found Reuben Crandall not guilty of all charges.

The Crandall trial was not Francis Scott Key's most shining moment. There is little doubt that in his zeal to prosecute Crandall (and, by extension, the Anti-Slavery Society), he trampled on the young doctor's constitutional rights.

Key "seems to have cherished deep malignity of purpose toward Dr. C. and to have spared no effort to procure his conviction," the abolitionist firebrand William Lloyd Garrison wrote in *The Liberator* about the trial. He continued:

> *Mr. Key is a leading manager of the American Colonization Society...* let not this fact be forgotten. Failing to prove that Dr. C. had circulated antislavery publications, he offered to prove that the prisoner was a manager of the American Anti-Slavery Society!
>
> What a horrible crime, if true! And how richly would Dr. C. deserve to be gibbeted, could the charge have been sustained!!
>
> But, it happened, he was neither an officer nor a member of the Society.... And this in a free country! At the Seat of Government!! In the city of *Washington!!!* The tyranny of a Nero was not worse than this.[47]

Reuben Crandall, a free man for the first time in eight months, spent the night of April 26 in the D.C. jail fearing retribution from angry antiabolitionists. Friends hustled him out of the jail that night. Just after midnight he took a stagecoach out of town, reaching his parents' house in Connecticut two days later.

The ordeal took a toll on his health. Suffering from a form of lung disease, most likely tuberculosis, Crandall tried recuperating in Connecticut. Late in 1836 he moved to Jamaica to see if the warm climate would do him good. Reuben Crandall died in Kingston, Jamaica, of consumption on January 17, 1838, at age thirty.

The Snow Riot mobs did not kill or maim any African Americans. After things calmed down, however, and following the verdicts in the Arthur Bowen and Reuben Crandall trials, life became significantly more difficult for Washington's free African Americans. An anonymous letter to the editor of the *National Intelligencer* expressed the sentiments of many white residents. "We have already too many free negroes and mulattoes in the city, and the policy of our corporate authorities should tend to the diminution of the insolent class," the letter said. "A motion is before the Common Council for prohibiting shop-licenses henceforth to this class of people. If they wish to live here, let them become subordinates and laborers as nature has designed."[48]

The local governments in Georgetown and Washington responded by enacting new laws on October 29 and November 9, 1836, that tightened their already restrictive Black Codes. Among other things, the new laws banned freed blacks from operating any businesses that required licenses, except for "licenses to drive carts, drays, hackney carriages." They also barred all unregistered free blacks who came to Washington from being granted a business license "for any purpose whatsoever."[49]

The 1836 ordinances also prohibited freed blacks from selling or bartering alcoholic beverages and—in a direct slap in the face of Beverly Snow—from owning "any tavern, ordinary, shop, porter-cellar, refectory or eating-house of any kind."

18

A FRIEND OF MEN
OF COLOR

I am still a slaveholder, and could not, without the greatest
inhumanity, be otherwise.

—*Francis Scott Key, 1838*

In the November 1835 term of the U.S. District Court, Francis Scott Key once again exhibited his lifelong devotion to law and order by prosecuting nineteen cases against men who took part in the Snow Riot in August. He won ten of those cases and lost nine; those convicted received fines but no jail time.[1]

In the March 1836 term, Key prosecuted one more case against seven additional Snow rioters: *United States v. Fenwick, et al.* The defendants included Andrew Laub, who witnesses said had led the rioters, and a former Washington constable named Alexander Beedle. The day-long trial took place on April 7, eight days before the start of the Reuben Crandall trial. Joseph Bradley, who would be Crandall's cocounsel, helped represent several of the accused rioters in the *Fenwick* case.

The jury found six defendants, including Laub and Beedle, guilty. Before sentencing, Judge William Cranch lectured the convicted rioters. "Civil society cannot exist without laws to protect the weak against the strong," he said. "When a mob is once raised, no one can tell where it will end, and all who assisted in raising it are guilty of all the consequences." Whereupon Cranch sentenced the men to six months in prison and a fine of fifty dollars plus court costs.[2]

Not long after the Crandall trial, in late May of 1836, Madison Jeffers, the Washington constable who had played prominent roles in the Crandall and Bowen cases and who moonlighted as a slave catcher, entered the home of Charles Bankhead, the secretary of the British legation to the United States. Jeffers seized a young African American man working as a paid domestic employee of the diplomat, contending that he was a runaway slave from Alabama. British Ambassador Henry Stephen Fox filed a formal complaint with the State Department, claiming that Jeffers's actions amounted to a breach of diplomatic privilege. Secretary of State John Forsyth responded by ordering U.S. Attorney Key to look into the matter; he promptly indicted Jeffers.

After a short trial on June 7, the court found Jeffers guilty of violating diplomatic privileges. His punishment was removal from office as a Washington, D.C., constable.

On June 22, 1836, tragedy struck the Key family when twenty-year-old Daniel Murray Key, a midshipman in the Navy, was killed in a duel with fellow midshipman John F. Sherburne just outside Washington. The family knew nothing of the affair until a carriage carrying Daniel's lifeless body arrived at their home on C Street on Capitol Hill.

Daniel Key's remains were "brought to his father's residence, which gave the family the first intimation of the heart-rending catastrophe," the *New York Courier*'s Washington correspondent reported. "Their house presented the most agonizing scene I ever witnessed."[3] Another correspondent described the Key household when "the still warm corpse" was taken home as "a scene of unalterable misery that would have melted hearts of stone."[4]

Sometime during the previous winter Daniel Key, who had joined the Navy at age seventeen in November of 1833, and John Sherburne returned to Washington following a Pacific cruise. Their duel stemmed from a personality clash between the two young men that had begun aboard ship. "Mr. Key had conceived a dislike for" Sherburne, a close friend of the latter, Thomas Mattingly, wrote, and "annoyed him with ceaseless insults."[5]

When the young midshipmen arrived at Hampton Roads in Virginia, Daniel Key challenged John Sherburne to a duel. Sherburne, "seeing no alternative—Mr. Key having challenged him—agreed to meet him,"

Mattingly wrote. But before anything happened, the Norfolk police arrested Daniel Key "and placed [him] under bond to keep the peace," as Mattingly put it. After his release, young Key returned to Washington. Sherburne left Norfolk for Baltimore, then came to Washington to visit his father, a high-ranking navy official.

The two young men crossed paths regularly in the nation's capital; every time they did, Key verbally accosted Sherburne. To try to defuse the situation, Sherburne sent his friend Mattingly to meet his tormentor. Key insisted they fight a duel to the death immediately.

That was Mattingly's version.

The Key family told a different story. "There had been an old quarrel between" Daniel Key and John Sherburne "at Norfolk when he first came in from sea," Francis Scott Key later wrote, "but he thought it was all over & had determined to have no more to do with him...till he was called on [by Mattingly]." Without "time to consider and without anyone to consult with, he agreed to meet him."[6]

Early that evening Daniel Key and John Sherburne rode out to Good Hope Tavern in Maryland just across the river from Washington. When Daniel Key arrived with his cousin Richard West and a physician, Dr. James Comb, Mattingly tried once again to convince him to call off the duel. Key refused.

The men faced each other and fired their pistols simultaneously. Both missed.

Again, Mattingly, according to his recounting, pleaded with young Key to end things to no avail. As the sun set over Washington, both men reloaded a second time and fired. Daniel Key took a bullet through the lower chest, Mattingly wrote. Twenty minutes later, he died on the spot where he fell to the ground.

Frank Key found comfort in his strongly held religious beliefs. "My dear child," he wrote to his daughter Anna in North Carolina four days after the duel, give "yourself up to his [God's] service & resign yourself fully to his will. In this and in all our troubles we shall find him our only comforter."[7]

Key coped with the loss of his son by throwing himself back into his work. Among the cases he prosecuted in 1836 was one in December against Richard H. White, accused of setting a fire in the U.S. Treasury building next to the White House. In that trial, Key had as assistant counsel his twenty-eight-year-old son John Ross Key.

Less than six months later, on May 21, 1837, John Ross Key died suddenly, from what the *National Intelligencer* called "a painful illness of a few days."

"Your mother's fears were awakened from the first," Francis Scott Key wrote to his daughter Anna four days later. "I saw no symptoms of danger for the first day or two of his illness. Still, I thought your dear brother might have to suffer much before he was revived."[8]

But the young man did not revive. His mourning parents, the *Intelligencer* said, "so lately and painfully bereaved of another promising son, have the sincere sympathy of every heart in their fresh and heavy affliction."[9]

"What we have suffered you can imagine," Key told Anna. "Your dear Mother can hardly yet realize our loss. She says it seems to her he is not dead—that he is gone somewhere & will return. Poor Virginia's agony cannot be described."

John Ross Key had married the former Virginia Ringgold in 1834. He left two young children, John Francis and Clarence, when he died.[10] To add to the tragedy, Virginia Ringgold Key was pregnant at the time of her husband's death. After she gave birth to her third son, John Ross Key Jr., in Hagerstown, Maryland, on July 16, 1837, she sent the baby to live with his parental grandparents in Washington.[11]

The grieving grandfather had written at least one will before the death of his third son. Following that tragic event, Francis Scott Key wrote another one that went into effect when he died in 1843. In it, Francis Scott Key named his son-in-law Charles Howard (his oldest daughter Elizabeth's husband) his executor and willed most of his significant estate to Polly and to their children and grandchildren.

In his will Key earmarked extra funds for "the education and maintenance" of the children "of my dear son John Ross Key." He explained to his other children that he made that disposition not because of "my want of equal affection for them, but to the greater necessities in case of my death of" John Ross Key's three young sons.[12]

He left his youngest daughter, Mary Alicia, who was fourteen when he wrote the will, $2,222, "so as to make for her a provision (as far as the funds may enable it to be made) equal to that which [her older sister Ellen, who was sixteen] now has." Key left his law library to his then nineteen-year-old son Philip Barton, "hoping he will make such use of it as will enable him to assist his younger brother & sisters & the children of his brother John."

As for his slaves, Key provided that they "serve my wife during her life" and that they be freed after her death—"unless (which I wish she would do) she should [choose] sooner to manumit them." There is no evidence that Polly Key manumitted any of the enslaved people she inherited.

Francis Scott Key spent his last five years in Washington working as a lawyer, remaining actively engaged with the American Colonization Society, faithfully serving Trinity Episcopal Church in Georgetown, attending to family matters in Washington and at Terra Rubra, and staying involved a variety of civic and charitable endeavors. Although his influence in the White House waned considerably with the election of Martin Van Buren in 1836, Key remained U.S. attorney for the District of Columbia.

He prosecuted scores of cases in those last years, including a good number involving issues related to slavery. On May 13, 1837, Key secured a conviction against Joseph Farrell, a free black man, for forging a certificate of freedom for an enslaved man named Sandy.[13]

Many of the other cases Key prosecuted had nothing to do with slavery. In September 1838, for example, he indicted a man named John Knott for stealing a dog valued at five dollars. In another September 1838 case Key went after John B. Henderson for counterfeiting Treasury notes. In that case, the famed orator subjected the jury to a two-hour concluding argument.[14]

In October 1838, Francis Scott Key engaged in an intense debate by letter with Reverend Benjamin Tappan, a Maine minister and a member of a group of northern clergymen that reached out to prominent southerners to exchange views on slavery. Key spelled out his views on slavery, colonization, and the races in a long, detailed letter he wrote to Tappan on October 8.

Key forcefully defended colonization, saying that Liberia was "flourishing," and "notwithstanding many difficulties, the coloured people have consented to remove to it, as fast as their establishment there could be prudently conducted."[15] In fact, Liberia was struggling at the time. "After twenty years of continued migration to the settlement," John Quincy Adams wrote in 1837, the "colonists were starving for want of bread."[16]

Key went on to say that he had seen "more indications of the favour of Providence towards [colonization] than any other," and that its "success is greater than that of any other similar enterprise ever undertaken." The "long-lost children of ill-fated Africa," he wrote hyperbolically, "will be restored to their fathers' land, bearing with them the blessings of religion and civilization, and thus 'Vindicate the ways of God to man.'"

Key went on to denounce abolitionists, calling their publications "dangerous and unnecessary." Slaveholders, he said, would never allow "an immediate and general emancipation, deeming it ruinous both to slaves and themselves." Key told Tappan that he had freed seven of his slaves and that they had "done pretty well" as freed persons, "supporting themselves comfortably and creditably." However, Key said, he feared that "age and infirmity" would cause them to suffer.

Yet, he argued, "I am still a slaveholder, and could not, without the greatest inhumanity, be otherwise." How was it humane to own another human being? Key used the example of his ownership of "an old slave, who has done no work for me for years. I pay his board and other expenses, and cannot believe that I sin in doing so."

Key pointed out that he had helped "several large families and many individuals" gain their freedom through the courts during his long legal career. But, Key said, in all but two instances, the freedom he "so earnestly sought for them was their ruin." He also pointed to a man in Maryland who had freed between two and three hundred of his slaves who then "crowded our cities, where their vices and idleness were notorious, and their sufferings extreme."

Expanding on that idea, Key said that a society filled with freed black people would be "a severer system of constraint than that of slavery." Freedmen, he said, "would constitute a distinct and inferior race of people, which all experience proves to be the greatest evil that could afflict a community."

In answer to Tappan's question asking if he believed the Bible condoned slaveholding, Key, in essence, said it did. Scripture, he said, "contains neither an express sanction nor an express prohibition on the subject."

In 1840, sixty-year-old Francis Scott Key owned eight slaves. He had earned a national reputation as a first-rate lawyer and as an ardent opponent of abolition. If "there is one man in the District of Columbia more obnoxious to the people than another on the question of abolition, it is [the] District Attorney, Mr. Key," Congressman John Minor Botts of Virginia pointed out.[17]

On January 1, 1841, lame duck President Van Buren—who had been soundly defeated by the ticket of William Henry Harrison and John Tyler in the 1840 presidential election—reappointed Francis Scott Key as U.S. attorney for Washington. Key's days in that post, however, were numbered.

After being administered the oath of office on March 1 by Chief Justice Roger B. Taney, President William Henry Harrison—who did not wear an overcoat or hat on the cold, rainy inaugural day—gave a nearly two-hour speech, the longest inaugural address in American history. In it, he vowed to end Jackson and Van Buren's extensive political patronage system. As Harrison put it: "Never with my consent shall an officer of the people, compensated for his services out of their pockets, become the pliant instrument of Executive will."

In a memo three weeks later, Harrison reiterated his promise not to countenance public officers who had campaigned in elections. That did not bode well for Frank Key, who had worked hard to get Andrew Jackson elected.

One "or two members of the bar are looking [at] the office of United States Attorney in this District, valued at about $10,000 year," the *U.S. Gazette* newspaper reported on March 24. "Mr. F.S. Key, the present incumbent, is an amiable and able man, and politics excepted, without reproach. But as he is within the rules laid down [by Harrison], his removal is anticipated, and his office sought with an avidity proportionate to its annual value."[18]

Frank Key was still in office on April 5, 1841, when he rose to speak at a court hearing in Alexandria, asking Judge James Dunlop to adjourn for two days to honor President Harrison, who had died the day before of pneumonia.[19] Key characterized Harrison's death as a "great and mysterious dispensation of Providence."[20]

President John Tyler did not replace Frank Key as U.S. attorney until July. In the interim, Key spent a good deal of time after the March District Court term on a long business trip. He went to New York and Alabama to represent clients in several real estate matters, primarily land title cases in Alabama. He also had been retained as counsel in what became known as the "Great Gaines Case," a long-running, complex lawsuit involving Myra Clark Gaines's effort to reclaim her father's vast Louisiana estate.[21]

Key arrived in New York four days after Harrison's death. Then, accompanied by his twenty-three-year-old son Philip Barton who had followed him into the law, he left on a trip west. Their riverboat landed in Cincinnati on April 22.

"We have a fine boat, good fare and pleasant company," Frank wrote to Polly that day. "The weather has been too cold for walking the deck and enjoying the scenery of this beautiful river. It has now become warmer and quite clear & we shall now be much on deck. Barton & I have a snug little stateroom with two beds & you can't think how comfortable we are."[22]

The father and son lawyers sailed down the Ohio River to Louisville and then headed west to St. Louis, a city Frank Key found to his liking. "I regret leaving this place as I should have liked to have seen more of it," he wrote to Polly that day. "It appears to be a large & splendid City. We have just dined at the Planter's house, which is a superb establishment, larger than the Astor House at New York."[23]

In June, after the father and son had returned to Washington, President John Tyler nominated Philip R. Fendall II of Alexandria to be U.S. attorney for Washington. "We regret that this…change is necessary," the *New York Tribune* editorialized. "The author of 'The Star-Spangled Banner' ought to be a Whig."[24]

"Mr. Key has fallen in bad company and consequently his noble ode could not save him," a Pennsylvania newspaper wryly commented. "All the Psalms and Hymns…availed him nothing; and thus the guillotine must work, despite the flowing numbers of the bard of Fort McHenry."[25]

Frank Key took the news philosophically. "I suppose you have not heard that Mr. Fendall is nominated as D.C. attorney in my place," he wrote to his thirteen-year-old son Charles. "We are all taking it very practically—not doubting but that it is for the best."[26]

Free of his government job, Frank Key at age sixty-two turned to working full time on his lucrative private legal practice. In the fall of 1841 he contemplated writing a book on criminal law. "As I shall probably have a little more leisure than heretofore," Key wrote to a friend in Philadelphia,

"I have been thinking of preparing some such work." He said he thought the book "would be useful & intend to produce a regularity and uniformity in criminal proceedings, which would be desirable."[27]

Key also said he was thinking of writing a book made up of letters "between myself and John Randolph with a short memoir of him by way of introduction."[28]

Neither book project came to fruition.

In October 1841, eyeing more legal business, Frank Key was admitted to practice law in Baltimore County. "May his residence among us be a peaceful and happy one," the *Baltimore Sun* enthused, "and his career prove as brilliant as the patriotism breathed in the words of his own undying verses to that flag that still waves 'o'er the land of the free and the home of the brave.'"[29]

In the following months Francis Scott Key spent a good deal of time in Baltimore where his oldest daughter, Elizabeth, and her husband, Charles Howard, lived with their eleven children. In December he delivered an address in that city entitled "Education as Applicable to Man and to Freemen" for the Maryland Institute of Education. In March of 1842, Key contemplated starting a "reading and writing" and riding school later that year at Pipe Creek.[30]

He paid a visit to his old friend Daniel Murray in April 1842. Murray was on his death bed at his Maryland farm near Elk Ridge. Key and Murray spent hours reminiscing about their time together at St. John's and sharing their deeply held religious convictions. Throughout his life, Key later wrote, Murray "was known as a warm, consistent Christian."

"When we first met," Murray told Key, "and you were a little boy, your good mother had taught you a hymn, which you used to repeat aloud every night...in bed." The hymn, Murray said, "made a remarkable and great impression on me, which was never effaced."

Murray told his old friend that he had "never gone to my rest at night without repeating to myself that hymn and praying."[31] Daniel Murray died on April 19, 1842, in his sixty-fourth year.

In early June, Francis Scott Key attended the funeral in Washington of William Costin, the widely respected leader of the free African American community in the nation's capital. An enormous crowd was there. A reporter counted more than seventy carriages filled with people, some of them white, followed by a long line of men on horseback, all of them

African Americans, with one exception. The one white rider was Francis Scott Key.

It "must be admitted," an abolitionist newspaper commented, "that for a distinguished white citizen of Washington to ride alone among a larger number of colored men in doing honor to the memory of a deceased citizen of color evinces an elevation of soul above the meanness of popular prejudice, highly honorable to Mr. Key's profession as a friend of men of color. He rode *alone*."[32]

Frank Key spent most of the month of December 1842 in Washington while Polly stayed at Terra Rubra. He set out on a business trip to Baltimore on January 7, 1843. After riding the thirty-plus miles north, he met Polly at the home of their daughter Elizabeth and her family on Mount Vernon Place in the center of the city.

"Lizzie, I have a feeling I never had before," Key told his eldest daughter, soon after he arrived.[33]

Francis Scott Key developed pleurisy that led to pneumonia. He seemed to rally on January 10, but the following day "became worse and continued gradually to sink through the day," Charles Howard later said. His mind was "constantly wandering and his ideas confused and incoherent....He only gave utterance to the wanderings of a disturbed imagination."[34]

Francis Scott Key died just before eight o'clock in the evening on January 11, 1843. He was sixty-three years old. His wife, Polly, and his two oldest daughters, Elizabeth and Maria, sat at his bedside when he breathed his last.

ONE OF THE BEST
MEN WHO EVER LIVED

Francis Scott Key's funeral took place at noon on January 14, 1843; he was set to rest in the Howard family vault in the graveyard at St. Paul's Episcopal Church in Baltimore, not far from his daughter's home. In 1866 his children and grandchildren decided to move his remains to Mount Olivet Cemetery in downtown Frederick, where his parents were buried. A small headstone was placed at his grave in a nondescript section of the cemetery.

In 1898 a huge monument topped with a statue of Key holding aloft a copy of "The Star-Spangled Banner" was dedicated inside the main entrance to the cemetery. Two years later, on May 18, 1890, the remains of Frank and Polly Key—who had died in 1859 at age 74 and was buried beside her husband—were exhumed and re-interred in a crypt at the base of the monument.

The best-known child of Frank and Polly Key, Philip Barton Key, followed his father into the law, became a prominent Washington attorney, and served as a U.S. attorney in Washington from 1846 until his death at age thirty-nine in 1859. Said death occurred in tabloid fashion when New York congressman Daniel Sickles shot and killed him in Lafayette Square. Key, a widower with four young children, was having an all-but-open affair with Sickles's wife Teresa. Sickles's trial famously resulted in a verdict of not guilty by reason of temporary insanity.

Elizabeth "Lizzie" Howard, Francis Scott Key's first born, was his last surviving child. She died on September 9, 1897, at age ninety-four. Her next youngest sister, Maria Steele, died on January 23, 1897, at age ninety-three. Lizzie Howard had eleven children, five of whom survived her; her sister Maria had six children; their sister Mary Alicia had four. Their younger sister, Ann Arnold Turner, had eleven children; their younger brother, Francis Scott Key Jr. had died at age fifty-nine in 1866, leaving a wife and nine children.

The most notable of the many Key family descendants was the writer Francis Scott Key Fitzgerald. F. Scott Fitzgerald's third-great-grandfather, John Key, was the son of Francis Scott Key's great-grandfather Philip Key. That made F. Scott Fitzgerald, the author, Francis Scott Key's second cousin, three generations removed.[1]

Francis Scott Key's heirs sold the family home in Georgetown in the mid-1850s. In subsequent years it was used as a hotel, restaurant, and a store that sold soft drinks. The entrepreneurs who owned the building in the late 1890s began calling it the "Key Mansion" to attract business. A group of preservation-minded citizens in Washington formed the Francis Scott Key Memorial Association in 1907 to purchase the place and turn it into a house museum in honor of the author of "The Star-Spangled Banner." The group leased the house for a time, but few people visited the unfurnished and decaying building. The association failed with its fund-raising effort and never bought the building.[2]

The federal government bought the entire block of M Street in 1931 with the intention of turning it into a riverside park. That never happened. The National Park Service took over management of the house in 1933. Preservation groups and the Park Service floated plans to restore the house, but nothing came of those efforts. In 1936, the Park Service tore down all the other structures on the block.

The house survived until March 1947, when it was dismantled to make way for a new ramp from M Street onto the Francis Scott Key Bridge. That bridge across the Potomac had opened in 1923, replacing the old Aqueduct Bridge, which dated from 1843. No historic marker is on the site of the former Key mansion today.

The Park Service had planned to reconstruct the house with materials from the original on the east side of the bridge. That never happened. Instead, a small park built by the Park Service in 1993 sits on that site with a bust of the man who lived nearby for twenty-five years. It's called Francis Scott Key Park and The Star-Spangled Banner Monument.

During his lifetime and up to the start of the Civil War, Francis Scott Key's "The Star-Spangled Banner" was one of many popular American patriotic airs. During the Civil War the tune became the unofficial national anthem of the North, and in the decades following the war the song grew in popularity nationwide.

Beginning in the late 1890s, the Army, Navy, and Marine Corps began using the song in ceremonies. In 1917 the Army and Navy officially named "The Star-Spangled Banner" the "national anthem of the United States" for all military ceremonies.

The first documented performance of the song at a sporting event took place in Chicago on September 5, 1918, during the first game of the World Series between the Chicago Cubs and the Boston Red Sox. The historic event came during the seventh-inning stretch. As the Cubs band played "The Star-Spangled Banner," the players and the nineteen-thousand-plus spectators stood, took off their hats, and sang along—much as they do today at sports contests.

"The Star-Spangled Banner" was played before opening-day games and each World Series game the following season, 1919, but not at any other regular-season games. That didn't happen until 1942, during World War II.

Members of Congress began introducing legislation to make "The Star-Spangled Banner" the national anthem in the early 1900s. Congress considered more than forty such bills and resolutions over the next two decades. The measures did not succeed for several reasons. First, some believed it inappropriate to have national anthem derived from an English "drinking" tune, especially after 1920 when Prohibition went into effect. Others objected because the melody was not written by an American. Another objection had to do with the difficulty of singing the song with its very wide range of notes. There also were arguments that Key's words were directed at Great Britain, which had become a close American ally. And some believed that the song was appropriate only as a martial air and not in times of peace.

An intensive lobbying effort by patriotic and veterans groups led by the American Legion and the Veterans of Foreign Wars won the day on behalf of Francis Scott Key's song. On January 31, 1930, the VFW presented the

House Judiciary Committee with a petition containing some five million signatures urging adoption of "The Star-Spangled Banner" as the national anthem.

The House approved a bill to do so on April 21, 1930; the Senate followed almost a year later, on March 3, 1931. That same day President Herbert Hoover signed into law a measure designating "The Star-Spangled Banner" as the national anthem of the United States, more than eight decades after the death of the man who wrote the words in 1814.

"Francis Scott Key was one of the best men that ever lived," his granddaughter Rebecca Key Turner Norwood told a newspaper reporter in 1898. "There were two things that he held dearer than all else in the world—his country and his God."

Norwood, who was twelve when her grandfather died, described him as "a quiet modest man" who "was not wont to talk of himself or what he had done. He was an intellectual man," she said, who every Christmas brought a box of books to his grandchildren.

He was a man "of most domestic tastes, and nothing pleased him more than to gather his children and grandchildren around him at family reunions." He was devoted to his grandchildren, she said, "and they in turn were devoted to him."[3]

God and country. Quiet and modest. Intellectual. Devoted to his children and grandchildren. Rebecca Norwood hit the essence of Francis Scott Key. He also was a spellbinding—if often long-winded—orator, a prolific amateur poet, a highly successful and renowned attorney, an Andrew Jackson intimate, and a Washington mover-and-shaker. He was a slave owner who condemned slave trafficking, represented freed men and women and slaves without charge, loathed abolitionists, and believed that sending freed blacks to Africa was the answer to ending slavery in the United States.

Francis Scott Key couldn't have been more wrong about colonization and slavery.[4] In nearly every other aspect of his full life, he acted with rectitude and integrity. Above all, for as long as the republic stands, he will be remembered for writing the words to the anthem that has stirred the hearts of Americans for two centuries.

APPENDIX

SELECTED FRANCIS SCOTT KEY FAMILY GENEALOGY

Francis Scott Key's great-grandparents:
Philip Key (1696–1764) and **Susanna Barton Gardiner** (1705–1742). They had seven children, including **Francis Key** (1731–1770).

John Ross (1696–1766) and **Alicia Arnold** (1700–1746). They had three children, including **Anne Arnold Ross** (1727–1811) and **Elizabeth Arnold Ross** (1730–1819).

FSK's grandparents:
Francis Key and **Anne Arnold Ross**. They had three children, **John Ross Key** (1754–1821), **Philip Barton Key** (1757–1815), and **Elizabeth Scott Key** (1759–1850).

FSK's parents:
John Ross Key and **Anne Phoebe Penn Dagworthy Charlton** (1756–1830). They had four children: Anne Charlton Key (1777, died in infancy), **Francis Scott Key** (1779–1843), Catherine Charlton Key (1781–1782), and **Anne Arnold Phoebe Charlton Key** (1783–1855).

Francis Scott Key married **Mary Tayloe Lloyd** (1784–1859). They had eleven children:

> **Elizabeth** Phoebe (1803–1897) married **Charles Howard**
> **Maria** Lloyd (1805–1897) married Henry Maynadier Steele
> **Francis** Scott Jr. (1806–1866) married Elizabeth Lloyd Harwood
> **John** Ross (1809–1837) married Virginia Ringgold
> **Ann** Arnold (1811–1884) married Daniel Turner
> **Edward** Lloyd (1813–1822)
> **Daniel** Murray (1816–1836)
> **Philip** Barton (1818–1859) married Ellen Swann
> **Ellen** Lloyd (1821–1884) married Simeon Frazier Blunt
> **Mary** Alicia (1823–1886) married George H. Pendleton
> **Charles** Henry Key (1827–1869) married Elizabeth Lloyd

Ann Arnold Phoebe Charlton Key married **Roger Brooke Taney** (1777–1864). They had seven children.

Note: Names in bold are mentioned prominently in the text.

ACKNOWLEDGMENTS

When I did the research for my book *Flag: An American Biography* ten years ago, I was surprised to learn that the most recent biography of Francis Scott Key had been published in 1937. I wrote two more books after *Flag* came out in 2005. When I began thinking about a subject for my next book, I again was surprised to see that no one had written a Key biography since the 1930s.

With the invaluable help of my friend and literary agent Joseph Brendan Vallely, I wrote a proposal for a twenty-first century biography. I wish to thank Joe and everyone at Palgrave Macmillan who saw merit in the idea. Many thanks to Laura Lancaster, to my excellent editor Elisabeth Dyssegaard, her assistant Tracey Lillis, production manager Donna Cherry, and the rest of the Palgrave team.

My first call went to Elizabeth Cromwell at the C. Burr Artz Library in Frederick, Maryland, Francis Scott Key's hometown. Thank you, Elizabeth, for your encouragement and for sharing your wide list of excellent contacts. That includes Mary Mannix, the manager of that library's Maryland Room, and her staff, who could not have been more helpful. Thanks, too, to Research Center Coordinator Rebecca Crago and Assistant Director Duane Doxzen at the Historical Society of Frederick County.

History Professors Bill Becker, Denver Brunsman, and Nemata Blyden at my alma mater, George Washington University, kindly took the time to steer me in the right Early Republic directions. Jefferson Morley and Steve Vogel, who have written more about Francis Scott Key than anyone in the last fifty years, graciously shared research information. Special thanks to Jerry McCoy, the head of Special Collections at the D.C. Public Library in Georgetown, for sharing his extensive knowledge about Key primary sources.

My thanks go also to Regina Rush at the Albert and Shirley Small Special Collections Library at the University of Virginia for her much-needed help, and to Suzana Chilaka at the Library of Congress's Manuscript

Division. Chris Haugh of the Tourism Council of Frederick County generously shared his extensive knowledge of Francis Scott Key's Frederick connections. Maria Day at the Maryland State Archives helped immeasurably. Thanks also to former Maryland State Archivist Ed Papenfuse for his advice and counsel.

I greatly appreciate the help I received from Adam Lewis and Anne McDonough of the Historical Society of Washington, D.C. for among other things opening the doors of the society's library to me. Catherine Dixon, the director of St. John's College's Greenfield Library, kindly gave me permission to use materials from the college's Francis Scott Key Collection. Thanks, too, to my friends at the Library of Virginia in Richmond, including Librarian of Virginia Sandy Treadway, Archives and Library Reference Manager Virginia Dunn, and former Library of Virginia Foundation Executive Director Mary Beth McIntire. My good friend Bill Fogarty very kindly helped me wade through complicated legal opinions in several Key cases.

I also benefited from advice and help from Robert Mangum at the National Archives in Washington; Cathy Baty at the Historical Society of Carroll County, Maryland; Robert Gudmestad at Colorado State University; Damon Talbot at the Maryland Historical Society; Scott Sheads at Fort McHenry; Marlene Young at the Delaplaine Foundation in Frederick; Christopher Pote at the Virginia Theological Seminary in Alexandria; Julie Randle at the Episcopal Diocese of Virginia in Richmond; James Goode, curator of the Albert H. Small Collection of Washingtoniana; Carolyn Spopinski Miller and Althea Riley at the Adams County Historical Society in Gettysburg, Pa.; Kenneth Cole at the Office of the Historian of the U.S. House of Representatives; and Lisa Jacobson at the Presbyterian Historical Society in Philadelphia.

Thanks, too, to my friends at the Middleburg Library in Loudoun County, Virginia, especially branch manager Sheila Whetzel, and to Anita Barrett, the Loudoun Library system's excellent interlibrary loan specialist. Thanks to my colleagues at Vietnam Veterans America national headquarters, especially my great editor and good friend Michael Keating. Thanks to Galen Schroeder for compiling a terrific index.

I've had much-appreciated support and encouragement from friends and family: Xande Anderer, Bernie and Linda Brien, Amoret Bruguiere, Cliff Boyle, Childs Burden, Quentin Butcher, Bob Carolla, Harriet and

David Condon, Liz Couture, Cathy Curtis, Larry Cushman, John Czaplewski, Diane Deitz, Terry Denbow, Benton Downer, Patrick Sheane Duncan, Russell Duncan, Bill and Sue Ferster, Carl Gray, John and Donna Hoffecker, Royce Kincaid, Evan Leepson, Peter and Ellen Leepson, Leslie Link, Treavor Lord, Hunt Lyman, Sandra and Joe Markus, Greg McNamee, Mike Morency, Vicki Moon, Dan Morrow, Tom and Ann Northrup, Angus Paul, Mike Powers, Steve Price, Susan Price, Dan and Margie Radovsky, Len Shapiro, Kathy Jo Shea, Terri Spencer, Jim Wagner, David Willson, B. P. Woodrow, Don and Mary Woodruff, and Walter Woodson.

Special thanks to my wife, Janna, for being a history book widow for too many months, and to my children, Cara and Devin, for their support and encouragement.

NOTES

INTRODUCTION A CLASSICAL SPEAKER

1. Unsigned letter to the editor, *Baltimore Federal Republican*, Oct. 7, 1811.
2. Francis Scott Key (FSK) letter to each of his children, undated, Maryland Historical Society, Francis Scott Key Papers, 1810–1845.
3. Clarence C. Wroth, "Francis Scott Key as a Churchman," *Maryland Historical Magazine* IV (1909): 154.
4. Rev. John T. Brooke, "Discourse on the Character of the Late Francis Scott Key, Esq.," *African Repository and Colonial Journal* 19 (1843): 149.
5. Stacy Schiff, "The Dual Lives of a Biographer," *New York Times*, Nov. 24, 2012.

1 A FAMILY OF LAWYERS

1. The best sources (in addition to the U.S. Census records and birth and death certificates) for details of the lives of Francis Scott Key's ancestors are: Christopher Johnston, "Key Family," *Maryland Historical Magazine* 3, no. 2 (June 1910): 194–200; Janie Warren Hollingsworth Lane, *Key and Allied Families* (Macon, GA.: J. W. Burke Co. Press, 1931), 55–68; Scottie Fitzgerald Smith, "The Colonial Ancestors of Francis Scott Key Fitzgerald," *Maryland Historical Magazine* 76, no. 4 (Winter 1981): 363–75; F. S. Key-Smith, "A Sketch of Francis Scott Key, with a Glimpse of His Ancestors," *Records of the Columbia Historical Society* 11 (1909): 71–87.
2. Historical Society of Frederick County, Key Family Papers, "Key, Philip, List of Negro Slaves, December 1763," MS 19, box 13, fol. 29.
3. *Maryland Gazette*, Dec. 14, 1752.
4. Alicia Ross to Anne Arnold Ross, undated, quoted in McHenry Howard, "Some Old English Letters," *Maryland Historical Magazine* 9 (March 1914): 153–55. McHenry Howard (1838–1923) was a grandson of FSK.
5. The 1790 U.S. Federal Census lists twenty-six slaves owned by John Ross Key, Esquire, in his Terra Rubra household.
6. John Ross Key to Francis Key, Sept. 19, 1770. Maryland Historical Society, Howard Papers, 1662–1919, MS 469, box 19.
7. *Muster Rolls and Other Records of Service of Maryland Troops in the American Revolution, 1775–1783* (Baltimore: Maryland Historical Society, 1900), 28; Francis C. Heitman, *Historical Register of Officers of the Continental Army During the War of the Revolution, April 1775 to December 1783* (Washington, D.C.: Rare Book Shop Publishing Co., 1914), 330.
8. A copy of John Ross Key's commission is in the Historical Society of Frederick County, Key Family Papers, box 13, fol. 38.
9. See J. Thomas Scharf, *History of Western Maryland*, vol. 2 (Philadelphia: L. H. Everts, 1882), 144.
10. Building his mansion in Washington, Philip B. Key was inspired by Woodley Lodge, Henry Addison's large country home in England. Key's house gave the name to the present-day Woodley Park section of Washington. The restored mansion at 3000 Cathedral Ave. NW sits inside the campus of the Maret School. See Al Kilbourne, *Woodley and Its Residents* (Charleston: Arcadia, 2008), 15–34.
11. Helen Hoban Rogers, ed., *Freedom & Slavery Documents in the District of Columbia* (Baltimore: Gateway Press, 2007), 2: 63.

12. Quoted in Johnston, "Key Family," 197.

13. The neighbor was identified only as "Mr. Hendon." Quoted in Nellie Eysler, "'The Star-Spangled Banner': An Hour with an Octogenarian," *Harper's New Monthly Magazine* 43 (July 1871): 255.

14. "To My Sister," in Rev. Henry V. D. Johns, ed. *Poems of the Late Francis S. Key* (New York: Robert Carter & Brothers, 1857), 37–40.

15. Elihu S. Riley, *"The Ancient City," History of Annapolis, in Maryland, 1649–1887* (Annapolis: Record Printing Office, 1887), 210.

16. FSK to Charles Henry Key, undated, quoted in the *Frederick News*, May 18, 1895. The letter likely was written in the early 1830s when Francis Scott Key was in his early fifties.

17. The 1800 U.S. Federal Census lists ten slaves owned by Upton Scott of Annapolis.

18. FSK letter, undated (ca. 1789), Maryland Historical Society, Howard Papers, 1662–1919, MS 469, box 19.

19. George Washington to the faculty of St. John's College, April 7, 1791, quoted in Philip R. Voorhees, "St. John's College—Annapolis, Md.," *University Magazine*, Jan. 1893, 229.

20. *The Papers of George Washington, Presidential Series, vol. 8, March 22, 1791-September 22, 1791,* ed. Mark A. Mastromarino (Charlottesville: University Press of Virginia, 1999), 311–12.

21. John McDowell delivered a short speech to the graduates in Latin, then offered a longer address in English, followed by the awarding of the degrees. The list of degrees conferred gave the graduates' first names in latinized form, including Danielis Murray, Robertus Goldsborough, Johannes Shaw, and Franciscus Key. Commencement address by John McDowell, 1796, St. John's College Archives Collection, Maryland State Archives, SC 5698-7-41.

2   ANNAPOLIS, FREDERICK TOWN, AND GEORGE TOWN

1. According to the 1800 Census, the population of Annapolis was 2,213. That number included 646 slaves and 273 free blacks.

2. FSK to John Leeds Kerr, Feb. 15, 1798, privately owned letter retrieved from www.liveauction-eers.com/item/2769475 on May 8, 2013.

3. FSK to John Leeds Kerr, July 13, 1799, ibid.

4. Samuel Tyler, ed., *Memoir of Roger Brooke Taney, LLD, Chief Justice of the Supreme Court of the United States* (Baltimore: John Murphy, 1872), 86.

5. "Mr. Hendon," as quoted in Nellie Eysler, "'The Star-Spangled Banner': An Hour with an Octogenarian," *Harper's New Monthly Magazine* 43 (July 1871): 255.

6. Maryland State Archives, St. John's College Archives, 1786–1826, *Minutes of the Board of Visitors and Governors,* MSA SC 5698-1-1, Oct. 15, 1800. See also *National Intelligencer,* Nov. 26, 1800.

7. "To Delia," in Rev. Henry V. D. Johns, ed. *Poems of the Late Francis S. Key* (New York: Robert Carter & Brothers, 1857), 83–84.

8. Thanks to Christopher Haugh, the Scenic Byway & Special Projects Manager for the Tourism Council of Frederick County (Maryland), for digging out and sharing the information on Cordelia Harris.

9. Frederick Douglass, *Narrative of the Life of Frederick Douglass, An American Slave* (Boston: Anti-Slavery Office, 1845), 9. Douglass's mother, Harriet Bailey, was a slave. His father was white, and there has been speculation that he was Douglass's master, Aaron Anthony, or perhaps Edward Lloyd IV or another member of the Lloyd family.

10. Douglass, *Narrative of the Life of Frederick Douglas,* 10–11.

11. "To Mary," *Poems of the Late Francis S. Key,* 81–82.

12. Rosalie Calvert to Charles J. Stier, Dec. 30, 1801, quoted in Margaret Law Callcott, ed., *Mistress of Riversdale: The Plantation Letters of Rosalie Stier Calvert, 1795–1821* (Baltimore: Johns Hopkins University Press, 1991), 31.

13. See Jesse J. Holland, *Black Men Built the Capitol: Discovering African-American History In and Around Washington, D.C.* (Guilford, CT: Globe Pequot, 2007), 28–29.

14. Northup was kidnapped on the streets of Washington in 1841. See Solomon Northup, *Twelve Years a Slave: Narrative of Solomon Northup* (London: Sampson, Low, Son & Co., 1853), 41–42.

15. Captain Basil Hall, *Travels in North America in the Years 1827 and 1828* (Edinburgh: Cadell and Co., 1830), 37–38.

16. Constance McLaughlin Green, *The Secret City: A History of Race Relations in the Nation's Capital* (Princeton, NJ: Princeton University Press, 1967), 42.

17. Ibid., 16–17.

18. *Special Report of the Commissioner of Education on the Condition and Improvement of Public Schools in the District of Columbia* (Washington, D.C.: Government Printing Office, 1871), 312.

19. Ibid., 312–13.

20. Abigail Adams to Mrs. William Smith, Nov. 21, 1800, quoted in Allen C. Clark, *Life and Letters of Dolly Madison* (Washington, D.C.: F. W. Roberts Press Co., 1914), 38.

21. Quoted in Gordon S. Wood, *Empire of Liberty: A History of the Early Republic, 1789–1815* (Oxford and New York: Oxford University Press, 2009), 289–290. Foster served in Washington as secretary to the British Legation of the United States from 1805 to 1807, and as Great Britain's minister plenipotentiary from 1811 to 1812.

22. The home that the Keys lived in was taken down in 1947 to make way for a new entrance onto the bridge over the Potomac, which was named in honor of Francis Scott Key. See Epilogue.

23. Barry Mackintosh, "The Loss of the FSK House: Was It Really?" 1981. Peabody Room, Washington, D.C., Public Library, vertical file.

24. See "FSK House," report by Robert Lyle of the District of Columbia Public Library in the collection of the Peabody Room, Georgetown Library. The Keys rented the house until Feb. 18, 1830, when they purchased it from the trustees of the estate of a previous owner.

25. In 1794, Bollman and Francis Huger of South Carolina tried to help the Marquis de Lafayette escape from prison in the Bohemian city of Olmütz. Lafayette had been imprisoned since 1792 by the Austrians for his antimonarchist actions during the French Revolution. The escape attempt failed, and Bollman and Huger were imprisoned for eight months before being released.

26. *Washington Federalist*, Feb. 4, 1807.

27. FSK to Marie West, March 6, 1808, *Papers of Francis Scott Key, 1808–1841*, Special Collections, University of Virginia Library, no. 6949.

3 NIL DESPERANDUM

1. John Randolph to Dr. John Brockenbrough, Feb. 11, 1821, quoted in William Cabell Bruce, *John Randolph of Roanoke, 1773–1833: A Biography Based Largely on New Material*, vol. 2 (New York: G. P. Putnam's Sons, 1922), 620.

2. *Hezekiah Wood v. John Davis and Others*, 11 U.S. 7 Cranch 271 (1812).

3. *Cincinnati Daily Gazette*, July 11, 1870.

4. Dorothy S. Provine, ed., *District of Columbia Free Negro Registers, 1821–1861* (Bowie, MD: Heritage Books, 1996), 214. The book contains abstracts from National Archives, Record Group 21, Records of U.S. District Courts, Manumission and Emancipation Record, 1821–1861.

5. Helen Hoban Rogers, ed., *Freedom & Slavery Documents in the District of Columbia*, vol. 2 (Baltimore: Gateway/Otterbay Press, 2007), 211.

6. *Mima Queen and Child, Petitioners for Freedom v. Hepburn*, 11 U.S. 290 (1813).

7. Unsigned letter to the editor, *Baltimore Federal Republican*, Oct. 7, 1811.

8. Report of the Lancaster Committee of Canterbury, Feb. 12, 1810, quoted in *The British System of Education: Being a Complete Epitome of the Improvements and Inventions Practised by Joseph Lancaster*...(Georgetown: Joseph Milligan, 1812), ix.

9. "Report of the Trustees of the Georgetown Lancaster School Society...," ibid., 122.

10. FSK to Mrs. Anne Phoebe Key, April 21, 1813, Special Collections, University of Virginia Library.

11. FSK to John Randolph, Nov. 27, 1813, quoted in Hugh A. Garland, *The Life of John Randolph of Roanoke*, vol. 2 (New York: D. Appleton, 1853), 27.

12. F. W. Thomas, *John Randolph of Roanoke, and Other Sketches of Character*...(Philadelphia: A. Hart, 1853), 14–17.

13. Several states held their 1812 congressional elections the following year; in Virginia, the vote did not occur until April 1813.

14. In his will, John Randolph named FSK one of the executors of his estate.

15. Quoted in Bruce, *John Randolph of Roanoke*, vol. 2, 620.

16. John Randolph to Dr. John Brockenbrough, circa 1821, quoted in Bruce, *John Randolph of Roanoke*, vol. 2, 620.

17. John Randolph to Dr. John Brockenbrough, Feb. 24, 1820, quoted in Garland, *The Life of John Randolph of Roanoke*, vol. 2, 134.

18. FSK to John Randolph, July 10, 1811, Maryland Historical Society, Howard Papers, box 19.

19. Thomas Jefferson to William Duane, Aug. 4, 1812, quoted in Paul Leicester Ford, ed. *The Writings of Thomas Jefferson*, vol. 11 (New York: G. P. Putnam's Sons, 1905), 265.

20. *History of Congress*, Annals of Congress, House of Representatives, 12th Congress, 1st Session, Dec. 1811, 534.

21. Quoted in Bruce, *John Randolph of Roanoke*, vol. 2, 382, 383.

22. *John Randolph: Correspondence, 1813*, Library of Virginia, Personal Papers collection, Accession 22636.

23. FSK to Polly Key, quoted in *Frederick News*, May 18, 1895. Excerpts from the letter also appear in an article *The Spirit of '76* magazine of Sept. 1894, 6.

24. "Southern Town Meeting," *Hampshire Gazette*, Aug. 26, 1812, 2.

25. The funeral took place on August 1. George Washington Parke Custis, a step-grandson of George Washington, not FSK, delivered the oration. See *Federal Republican*, Aug. 3 and 9, 1812; and Grace Dunlop Ecker, *A Portrait of Old George Town* (Richmond, VA: Dietz Press, 1951), 307.

26. John Randolph to FSK, May 10, 1813, quoted in Garland, *Life of John Randolph of Roanoke*, vol. 2, 12.

27. Ibid., 13.

28. Ibid., 14.

29. FSK to Mrs. Anne Phoebe Key, April 21, 1813, Special Collections, University of Virginia Library.

30. FSK to John Randolph, May 14, 1813, Maryland Historical Society, Howard Papers, box 19.

31. FSK to John Randolph, Aug. 30, 1813, quoted in Garland, *Life of John Randolph of Roanoke*, vol. 2, 19.

32. Ibid., 23.

4 PIETY AND PATRIOTISM

1. FSK to John Randolph, Nov. 27, 1813, quoted in Hugh A. Garland, *The Life of John Randolph of Roanoke*, vol. 2 (New York: D. Appleton, 1853), 27.

2. FSK to John Ross Key, Nov. 27, 1813, Maryland Historical Society, Howard Papers, box 19.

3. FSK to Anne Phoebe Key, Dec. 27, 1813, Special Collections, University of Virginia Library.

4. John Randolph to Josiah Quincy, Dec. 11, 1813, quoted in William Cabell Bruce, *John Randolph of Roanoke, 1773–1833: A Biography Based Largely on New Material*, vol. 1 (New York: G. P. Putnam's Sons, 1922), 404.

5. FSK to Anne Phoebe Key, Jan. 2, 1814, Special Collections, University of Virginia Library.

6. *Northern Whig*, Jan. 4, 1814, 3.

7. "Fatal Duel," *Rutland Herald*, July 5, 1836.

8. *Boston Daily Advertiser*, March 4, 1814.

9. "The Oration of Honorable Francis Scott Key, February 22, 1814" in William Buckner McGroarty, ed., *Washington: First in the Hearts of His Countrymen: Orations...* (Richmond: Garrett & Massie, 1932), 217–35.

10. FSK to John Randolph, Feb. 26, 1814, Maryland Historical Society, Howard Papers, 1662–1919, box. 19.

11. FSK to Rev. Dr. James Kemp, April 4, 1814, quoted in Clarence C. Wroth, "Francis Scott Key as a Churchman," *Maryland Historical Magazine* IV (1909), 156.

12. *The American Weekly Messenger or Register of State Papers, History and Politics, 1814–1815*, vol. 2 (Philadelphia: John Conrad, 1815), 263.

13. "Letter from the Chesapeake," *New York Evening Post*, June 4, 1814.

14. See Edward S. Delaplaine, *Francis Scott Key: Life and Times* (New York: Biography Press, 1937), 91–92.

15. "The Patuxent," *Federal Republican*, July 13, 1814, account written by "A Militia Man."

16. FSK to Mrs. A. T. Key, Maryland State Archives, Bartow Collection, MSA Sc 1105-1-1.

17. FSK to John Randolph, July 3, 1814, Maryland Historical Society, Howard Papers, 1662–1919, box. 19.

18. Elizabeth Maynadier to Anne Key, August 9, 1814, letters to Mrs. John Ross Key and Anna Taney, 1814 and 1834, Special Collections, University of Virginia Library, MSS 5107.

19. Samuel Tyler, ed. *Memoir of Roger Brooke Taney, LLD, Chief Justice of the Supreme Court of the United States* (Baltimore: John Murphy, 1872), 110. Taney, writing more than four decades after the fact, claimed that he went to Georgetown from his home in Frederick to "try to persuade Mrs. Key to come away with her children, and stay with me or with Mr. Key's father until the danger was over." FSK's letter of August 22, however, contains no mention of his brother-in-law and indicates that his children already were in Terra Rubra with his parents.

20. FSK to his mother, Aug. 22, 1814, Maryland Historical Society, Howard Papers, 1662–1919, box. 19.

5 A CITIZEN OF THE HIGHEST RESPECTABILITY

1. G. R. Gleig, *The Campaigns of the British Army at Washington and New Orleans in the Years 1814–1815*, 3rd ed. (London: John Murray, 1828), 114.

2. If Madison had come under fire at Bladensburg, he would have been the first sitting American president to do so. Abraham Lincoln was fired upon in a war while he was in office. On July 12, 1864, Lincoln stood on a parapet at Fort Stevens in northwest Washington, D.C. as Confederate forces under Gen. Jubal Early attacked the city. An enemy sniper wounded a Union Army surgeon standing next to Lincoln. See Marc Leepson, *Desperate Engagement: How a Little-Known Civil War Battle Saved Washington, D.C., and Changed American History* (New York: Thomas Dunne Books, 2007), 198–203.

3. G. R. Gleig, *A Subaltern in America: Comprising His Narrative of the Campaign of the British Army at Baltimore, Washington, etc. during the Late War* (Baltimore: Carey, Hart, 1833), 67.

4. Mary Barney, *Biographical Memoir of the Late Commodore Joshua Barney* (Boston: Gray & Bowen, 1832), 266.

5. Gleig, *The Campaigns…*, 125.

6. For an analysis of the casualty figures, see Anthony S. Pitch, *The Burning of Washington: The British Invasion of 1814* (Naval Institute Press, 1998), 85.

7. "Narrative of General Winder, Sept. 26, 1814," *American State Papers, Military Affairs*, vol. 1, 1789–1819, 557.

8. See Walter Lord, *The Dawn's Early Light* (New York: W.W. Norton, 1972), 114–115.

9. FSK to Major George Peter, Oct. 17, 1814, Peter Family Papers, CA. 1700–1897, Special Collections, University of Virginia Library, accession 7605–1, box 3.

10. FSK to his mother, Sept. 2, 1814, quoted in Edward S. Delaplaine, *Francis Scott Key: Life and Times* (New York: Biography Press, 1937), 153–154. Delaplaine included a transcript of the entire letter in an article he wrote in the *Frederick Post* (Maryland), Sept. 14, 1972.

11. Paul Jennings, *A Colored Man's Reminiscences of James Madison* (Brooklyn: George C. Bradley, 1865), 10–11.

12. The original copy of the letter has disappeared. Historians believe that Dolley Madison wrote it after the fact, but they still regard it as an accurate depiction of the dramatic events in the White House on Aug. 23–24, 1814. See David B. Mattern, "Dolley Madison Has the Last Word: The Famous Letter," *Journal of the White House Historical Association*, Fall 1998, 38–43.

13. Sir Henry George Wakelyn Smith, ed., *The Autobiography of Lieutenant-General Sir Harry Smith* (London: J. Murray, 1901).

14. Francis Dodge to his wife, Aug. 26, 1814, quoted in Grace Dunlop Ecker, *A Portrait of Old George Town* (Richmond, Va.: Dietz Press, 1951), 235.

15. FSK to his father, Sept. 2, 1814, quoted in *Frederick Post*, Sept. 14, 1972.

---

16. Roger B. Taney letter to Charles Howard, March 12, 1856, quoted in Samuel Tyler, ed., *Memoir of Roger Brooke Taney* (Baltimore: John Murphy, 1872), 111.
17. Quoted in *Baltimore Sun*, July 14, 1849.
18. It's unclear whether or not FSK met with Madison personally or if the president simply told Mason that he wanted FSK to do the job.
19. Lord, *The Dawn's Early Light*, 241–42.
20. General John Mason to Major General Robert Ross, Sept. 2, 1814, National Archives, Naval Records Collection of the Office of Naval Records and Library, Record Group 45.
21. FSK to his mother, Sept. 2, 1814, quoted in Edward S. Delaplaine, *Francis Scott Key: Life and Times* (New York: Biography Press, 1937), 153.

6   A BEAUTIFUL AND ANIMATING EFFUSION

1. FSK to John Randolph, Oct. 5, 1814, Maryland Historical Society, Howard Papers, box 19.
2. Skinner's account, "Incidents of the War of 1812," was published in the *Baltimore Patriot*, May 23, 1849, in the *National Intelligencer*, June 4, 1849, and in the *Maryland Historical Magazine* 32, no. 4, Dec. 1937, 340–47. Steve Vogel's *Through the Perilous Fight: Six Weeks That Saved the Nation* (New York: Random House, 1813) contains a comprehensive account of the entire Battle of Baltimore.
3. Major General Robert Ross to General Mason, Sept. 7, 1814, National Archives, Record Group 45.
4. Scott Sheads, Fort McHenry ranger and historian, quoted in Ken Iglehart, "200 Years: The War of 1812," *Baltimore Magazine*, June 2012.
5. Henry Wheaton Papers, 1786–1926, Brown University, John Hay Library.
6. See, for example, "Baltimore and Maryland Were to the Front in the War of 1812," Part I of the Official Program of the National Star-Spangled Banner Centennial, 1914, 17.
7. Edward Codrington to his wife, Sept. 10, 1814, in Jane Bourchier, ed., *Memoir of the Life of Admiral Sir Edward Codrington with Selections from His Public and Private Correspondence* (London: Longmans, Green, 1873), 319–20.
8. Elizabeth Maynadier to Anne Key, Sept. 12, 1814, Letters to Mrs. John Ross Key and Anna Taney, 1814 and 1834, Special Collections, University of Virginia Library.
9. Quoted in Walter Lord, *The Dawn's Early Light* (New York: W.W. Norton, 1972), 251.
10. G. R. Gleig, *The Campaigns of the British Army at Washington and New Orleans in the Years 1814–1915*, 3rd ed. (London: John Murray, 1828), 177–78.
11. David Brown, *Diary of a Soldier, 1805–1827* (Ardrossan, Scotland: A Guthrie, 1934), 29. Also see Vogel, *Through the Perilous Fight*, 332–33.
12. Quoted in Pitch, *The Burning of Washington: The British Invasion of 1814* (Naval Institute Press, 1998), 211.
13. G. R. Gleig, *The Campaigns of the British Army*, 106.
14. Quoted in *Niles' Weekly Register*, Oct. 1, 1814, 40.
15. Captain Joseph H. Nicholson to Secretary of State James Monroe, Sept. 17, 1814, Library of Congress, *Joseph Hopper Nicholson Papers*. Also see Lonn Taylor, Kathleen M. Kendrick, and Jeffrey L. Brodie, *The Star Spangled Banner: The Making of an American Icon* (New York: Smithsonian Books, 2008), 26.
16. Quoted in "Naval Recollection of the Late American War," *United States Journal and Naval and Military History Magazine*, April 1841, Part 1, 463.
17. *Salem Gazette* (Massachusetts), Sept. 28, 1814.
18. "Attack Upon Baltimore," *Niles' Weekly Register*, Sept. 24, 1814, 24.
19. *United States Journal and Naval and Military History Magazine*, 463.
20. The victory at New Orleans came two weeks after this country and Britain had signed the Treaty of Ghent, officially ending the war.
21. The letter, dated Sept. 17, 1814, appeared in the Boston newspaper *The Yankee* on September 30.
22. The August 6, 1834, speech is paraphrased in Rev. Henry V. D. Johns, ed., *Poems of the Late Francis S. Key* (New York: Robert Carter & Brothers, 1857), 195–203, and quoted in Edward S. Delaplaine, *Francis Scott Key: Life and Times* (New York: Biography Press, 1937), 379–381.

23. Elizabeth Maynadier to Anne Key, Oct. 27, 1814, *Letters to Mrs. John Ross Key…*, Special Collections, University of Virginia Library.

24. *National Intelligencer*, Dec. 12, 1814, reprinted in the Baltimore *American and Commercial Daily Advertiser*, Dec. 22, 1814.

25. *Philadelphia Press*, Aug. 1, 1881.

26. See Roland Greene, ed., *Princeton Encyclopedia of Poetry and Poetics*, 4th ed. (Princeton, NJ: Princeton University Press, 2012), 1483.

27. Baltimore *American and Commercial Daily Advertiser*, Dec. 14, 1805.

28. Quoted in Megan Gambino, "Document Deep Dive: The Musical History of 'The Star-Spangled Banner,'" *Smithsonian Magazine*, Smithsonianmag.com, June 13, 2012.

29. See Marc Leepson, *Flag: An American Biography* (New York: Thomas Dunne Books, 2005), 59–75.

30. Walter Lord, "Mysteries of American History," *American Heritage*, Dec. 1990.

7   A USELESS, PERNICIOUS, DANGEROUS PORTION OF THE POPULATION

1. FSK to John Randolph, Oct. 5, 1814, and Nov. 13, 1814, MS 469, Maryland Historical Society, Howard Papers, 1662–1919, box 19.

2. FSK to Mrs. Anne Phoebe Key, Dec. 4, 1814, Special Collections, University of Virginia Library.

3. Library of Congress, *U.S. Congressional Documents and Debates, 1774–1875*, *Annals of Congress*, House of Representatives, 12th Congress, 1st Session, 450–51.

4. FSK to Mrs. Anne Phoebe Key, Jan. 20, 1816, Special Collections, University of Virginia Library.

5. *Gettings v. Burch's Administratrix*, 13 U.S. 372 (1815).

6. FSK to Mrs. Anne Phoebe Key, Dec. 24, 1814, Special Collections, University of Virginia Library.

7. Key quoted by John Randolph in his May 29, 1815, letter to John Brockenbrough, in Hugh A. Garland, *The Life of John Randolph of Roanoke*, vol. 2 (New York: D. Appleton, 1853), 65.

8. FSK to Mrs. Anne Phoebe Key, Dec. 24, 1814, Special Collections, University of Virginia Library.

9. *Georgetown Federal Republican*, July 19, 1815.

10. "Philip Barton Key, Who Departed This Life July the 18th 1815," in Henry V. D. Johns, ed. *Poems of the Late Francis S. Key*, 125.

11. Quoted in Elizabeth Hesselius Murray, *One Hundred Years Ago: or, The Life and Times of Rev. Walter Dulany Addison, 1769–1848* (Baltimore: W. Jacobs, 1895), 172.

12. See Anna Key Bartow, "Recollections of Francis Scott Key," *Modern Culture* 13 (Sept. 1900 to Feb. 1901), 205.

13. FSK to Mrs. Anne Phoebe Key, June 22, 1816, Special Collections, University of Virginia Library.

14. *Reports of Cases Argued and Determined in the General Court and Court of Appeals of the State of Maryland* (Annapolis: Jonas Green, 1827), 398.

15. Key biographer Edward Delaplaine called that case an example of FSK appearing in court "to fight for the ownership of slaves as though they were mere articles of merchandise." Edward A. Delaplaine, *Francis Scott Key: Life and Times* (New York: Biography Press, 1937), 193.

16. Henry Barnard, ed., *The American Journal of Education*, vol. 2 (Hartford: Office of the American Journal of Education, 1870) 298. Also see "History of Schools for the Colored Population in the District of Columbia," U.S. Office of Education, 1869.

17. *Negress Sally Henry by William Henry, her father and next friend v. Ball*, 14 US 1 (1816).

18. *Negro John Davis, et al v. Wood*, 14 US 6 (1816); see ch. 3.

19. *Annals of Congress*, 14th Congress, 1st Session, House of Representatives, March 1, 1816, 1115–16.

20. National Archives, *Records of the U.S. House of Representatives, 1789–1989*, Ch. 33, Record Group 223, Deposition of FSK, April 22, 1816, "Records of the Select Committee to Inquire Into the Existence of an Inhuman and Illegal Traffic in Slaves in the District of Columbia."

Also see Carol Wilson, *Freedom at Risk: The Kidnapping of Free Blacks in America—1780–1865* (Lexington: University Press of Kentucky, 1994), 70.

21. Jesse Torrey, *A Portraiture of Domestic Slavery in the United States* (Philadelphia: published by author, 1817), 52.

22. Henry Louis Gates, Jr. and Evelyn Brooks Higginbotham, eds., *African American Lives* (New York: Oxford University Press, 2004), 200–201.

23. Letters published in *American State Papers: Documents, Legislative and Executive, of the Congress of the United States From the First Session of the First to the Second Session of the Tenth Congress*, vol. 1 (Washington, D.C.: Gales and Seaton, 1834), 464–67.

24. Charles Fenton Mercer, "An Address to the American Colonization Society at their 36th annual meeting in the city of Washington on the 18th January 1853," Cornell University Library (1854). Also see Douglas R. Egerton, *Charles Fenton Mercer and the Trial of National Conservatism*. (Jackson, MS, and London: University Press of Mississippi, 1989), 107–12.

25. Quoted in Isaac V. Brown, *Biography of the Rev. Robert Finley....* (Philadelphia: John W. Moore, 1857), 142.

26. Quoted in *The National Intelligencer*, Dec. 24, 1816, reprinted in "Colonization of Free People of Colour," U.S. House of Representatives, 19th Congress, 2nd Session, March 3, 1827, Report No. 101, 25–26.

27. "Origin, Constitution, and Proceedings of the American Society for Colonizing the Free People of Colour of the United States," vol. 1, 1816, American Colonization Society Papers, Library of Congress, 4.

8   A CLASS OF VERY DANGEROUS PEOPLE

1. "Colonizing the Free Blacks," *Independent American*, July 30, 1817.

2. *Federal Republication and Baltimore Telegraph*, reprinted in *Massachusetts Spy*, July 16, 1917.

3. W. B. Hodgeson to FSK, Aug. 1, 1817. Maryland Historical Society, Francis Scott Key Vertical File.

4. *First Annual Report of the American Society for Colonizing the Free People of Color...* (Washington, D.C.: D. Rapine, 1818), 15.

5. American Colonization Society, *The African Repository and Colonial Journal*, vol. 9 (Washington, D.C.: James C. Dunn, 1834), 266.

6. Quoted in *Georgetown National Messenger*, Feb. 25, 1818.

7. See William A. R. Goodwin, *History of the Theological Seminary in Virginia and Its Historical Background* (New York: Edwin S. Gorham, 1923), vol. 1:122, 202, 514; vol. 2:46, 53.

8. John Randolph to FSK, Sept. 7, 1818, quoted in Hugh A. Garland, *The Life of John Randolph of Roanoke*, vol. 2 (New York: D. Appleton, 1853), 99.

9. FSK to Rev. William Meade, Sept. 29, 1818, Special Collections, University of Virginia Library.

10. FSK to Bishop James Kemp, October 17, 1818, quoted in "Francis Scott Key as a Churchman," *Maryland Historical Magazine* IV (1909), 165.

11. "Colonization of Free People of Colour," Report No. 101, 19th Congress, 2nd Session, House of Representatives, March 3, 1827, 11.

12. *Statutes at Large of the United States of America, 1789–1873*, vol. 3 (1845), 533.

13. Quoted in Paul E. Teed, *John Quincy Adams: Yankee Nationalist* (Hauppauge, NY: Nova Science, 2011), 138.

14. *John Quincy Adams Diary*, Adams Family Papers, Massachusetts Historical Society, March 12, 1819, 60.

15. Ibid., 59.

16. George Smith (writing as "Clericus"), *Facts Designed to Exhibit Real Character and Tendency of the American Colonization Society* (Liverpool: Egerton Smith, 1833), 5–6.

17. FSK to Rev. William Meade, no date, quoted in Edward S. Delaplaine, *Francis Scott Key: Life and Times* (New York: Biography Press, 1937), 203.

18. See Douglas R. Egerton, *Charles Fenton Mercer and the Trial of National Conservatism* (Jackson, MS, and London: University Press of Mississippi, 1989), 32.

19. FSK to Rev. William Meade, quoted in Delaplaine, *Francis Scott Key: Life and Times*, 203–204.

20. In a Dec. 17, 1819, message to Congress. See *Annals of Congress*, U.S. Senate, 16th Congress, 1st Session, 30–31.

21. Helene Cooper, *The House at Sugar Beach: In Search of a Lost African Childhood* (New York: Simon & Schuster, 2009), 31–32.

22. John Randolph to FSK, May 3, 1819, quoted in Garland, *The Life of John Randolph of Roanoke*, vol. 2, 105.

23. FSK to John Randolph, July 21, 1819, Maryland Historical Society, Howard Papers, MS 469, box 19.

24. FSK to John Randolph, Aug. 16, 1819, ibid.

25. *Alexandria Gazette*, Oct. 6, 1819.

26. FSK to Dr. William B. Tyler, Nov. 28, 1819, Historical Society of Frederick County, Key Family Papers, MS 19, box 13, folder 17.

9 A STORMY TUMULT OF FEELING

1. Quoted in the *Norfolk, Virginia, American Beacon*, Jan. 19, 1820.

2. *Annals of Congress*, 16th Congress, 1st Session, Feb. 1, 1820, 1047.

3. Thomas Jefferson to William Short, April 13, 1820, Library of Congress, *The Thomas Jefferson Papers Series 1, General Correspondence, 1651–1827*.

4. John Randolph to Dr. John Brockenbrough, Feb. 24, 1820, quoted in Hugh A. Garland, *The Life of John Randolph of Roanoke*, vol. 2 (New York: D. Appleton, 1853), 34.

5. "Valuable Property For Sale," *National Messenger*, April 5, 1820.

6. Ad in the *Daily National Intelligencer*, Oct. 31, 1820.

7. Quoted in, among other newspapers, *Patron of Industry*, Feb. 21, 1821.

8. *Washington Gazette*, Oct. 19, 1821.

9. George Smith, *Facts Designed to Exhibit Real Character and Tendency of the American Colonization Society* (Liverpool: Egerton Smith, 1833), 16.

10. Quoted in G. B. Stebbins, ed., *Facts and Opinions Touching the American Colonization Society: Views of Wilberforce, Clarkson, and Others, and Opinions of Free People of Color of the United States* (Boston: John. P. Jewett, 1853), 171–72.

11. William Lloyd Garrison, "Thoughts on African Colonization...," 1832, 25.

12. "Drowning of Edward Key," Historical Society of Frederick County, Francis Scott Key Family Vertical File. The entry in this file is a typed transcription; it is quoted in Edward S. Delaplaine, *Francis Scott Key: Life and Times* (New York: Biography Press, 1937), 222–29, as coming from FSK's diary. No historian, archivist, or researcher has been able to find the original FSK diary referred to by Delaplaine.

13. John Earle Uhler, "The Delphian Club: A Contribution to the Literary History of Baltimore in the Early Nineteenth Century," *Maryland Historical Magazine* 20 (Dec. 1925), 307.

14. Delaplaine, *Francis Scott Key: Life and Times*, 231. The poem also appears, without attribution, in David Lehman, ed., *The Best American Erotic Poems: From 1800 to the Present* (New York: Scribner, 2008), 1.

15. *Negro William Jordan v. Lemuel Sawyer*, U.S. Circuit Court for the District of Columbia, April term, 1823.

16. Quoted in *Baltimore Sun* obituary of Maria Lloyd Key Steele, Jan. 26, 1897.

17. The report was published in, among other newspapers, *Augusta, Georgia, Chronicle*, July 23, 1823, and *Boston Recorder*, Aug. 9, 1823.

10 A VIGOROUS AND WELL-CULTIVATED INTELLECT

1. U.S. Supreme Court, 23 U.S. 10 Wheat. 66 (1825)

2. Henry S. Foote, *A Casket of Reminiscences* (Washington, D.C.: Chronicle Publishing, 1874), 12–13.

3. See John T. Noonan, Jr., *The Antelope: The Ordeal of the Recaptured Africans in the Administrations of James Monroe and John Quincy Adams* (Berkeley: University of California Press, 1977), 97.

4. B. R. Curtis, *Reports of Decisions in the Supreme Court of the United States*, vol. 6 (Boston: Little Brown, 1855), 340.
5. *Argument of John Quincy Adams Before the Supreme Court...In the Case of United States, Appellants, vs. Cinque, and Others, Captured in the Schooner Amistad...Delivered on the 24th of February and the 1st of March, 1841* (New York: S. W. Benedict, 1841), 115.
6. Charles Warren, *The Supreme Court in United States History*, vol. 2 (New York: Little Brown, 1922), 45.
7. *Register of Debates*, 18th Congress, 2nd Session, 527.
8. See Diane Windham Shaw, "Lafayette and Slavery," *Lafayette Alumni News Magazine*, Winter 2007, and Marc Leepson, *Lafayette: Lessons in Leadership from the Idealist General* (New York: Palgrave Macmillan, 2011), 120–21.
9. *The Eighth Annual Report of the American Society for Colonizing the Free People of Color...* (Washington, D.C.: James C. Dunn, 1825), 3–4.
10. *Daily National Intelligencer*, May 25, May 30, May 31, June 1, and June 3, 1825.
11. Quoted in *Baltimore Patriot*, Jan. 11, 1826.
12. John Randolph to Dr. John Brockenbrough, Jan. 30, 1826, quoted in Hugh A. Garland, *The Life of John Randolph of Roanoke*, vol. 2 (New York: D. Appleton, 1853), 265.
13. John Randolph to Dr. John Brockenbrough, Feb. 20, 1826, ibid., 266.
14. Charles Francis Adams, ed., *Memoirs of John Quincy Adams*, vol. 9 (Philadelphia: J. B. Lippincott, 1876), 437, diary entry of Nov. 30, 1837.
15. Quoted in *First Annual Report of the Board of Managers of the New-England Anti-Slavery Society* (Boston: Garrison & Knapp, 1833), 36.
16. Ibid., 39.
17. Quoted in Garland, *Life of John Randolph*, 260.
18. Quoted in *Canton Repository* (Ohio), Nov. 30, 1826.
19. See David Eltis, "The Abolition of the Slave Trade," New York Public Library, Schomburg Center for Research in Black Culture, 2007.
20. Francis S. Key, *A Discourse on Education* (Annapolis: Maryland Gazette, 1827), 23.

11   A FRIEND OF PEACE

1. See William Safire, *Safire's Political Dictionary* (New York: Oxford University Press, 2008), 373–74: "Jackson's frontier coterie was the first designated as the 'kitchen' cabinet," Safire wrote, "presumably because of his and their reputation for unpolished manners."
2. Quoted in *The African Repository and Colonial Journal*, Feb. 1828 (3:12), 353–56.
3. *Daily National Intelligencer*, Nov. 28, 1828.
4. Ibid., Jan. 3, 1829.
5. Quoted in the *National Intelligencer*, June 13, 1825. Also see Wilhemus Bogart Bryan, *A History of the National Capital, 1815–1878*, vol. 2 (New York: Macmillan, 1916), 40.
6. Arthur J. Stansbury, in *Arthur's Home Gazette*, May 1851.
7. Fletcher Webster, ed., *The Private Correspondence of Daniel Webster*, vol. 1 (Boston: Little, Brown, 1857), 473.
8. Gaillard Hunt, ed., *The First Forty Years of Washington Society Portrayed by the Family Letters of Mrs. Samuel Harrison Smith (Margaret Bayard) from the Collection of Her Grandson, J. Henley Smith* (New York: Charles Scribner's Sons, 1906), 296, 293–94.
9. See "Case of Tobias Watkins," *Niles' Weekly*, July 25, 1829.
10. Andrew Jackson to Samuel Delucenna Ingham, Nov. 10, 1829, Daniel Feller et al., eds., *The Papers of Andrew Jackson*, vol. 7 (Knoxville: University of Tennessee Press, 2007), 545.
11. Eaton was twenty-eight when, at Andrew Jackson's behest, the Tennessee Legislature named him to fill the seat of a senator who had resigned. That made Eaton the youngest man ever to serve in the U.S. Senate.
12. Hunt, ed., *The First Forty Years of Washington Society*, 252.
13. Ibid.
14. Feller et al., eds., *The Papers of Andrew Jackson*, vol. 7, 415.
15. Andrew Jackson to Ezra Stiles Ely, March 23, 1829, ibid., 113.

16. Quoted in Claude G. Bowers, *The Party Battles of the Jackson Period* (Boston, New York: Houghton Mifflin, 1922), 25.

17. Ibid., 420, 414.

18. Charles Francis Adams, ed., *Memoirs of John Quincy Adams*, vol. 8 (Philadelphia: J. B. Lippincott, 1874–1877), 164, diary entry, Feb. 6, 1830.

19. Ezra Stiles Ely to Andrew Jackson, March 18, 1829, in Feller et al., eds., *The Papers of Andrew Jackson*, vol. 7, 103.

20. Quoted in James Parton, *Life of Andrew Jackson* (New York: Mason Brothers, 1860), 186.

21. Ibid., 204.

22. Jackson later named Eaton territorial governor of Florida and ambassador to Spain. Jackson nominated Van Buren to be ambassador to England, but the Senate, on a tie-breaking vote by Vice President Calhoun, rejected the nomination.

23. FSK to Robert B. Taney, June 14, 1831, quoted in Samuel Tyler ed., *Memoir of Roger Brooke Taney, LLD, Chief Justice of the Supreme Court of the United States* (Baltimore: John Murphy, 1872), 169.

24. Jackson's "kitchen cabinet" also included his close friends and strong political supporters William Berkeley Lewis, Amos Kendall, and Isaac Hill; newspaper editors Francis Preston Blair and Duff Green; and Jackson's nephew and private secretary, Andrew Donelson.

12   A PARTICULAR FRIEND OF THE PRESIDENT

1. *Rights of All*, October 19, 1829.

2. *National Gazette* (Philadelphia), Oct. 24, 1829.

3. Letter to *Daily National Intelligencer*, April 13, 1829.

4. *Negro Harry Quando v. Claggett*, William Cranch, *Reports of Cases Civil & Criminal in the U.S. Circuit Court of the District of Columbia from 1804 to 1841*, vol. 4 (Boston: Little Brown, 1852), 17.

5. The cost of the funeral was $42: $22 for making the coffin and $20 for the hearse. *F. S. Key Legal Papers, 1812–1966*, "Receipts, general," Maryland Historical Society, Special Collections, MS 3009.

6. Thomas Jefferson and John Adams both died on July 4, 1826, the fiftieth anniversary of the founding of the Republic.

7. Reprinted in *National Gazette of Philadelphia*, July 9, 1831.

8. *New York Commercial Advertiser*, July 1, 1831.

9. *Oration Delivered by Francis S. Key, Esq. in the Rotunda of the Capitol of the United States on the 4th of July, 1831* (Washington, D.C., 1831), 7.

10. Ibid.

11. Quoted in *New York Evening Post*, July 11, 1831.

12. Jackson's remark, which he gave as a toast at the annual Jefferson Day Dinner on April 13, 1830, at Brown's Hotel in Washington, was reported in *Niles' Weekly Register* of April 24 as "Our *federal* union; it *must be preserved*."

13. *U.S. Congressional Documents and Debates, 1774–1875,* Elliot's Debates, vol. 4, p. 585.

14. Henry Clay to William Jarvis, Aug. 3, 1833, Gilder Lehrman Institute of History, Collection No. GLC03307.

15. FSK to Thomas Charlton, Nov. 1832, quoted in Edward S. Delaplaine, *Francis Scott Key: Life and Times* (New York: Biography Press, 1937), 320.

16. William Lloyd Garrison, "Thoughts on African Colonization...," in *Selections from the Writings of W. L. Garrison* (Boston: R. F. Wallcut, 1852), 23–24.

17. Mary Kay Ricks, *Escape of the Pearl: The Heroic Bid for Freedom on the Underground Railroad* (New York: William Morrow, 2007), 397.

18. Dorothy S. Provine, ed., *District of Columbia Free Negro Registers, 1821–1861* (Bowie, MD: Heritage Books, 1996), 195–96. Also see National Archives Record Group 21, Records of U.S. District Courts, *Manumission and Emancipation Record, 1821–1861*, vol. 2, Register no. 916, 163.

19. Ibid., 199–200.

20. Adams County Historical Society, Gettysburg, Pa., *Clem Johnson Manumission Papers*, Family File—Clem Johnson, 1831. Also see Jefferson Morley, *Snow-Storm in August: Washington City, Francis Scott Key and the Forgotten Race Riot of 1835* (New York: Doubleday, 2012), 60–61.
21. Quoted in *Gettysburg Star & Sentinel* (Pennsylvania), March 15, 1888.
22. FSK to Charles Howard, May 19, 1832, Maryland Historical Society, *Howard Papers*, box 19.
23. FSK to Charles Howard, May 21, 1832, ibid.
24. FSK to Elizabeth Howard, May 22, 1832.

13   A RANK JACKSON MAN

1.   Quoted in *The Federal Cases Comprising Cases Argued and Determined in the Circuit and District Courts of the United States* (St. Paul: West Publishing, 1896), 380.
2.   Both letters are reprinted in *Gales & Seaton's Register of Debates in Congress*, 22nd Congress, 1st Session, House of Representatives, "Case of Samuel Houston," April 19, 1832, 2571.
3.   Grundy had won a special election in 1829 to fill the Senate seat vacated when Jackson appointed John Eaton secretary of war.
4.   Testimony before the House, April 23, 1832, *Journal of the House of Representatives*, vol. 25 (April 23, 1832), 637.
5.   William Stanbery to the Hon. Andrew Stevenson, Speaker of the House of Representatives, April 14, 1832, printed as House of Representatives Document 210, 22nd Congress, 1st Session, April 18, 1832.
6.   Testimony before the House, *Gales & Seaton's Register of Debates in Congress*, "Case of Samuel Houston," April 19, 1832, 2572.
7.   *Journal of the House of Representatives of the United States, 1831–1832*, April 14, 1832, 592.
8.   Andrew Jackson to Anthony Butler, April 19, 1832 in John Spencer Bassett, ed., *Correspondence of Andrew Jackson*, vol. 4 (Washington, D.C.: Carnegie Institution, 1926), 436. Also see H. W. Brands, *Andrew Jackson: His Life and Times* (New York: Doubleday, 2005), 507–08.
9.   See Charles H. Ambler, *The Life and Diary of John Floyd* (Richmond: Richmond Press, 1918), 185.
10. Statement, April 18, 1832, before the House of Representatives, *Gales & Seaton's Register*, "Case of Samuel Houston," April 18, 1832, 2562, 2568.
11. Unsigned "Private Correspondence," *Frankfort, Kentucky, Argus*, May 2, 1832.
12. *Gales & Seaton's Register*, April 26, 1832, 2597.
13. Ibid., 2599.
14. *Frankfort Argus*, May 2, 1832.
15. Dispatch from the Washington correspondent of the *United States Gazette*, reprinted in the *Alexandria Gazette*, May 1, 1832.
16. *United States Gazette*, reprinted in the *Alexandria Gazette*, May 1, 1832.
17. *Cincinnati Gazette*, reprinted in the *Alexandria Gazette*, "Bank Lawyers," Aug. 22, 1832.
18. *Gales & Seaton's Register*, May 7, 1832, 2821.
19. Ibid, May 11, 1832, 3014.
20. *Hampshire Gazette*, May 2, 1832.
21. William Cranch, *Reports of Cases Civil & Criminal in the U.S. Circuit Court of the District of Columbia from 1804 to 1841*, vol. 4, *United States v. Houston* (Boston: Little Brown, 1852), 268.
22. Cranch, ibid., 261.
23. James Parton, *Life of Andrew Jackson*, vol. 3 (New York: Mason Brothers, 1860), 391.
24. George W. Pascal, "The Last Years of Sam Houston," *Harper's Monthly Magazine*, 32:191 (April 1866), 631.

14   THE PROSECUTOR

1.   John Thompson Mason was the first U.S. attorney in Washington. He served for just a few months in 1801 and was succeeded by Walter Jones, who held the office for twenty years.
2.   See George Watterston, *A New Guide to Washington* (Washington, D.C.: Robert Farnham, 1842), 166–67.

3. According to the U.S. Census, the population of Washington, D.C., in 1830 was 30,261, including 9,109 African Americans, of whom 4,604 were freed blacks and 4,505 were slaves.

4. *United States v. John W. Prout*, in William Cranch, *Reports of Cases Civil and Criminal in the United States Circuit Court of the District of Columbia, 1801 to 1841*, vol. 4 (Boston: Little, Brown, 1852), 302.

5. *The Sixteenth Annual Report of the American Society for the Colonization of Free People of Colour of the United States* (Washington, D.C.: James C. Dunn, 1833), xxii.

6. Hugh A. Garland, *Life of John Randolph of Roanoke*, vol. 2 (New York: D. Appleton, 1853), 149–150.

7. Washington Irving to Peter Irving, May 17, 1833, quoted in Pierre M. Irving, *The Life and Letters of Washington Irving*, vol. 2 (New York: Putnam and Sons, 1883), 175.

8. *Ex parte Pleasants*, in Cranch, *Reports of Cases Civil and Criminal in the United States Circuit Court, 1801 to 1841*, vol. 4, 323.

9. *Genius of Universal Emancipation* 3, no. 8 (June 1833), 127.

10. National Archives, *Circuit Court for the District of Columbia, Case Papers 1802–1863*, Docket Book, vol. 70, Records Group 21. Also see Jefferson Morley, *Snow-Storm in August: Washington City, Francis Scott Key, and the Forgotten Race Riot of 1835* (New York: Nan A. Talese/Doubleday, 2012), 80–82.

11. See, for example, *Daily National Intelligencer*, Sept. 26, 1833.

12. See, for example, *Hagerstown, Maryland Torch Light*, Oct. 24, 1833.

13. FSK to anonymous, Jan. 21, 1835, Key papers, Special Collections, University of Virginia Library.

14. Morley, *Snow-Storm in August*, 69. The author wishes to thank Jefferson Morley for generously sharing his extensive research on FSK's work as U.S. attorney.

15. Letter to the Editor, *Philadelphia Commercial Herald*, published in *Daily National Intelligencer*, Nov. 12, 1833.

16. National Archives, *Circuit Court for the District of Columbia, Case Papers*, 1802–63.

17. Cranch, *Reports of Cases Civil and Criminal in the United States Circuit Court of the District of Columbia, 1801 to 1841*, vol. 4, 338.

18. "Madam on the Mall," Smithsonian Institution, Architectural History & Historic Preservation Division web site, retrieved May 4, 2013, www.si.edu/oahp/madam.

15 MINISTER TO ALABAMA

1. Francis Paul Prucha, *The Great Father: The United States Government and the American Indians*, vol. 1 (Lincoln: University of Nebraska Press, 1984), 222.

2. Quoted in Thomas Chalmers McCorvey, "The Mission of Francis Scott Key to Alabama in 1833," *Alabama Historical Society Transactions* 4 (1904), 150.

3. *Niles' Weekly Register*, Oct. 26, 1833, 142.

4. Ibid.

5. Editorial in *Huntsville Democrat*, Jan. 23, 1834.

6. Ibid., 144.

7. *Tuscaloosa State Rights Expositor*, quoted in McCorvey, "The Mission of Francis Scott Key...," 151.

8. *Niles' Weekly Register*, Jan. 11, 1834, 329.

9. Printed in, among other newspapers, the *Richmond Enquirer*, Nov. 9, 1833.

10. FSK to Roger Brooke Taney, Nov. 6, 1833, *Maryland Historical Magazine*, 44:4 (1949), 290.

11. FSK to Ellen Key, Nov. 7, 1833, Historical Society of Frederick County, Francis Scott Key, vertical file.

12. FSK to Roger Brooke Taney, Nov. 14, 1833, *Maryland Historical Magazine*, vol. 5 (March 1910), 29.

13. *Executive Letterbook G*, Alabama Department of Archives and History, vol. 4, 665. Also see John T. Ellisor, *The Second Creek War: Interethnic Conflict and Collusion on a Collapsing Frontier* (Lincoln: University of Nebraska Press, 2010), 91–92.

14. Published in, among other places, *National Gazette*, Jan. 14, 1834.

15. McCorvey, "The Mission of Francis Scott Key…," 159.
16. Both poems appeared in, among other newspapers, *Alexandria Gazette*, April 2, 1834. They also are included in *Poems of the Late Francis S. Key, Esq.*, pp. 41–48. The original letters containing the poems are in the Papers of Francis Scott Key, 1821–1841, Special Collections, University of Virginia Library, 6949-A.
17. Jefferson Morley, *Snow-Storm in August: Washington City, Francis Scott Key, and the Forgotten Race Riot of 1835* (New York: Nan A. Talese/Doubleday, 2012), 74.
18. Edward S. Delaplaine, *Francis Scott Key: Life and Times* (New York: Biography Press, 1937), 357.
19. McCorvey, "The Mission of Francis Scott Key…," 160.

16 AN INCORRUPTIBLE PATRIOT

1. William Cranch, *Reports of Cases Civil and Criminal in the United States Circuit Court of the District of Columbia, from 1801 to 1841*, vol. 4 (Boston: Little, Brown, 1852), 423.
2. Ibid., 446.
3. Ibid., 451.
4. Ibid., 431, 457.
5. *National Gazette*, Aug. 30, 1834.
6. Francis S. Key, *The Power of Literature and Its Connexion with Religion: An Oration* (Bristol, PA: Bristol College Press, 1834), 3–4.
7. "Dinner to Mr. Taney," *Baltimore Patriot*, Aug. 15, 1834, reprinted from *Frederick Examiner*, Aug. 13, 1834.
8. *Richmond Enquirer*, Aug. 12, 1834.
9. Key's words come from a newspaper account of the speech reported in the third person, see Edward S. Delaplaine, *Francis Scott Key: Life and Times* (New York: Biography Press, 1937), 379–80.
10. *Alexandria Gazette*, Aug. 12, 1834.
11. *New York American*, Oct. 10, 1834.
12. See Robert A. Diamond, ed., *Congressional Quarterly's Guide to U.S. Elections* (Washington, D.C.: Congressional Quarterly, 1975), 560, 564.
13. Quoted in "Tract Meeting—Communicated," *Daily National Intelligencer*, Dec. 31, 1834.
14. FSK to Roger B. Taney, Jan. 30, 1825, Maryland Historical Society, Howard Papers, MS 469, box 19.
15. Thomas Hart Benton, *Thirty Years' View or, A History of the Working of the American Government, from 1820 to 1850*, vol. 1 (New York. D. Appleton, 1856), 521.
16. *New York Evening Post*, Feb. 2, 1835.
17. *Alexandria Gazette*, Jan. 31, 1835.
18. Harriet Martineau, *Restrospect on Western Travel* (London: Saunders & Otley, 1838), 162.
19. Charles Francis Adams, ed., *Memoirs of John Quincy Adams*, vol. 9 (Philadelphia: J. B. Lippincott, 1874–1877), 229.
20. *Rhode Island Republican*, Feb. 11, 1835.
21. Poindexter spoke at a dinner given for him in Philadelphia on March 27, 1835; his comments were published in their entirety in the *Daily National Intelligencer*, April 15, 1835.
22. *Alexandria Gazette*, March 4, 1835.
23. Charles Francis Adams, ed., *Memoirs of John Quincy Adams*, vol. 9 (Philadelphia: J. B. Lippincott, 1874–1877), 230.
24. Quoted in *New York Evening Post*, Feb. 5, 1835.
25. Quoted in *Richmond Whig*, Feb. 13, 1835.
26. Ibid.
27. *National Intelligencer*, as reported in "Trial of Richard Lawrence," *Niles' Register*, April 18, 1835, 119.
28. Quoted in New York *Journal of Commerce* and reprinted in many other newspapers, including the Norwich, CT, *Courier*, April 22, 1835.
29. *National Intelligencer*, as reported in "Trial of Richard Lawrence," *Niles' Register*, April 18, 1835, 121.
30. Ibid.

17   AN ALARMING STATE OF DISORDER

1. Quoted in James Parton, *Life of Andrew Jackson*, vol. 3 (New York: Mason Brothers, 1860), 587.
2. *Journal of the Senate*, 24th Congress, 1st session, Dec. 8, 1835, 31.
3. Quoted in *The Trial of Reuben Crandall, M.D., Charged with Publishing Seditious Libels...* (New York: H. R. Piercy, 1836), 9. No word-for-word transcripts from the Crandall trial exist. However, the publication cited above and two others published in 1836 contain extensive notes by different anonymous reporters on the eleven-day trial. The others are *The Trial of Reuben Crandall, M.D., Charged with Publishing and Circulating Seditious and Incendiary Papers, &c...* (Washington, D.C.) and "A Part of a Speech Pronounced by Francis S. Key, Esq. on the Trial of Reuben Crandall, M.D. Before the Court of the District of Columbia..." *African Repository and Colonial Journal*, vol. 12, Nov. 1836. They are cited below as New York transcript, Washington transcript, and *African Repository* respectively.
4. According to the warrant, see Jefferson Morley, *Snow-Storm in August: Washington City, Francis Scott Key, and the Forgotten Race Riot of 1835* (New York: Nan A. Talese/Doubleday, 2012), 139.
5. Washington transcript, 44.
6. New York transcript, 33.
7. Washington transcript, 19–20.
8. New York transcript, 27.
9. Reuben Crandall to his father, Jan. 26, 1836, quoted in Marvis Olive Welch, *Prudence Crandall: A Biography* (Manchester, Conn.: Jason Publishers, 1983), 117.
10. Washington transcript, 5.
11. Anna Maria Brodeau Thornton Papers, 1793–1861, Manuscript Division, Library of Congress, vol. 1, 32. The fullest account by far of the Reuben Crandall and Arthur Bowen sagas is contained in Jefferson Morley's *Snow-Storm in August*, which also goes into great detail about the race riot that took place in Washington on August 13–14 and FSK's prosecution of Bowen and Crandall. In Edward Delaplaine's 1937 biography, *Francis Scott Key: Life and Times*, the author does not mention Bowen or the Snow Riot and gives the Crandall affair one paragraph in which he describes the young botanist as "an Abolitionist agitator" (p. 446).
12. Anna Maria Brodeau Thornton Papers, vol. 1, 931. Also see Morley, *Snow-Storm in August*, 135.
13. John G. Sharp, ed., *The Diary of Michael Shiner Relating to the History of the Washington Navy Yard 1813–1869* (Concord, CA: Hannah Morgan Press, 2011), 61. Spelling and punctuation are corrected in the quote.
14. Ibid., 62.
15. Anna Maria Brodeau Thornton Papers, vol. 1, 931.
16. Ibid., 932.
17. *Boston American Traveler*, Aug. 18, 1835.
18. Undated August 1835 letter to one of her children, quoted in Joseph Seaton, *William Winston Seaton of the "National Intelligencer": A Biographical Study* (Boston: James R. Osgood, 1871), 217.
19. Quoted in the *Richmond Inquirer*, Aug. 14, 1835.
20. *Washington Globe*, Aug. 14, 1835.
21. Morley, *Snow-Storm in August*, 152.
22. *Washington Globe*, August 14, 1835.
23. Undated August 1835 letter to one of her children, quoted in Joseph Seaton, *William Winston Seaton of the "National Intelligencer": A Biographical Study* (Boston: James R. Osgood, 1871), 217.
24. *National Intelligencer*, Aug. 15, 1835.
25. Quoted in *Georgetown Metropolitan*, Dec. 11, 1835.
26. Ibid.
27. Ibid.
28. Anna Maria Brodeau Thornton Papers, vol. 2, 960.
29. *Georgetown Metropolitan*, Feb. 24, 1836.
30. Ibid.

31. Reuben Crandall to his father, Jan. 26, 1836, in Welch, *Prudence Crandall: A Biography*, 117.
32. Ibid.
33. Washington transcript, 46.
34. "Crandall's Trial," *Hampshire Gazette* (Northampton, MA), May 4, 1836.
35. *African Repository*, 9.
36. *United States v. Reuben Crandall*, William Cranch, *Reports of Cases Civil and Criminal in the United States Circuit Court of the District of Columbia, from 1801 to 1841*, vol. 4 (Boston: Little, Brown, 1852), 684.
37. *African Repository*, 5.
38. "Trial of Reuben Crandall," *New York Spectator*, April 21, 1836.
39. Washington transcript, 43.
40. Ibid., 41.
41. Ibid., 43.
42. Ibid., 44.
43. New York transcript, 49.
44. Neil S. Kramer, "The Trial of Reuben Crandall," *Records of the Columbia Historical Society*, vol. 50 (1980), 138.
45. *African Repository*, 46.
46. Washington transcript, 48.
47. William Lloyd Garrison, "Acquittal of Dr. Crandall," *Liberator*, May 7, 1836, 75.
48. See Constance McLaughlin Green, *The Secret City: A History of Race Relations in the Nation's Capital* (Princeton: Princeton University Press, 1967), 37.
49. Worthington G. Snethen, *The Black Code of the District of Columbia in Force September 1, 1848* (New York: The A. & F. Anti-Slavery Society, 1848), 45.

18   A FRIEND OF MEN OF COLOR

1. See Jefferson Morley, *Snow-Storm in August: Washington City, Francis Scott Key, and the Forgotten Race Riot of 1835* (New York: Nan A. Talese/Doubleday), 185, 208–210.
2. *United States v. Fenwick*, William Cranch, *Reports of Cases Civil and Criminal in the United States Circuit Court of the District of Columbia, from 1801 to 1841*, vol. 4 (Boston: Little, Brown, 1852), 675–681.
3. Reprinted in *New York Commercial Advertiser*, June 24, 1836.
4. "Correspondence of the *Commercial Advertiser*," reprinted in *Rutland Herald* (Vermont), July 5, 1836.
5. Thomas Mattingly, John Sherburne's second in the duel, wrote a detailed account of the affair in the *Memphis Avalanche* in 1859. It was reprinted in *National Era*, May 12, 1859.
6. FSK to Anna Key Turner, June 26, 1836, *Papers of the Key, Cutts and Turner Families, 1808–1859*, Special Collections, University of Virginia Library.
7. Ibid.
8. FSK to Anna Key Turner, May 25, 1837, ibid.
9. *National Intelligencer*, May 22, 1837.
10. Janie W. H. Lane, *Key and Allied Families* (Macon, GA: Press of the J. W. Burke Co., 1931), 61.
11. John Ross Key Jr. became an artist of some renown in Washington. Among his paintings is a romanticized oil of the Key house in Georgetown that hangs today in a hallway outside the Diplomatic Reception Rooms of the U.S. State Department.
12. Francis Scott Key Will, 1837, Maryland Historical Society, Special Collections, vertical file.
13. *United States v. Negro Joseph Ferrell*, Cranch, *Reports of Cases Civil and Criminal…*, vol. 5, 311–12.
14. Account in *Alexandria Gazette*, Sept. 22, 1838.
15. FSK to Rev. Benjamin Tappan, *Colonization Herald and General Register*, vol. 1 (June 1839), 254.
16. Diary entry, Nov. 30, 1837, in Charles Francis Adams, ed., *Memoirs of John Quincy Adams*, vol. 9 (Philadelphia: J. B. Lippincott, 1874–1877), 438.
17. *Daily National Intelligencer*, Sept. 12, 1840.

18. Reprinted in the *Alexandria Gazette*, May 29, 1841.

19. Harrison died at age 68, the first American president to die in office. Although Harrison had spoken hatless and coatless for nearly two hours in the rain and cold at his inauguration a month earlier, the consensus of medical opinion today is that the pneumonia was not caused by his exposure to the elements.

20. Quoted in the *Alexandria Gazette,* April 5, 1841.

21. The Gaines case—the longest-running in the history of the American court system—began in Louisiana in 1834 and did not end until a Supreme Court ruling in 1891, six years after Myra Clark Gaines's death. The case came before the U.S. Supreme Court seventeen times in various guises, and before the Louisiana Supreme Court five times. See Elizabeth Urban Alexander, *Notorious Woman: The Celebrated Case of Myra Clark Gaines* (Baton Rouge: Louisiana State University Press, 2004).

22. Quoted in Weybright, 281–282.

23. FSK to Polly Key, April 26, 1841, Papers of Francis Scott Key, Special Collections, University of Virginia Library.

24. June 24, 1841.

25. *Harrisburg Watchman*, July 24, 1841.

26. FSK to Charles Key, June 19, 1841, Papers of Francis Scott Key, Special Collections, University of Virginia Library.

27. FSK to Dr. J. K. Mitchell, Sept. 25, 1841, ibid.

28. Ibid.

29. *Baltimore Sun*, Oct. 23, 1841.

30. FSK letter to his nine-year-old granddaughter Ellen Turner, published in *Philadelphia Press*, Aug. 1, 1881.

31. "Daniel Murray, Late Lieutenant in the American Navy," *Maryland Historical Magazine* 20 (1925), 200–201.

32. *The Emancipator*, reprinted in *Massachusetts Spy*, June 15, 1842.

33. McHenry Howard to Mrs. K. Mackenzie Brevett, May 8, 1912, Howard Papers, 1662–1919, Maryland Historical Society.

34. Charles Howard to Daniel Turner, Jan. 12, 1843, Special Collections, University of Virginia Library.

EPILOGUE   ONE OF THE BEST MEN WHO EVER LIVED

1. See Scottie Fitzgerald Smith, "The Colonial Ancestors of Francis Scott Key Fitzgerald," *Maryland Historical Magazine* 76:4 (Winter 1891), 363–75.

2. See Barry Mackintosh, "The Loss of the Francis Scott Key House: Was It Really?" Peabody Room, Georgetown Library, vertical file, 1981.

3. Quoted in *New York Times*, July 11, 1898.

4. The American Colonization Society sent some 15,000 African Americans to Liberia. When the Civil War started in 1861, there were nearly four million enslaved people in the United States.

BIBLIOGRAPHY

BOOKS

Berlin, Ira. *Many Thousands Gone: The First Two Centuries of Slavery in North America*. Cambridge, MA: Belknap Press of Harvard University Press, 1998.

Boyle, Esmeralda, *Biographical Sketches of Distinguished Marylanders*. Baltimore: Kelly, Piet & Co., 1877.

Brands, H. W. *Andrew Jackson: His Life and Times*. New York: Doubleday, 2005.

Bryan, Wilhelmus Bogart. *A History of the National Capital, 1815–1878*, vol. 2. New York: Macmillan, 1916.

Brooke, John. T. *A Sketch of the Character of the Late Francis Scott Key, Esq*. Cincinnati: Wilson & Drake, 1843.

Bruce, William Cabell. *John Randolph of Roanoke, 1773–1822: A Biography Based Largely on New Material*. New York: G. P. Putnam's Sons, 1922.

Burin, Eric. *Slavery and the Peculiar Solution: A History of the American Colonization Society*. Gainesville: University Press of Florida, 2005.

Cranch, William. *Reports of Cases Civil and Criminal in the United States Circuit Court of the District of Columbia, From 1801 to 1841*, vols. 4 and 5. Boston: Little, Brown and Co., 1852.

Delaplaine, Edward S. *Francis Scott Key: Life and Times*. New York: Biography Press, 1937.

Ecker, Grace Dunlop. *A Portrait of Old George Town*. Richmond, VA: Dietz Press, 1951.

Egerton, Douglas R. *Charles Fenton Mercer and the Trial of National Conservatism*. Jackson: University Press of Mississippi, 1989.

Ellison, John T. *The Second Creek War: Interethnic Conflict and Collusion on a Collapsing Frontier*. Lincoln: University of Nebraska Press, 2010.

Foote, Henry S. *A Casket of Reminiscences*. Washington, D.C.: Chronicle Publishing, 1874.

Fox, Early Lee, *The American Colonization Society: 1817–1840*. Baltimore: Johns Hopkins University Press, 1919.

Garland, Hugh A. *The Life of John Randolph of Roanoke*. New York: D. Appleton & Co., 1853.

Green, Constance McLaughlin. *Washington: Village and Capital, 1800–1878*. Princeton: Princeton University Press, 1962.

Higgins, Edwin. *The National Anthem: "The Star-Spangled Banner," Francis Scott Key, and Patriotic Lines*. Baltimore: Williams & Wilkins, 1898.

Howe, Daniel Walker. *What Hath God Wrought: The Transformation of America, 1815–1848*. Oxford: Oxford University Press, 2009.

Hunt, Gaillard, ed. *From the First Forty Years of Washington Society Portrayed by the Family Letters of Mrs. Samuel Harrison Smith (Margaret Bayard) from the Collection of Her Grandson, J. Henley Smith*. New York: Charles Scribner's Sons, 1906.

Johnson, David. *John Randolph of Roanoke*. Baton Rouge: Louisiana State University Press, 2012.

Jordan, Winthrop D. *White Over Black: American Attitudes Toward the Negro, 1550–1812*. Chapel Hill: University of North Carolina Press, 1968.

Key, Francis S. *A Discourse on Education*. Annapolis: Office of the Maryland Gazette, 1827.

Key, Francis Scott. *The Power of Literature and Its Connexion with Religion*. Bristol, Conn.: Bristol College Press, 1834.

Key-Smith, F. S. *Francis Scott Key, Author of the Star Spangled Banner: What Else He Was and Who*. Washington, D.C.: Key-Smith & Co., 1911.

Lancaster, Joseph. *The British System of Education*. Washington, D.C.: Joseph Milligan and William Cooper, 1812.

Lane, Janie Warren Hollinsgworth. *Key and Allied Families*. Macon, GA: Press of the J.W. Burke Co., 1931.

Leepson, Marc. *Flag: An American Biography*. New York: Thomas Dunne Books, 2005.

Lessem, Harold I., and George C. MacKenzie. *Fort McHenry National Monument and Historic Shrine*. Washington, D.C.: National Park Service, Historical Handbook Series 5, 1961.

Lewis, Walker. *Without Fear or Favor: A Biography of Chief Justice Roger Brooke Taney*. Boston: Houghton Mifflin, 1965.

Lord, Walter. *The Dawn's Early Light*. New York: W.W. Norton, 1972.

Marszalek, John F. *The Petticoat Affair: Manners, Mutiny, and Sex in Andrew Jackson's White House*. Baton Rouge: Louisiana State University Press, 2000.

Meyer, Sam, *Paradoxes of Fame: The Francis Scott Key Story*. Annapolis, MD: Eastwind, 1995.

Molotsky, Irvin. *The Flag, the Poet & the Song: The Story of the Star-Spangled Banner*. New York: Dutton, 2001.

Morley, Jefferson. *Snow-Storm in August: Washington City, Francis Scott Key, and the Forgotten Race Riot of 1835*. New York: Nan A. Talese/Doubleday, 2012.

Newman, Richard S. *The Transformation of American Abolitionism: Fighting Slavery in the Early Republic*. Chapel Hill: University of North Carolina Press, 2001.

Owen, Thomas McAdory, ed. *Transactions of the Alabama Historical Society, 1899–1903*. Montgomery: Alabama Historical Society, 1904.

Parton, James. *Life of Andrew Jackson*. New York: Mason Brothers, 1860.

Peden, Henry C. Jr. *Revolutionary Patriots of Frederick County, Maryland*. Westminster, MD: Family Line Publications, 1995.

Pitch, Anthony S. *The Burning of Washington: The British Invasion of 1814*. Annapolis, MD: Naval Institute Press, 1998.

Scharf, Thomas J. *History of Western Maryland: Being a History of Frederick, Montgomery, Carroll, Washington, Allegany, and Garrett Counties from the Earliest Period to the Present Day*. Philadelphia: L.H. Everts, 1882.

Smith, Gene Allen. *The Slaves' Gamble: Choosing Sides in the War of 1812*. New York: Palgrave Macmillan, 2013.

Staudenraus, P. J. *The African Colonization Movement, 1816–1865*. New York: Columbia University Press, 1961.

Steiner, Bernard C. *Life of Roger Brooke Taney, Chief Justice of the United States Supreme Court*. Baltimore: Williams & Wilkins, 1922.

Svejda, George J., *History of the Star Spangled Banner from 1814 to the Present*. Washington, D.C.: National Park Service, Division of History, Office of Archeology and Historic Preservation, Feb. 28, 1969.

Taylor, Lonn. *The Spangled Banner: The Flag That Inspired the National Anthem*. New York: Harry N. Abrams, 2000.

Taylor, Lonn, Kathleen M. Kendrick, and Jeffrey L. Brodie. *The Star-Spangled Banner: The Making of an American Icon*. New York: Smithsonian Books, 2008.

The Trial of Reuben Crandall, M.D., Charged with Publishing Seditious Libels by Circulating the Publications of the American Anti-Slavery Society...New York: H.R. Piercy, 1836.

The Trial of Reuben Crandall, M.D., Charged with Publishing and Circulating Seditious and Incendiary Papers, &c in the District of Columbia With the Intent of Exciting Service Insurrection...Washington, D.C., 1836.

Tyler, Samuel, ed. *Memoir of Roger Brook Taney, LLD, Chief Justice of the Supreme Court of the United States*. Baltimore: John Murphy & Co., 1872.

Vogel, Steve. *Through the Perilous Fight: Six Weeks That Saved the Nation*. New York: Random House, 2013.

Welch, Marvis Olive. *Prudence Crandall: A Biography*. Manchester, CT: Jason Publishers, 1983.

Weybright, Victor. *Spangled Banner: The Story of Francis Scott Key*. New York: Farrar and Rinehart, 1935.

Wilentz, Sean. *The Rise of American Democracy: Jefferson to Lincoln*. New York: Norton, 2005.

Wood, Gordon S. *Empire of Liberty: A History of the Early American Republic, 1789–1815.* Oxford: Oxford University Press, 2009.
Youngberg, H. Ray. *Ancestors and Descendants of Francis Scott Key, Lawyer and Poet.* Wilmington, NC: Youngberg, 1998.

ARTICLES

American Colonization Society. *The African Repository and Colonial Journal*, various issues.
Bartow, Anna Key. "Recollections of Francis Scott Key." *Modern Culture* 13 (Sept.1900).
Berlin, Jean V. "A Mistress and a Slave: Anna Maria Thornton and John Arthur Bowen." *Proceedings of the South Carolina Historical Association*, 1990.
Didier, Eugene L. "Francis Scott Key as a Lawyer," *Green Bag* 16, no. 5 (May 1904).
Egerton, Douglas R. "Its Origin Is Not a Little Curious: A New Look at the American Colonization Society." *Journal of the Early Republic* 5 (Winter 1985).
Eysler, Nellie. "The Star-Spangled Banner: An Hour with an Octogenarian," *Harper's New Monthly Magazine* 43, no. 254 (June 1871).
Ford Jr., Lacy K. "Reconfiguring the Old South: 'Solving' the Problem of Slavery, 1787–1838." *Journal of American History* 95, no.1 (2008).
Kramer, Neil S. "The Trial of Reuben Crandall," *Records of the Columbia Historical Society, Washington, D.C.*, 50 (1980).
Lichtenwanger, William, "The Music of 'The Star-Spangled Banner.'" *Quarterly Journal of the Library of Congress*, July 1977.
Magruder Jr., Caleb Clark. "Dr. William Beanes, the Incidental Cause of the Authorship of the Star-Spangled Banner." *Records of the Columbia Historical Society, Washington, D.C.* 22 (1919).
Maryland Historical Magazine, various issues.
Owsley Jr., Frank L. "Francis Scott Key's Mission to Alabama in 1833." *Alabama Review* 23 (July 1970).
Sherwood, Henry Noble. "Formation of the American Colonization Society." *Journal of Negro History* 3 (July 1917).
Shippen, Rebecca Lloyd. "The Original Manuscript of 'The Star-Spangled Banner.'" *Pennsylvania Magazine of History and Biography* 25 (1901–02).
Smith, F. S. Key. "A Sketch of Francis Scott Key, with a Glimpse of His Ancestors." *Records of the Columbia Historical Society, Washington, D.C.* 11 (1909).

ARCHIVAL MATERIAL

Anna Maria Brodeau Thornton Papers, 1793–1871. Manuscript Division, Library of Congress.
Edward S. Delaplaine Collection. Historical Society of Frederick County.
F. S. Key Legal Papers, 1812–1966. Maryland Historical Society.
F. S. Key Papers, 1810–1845. Maryland Historical Society.
Howard Papers, 1662–1919. Maryland Historical Society.
Key Family Papers. Historical Society of Frederick County.
Key Family Papers Collection. Maryland State Archives.
Maryland State Colonization Society Papers, 1827–1871. Maryland Historical Society.
Papers of Francis Scott Key, 1808–1841. Special Collections, University of Virginia Library.
Papers of the Key, Cutts, and Turner Families, 1808–1859. Special Collections, University of Virginia Library.
Slaves and the Courts, 1740–1860. Library of Congress.
Washington, D.C. Circuit Court for the District of Columbia Case Papers, 1802–1863. National Archives of the United States.

INDEX

Abbreviation FSK stands for Francis Scott Key. Names identified with a familial relationship indicate relationship to FSK. Page numbers for Endnotes contain both chapter and note designation (e.g. 209n2:25 indicates Page 209, Chapter 2, Note 25).